Master the Art of Perspective Drawing

Olivia D. Turner

<u>*Funny helpful tips:*</u>

Engage with books that promote a growth mindset; they foster a belief in personal evolution and potential.

Stay agile in business strategies; adaptability ensures resilience.

Master the Art of Perspective Drawing : Unlock Your Artistic Potential with Proven Techniques for Creating Realistic and Captivating Drawings

Life advices:

Ensure your training gear is appropriate; the right shoes and attire can prevent injuries and improve performance.

Seek feedback regularly; it's a tool for growth and self-improvement.

Introduction

This is an excellent guide that introduces aspiring artists to the fundamental concepts of perspective drawing. With a focus on common areas and various architectural elements, this guide empowers beginners to create compelling and realistic drawings.

The guide starts by covering the basics of perspective drawing, introducing the concept of vanishing points and horizon lines, which are essential for creating the illusion of depth and space in drawings. It then delves into more complex topics like foreshortening and proportion, which are crucial for accurately representing objects in different perspectives.

The first section, "Perspective Drawing: Common Area," provides step-by-step instructions on drawing simple indoor spaces, like a room or a living area. Readers learn how to place objects in relation to the vanishing points and how to create the illusion of depth and three-dimensionality.

Moving on, the guide explores more challenging scenarios, such as "Perspective Drawing: Hallway Look Through," where the artist learns how to draw a hallway from one end, looking through to the other. This exercise helps improve the artist's understanding of depth and the relationship between different elements in a drawing.

"Perspective Drawing: Loft Hideaway" offers a creative challenge, encouraging artists to draw a loft with intricate details and unique perspectives. The step-by-step instructions help beginners gain confidence and hone their skills.

The guide also ventures outside, exploring "Perspective Drawing: Exterior Building." Drawing a building from an exterior viewpoint involves understanding the angles and perspectives of various architectural elements, such as windows, doors, and roofs.

Next up is "Perspective Drawing: Alleyway," where artists learn to draw urban landscapes with converging lines and captivating compositions. This exercise allows them to experiment with different textures and lighting effects.

"Perspective Drawing: Estate Overview" provides an opportunity to draw a more extensive scene, like an estate or a large compound. The artist learns to incorporate various elements into a cohesive and visually appealing composition.

The guide further explores "Perspective Drawing: Industrial Building," challenging artists to draw complex structures with precision and accuracy. Drawing industrial buildings involves paying attention to small details, such as pipes, beams, and machinery.

Moving back indoors, "Perspective Drawing: Storefront" focuses on drawing commercial spaces and showcases how perspective can be applied to various architectural styles.

The guide continues to present more advanced challenges, such as "Drawing: Industrial Exterior" and "Drawing: Corporate Building." These exercises push beginners to refine their skills, paying attention to finer details and mastering the art of perspective drawing.

In conclusion, this is a comprehensive guide that provides a structured approach to perspective drawing, enabling beginners to grasp the foundational concepts and progress to more complex and visually stunning drawings. With step-by-step instructions and creative challenges, this guide is an invaluable resource for aspiring artists seeking to improve their drawing skills and create realistic and captivating perspective drawings.

Contents

First Perspective Drawing: Common Area

For the first drawing in this series we're going to start with a a perspective drawing of a common area. A simple room with a couch, a window and curtains with pictures on the walls and a tv against one of the walls as well. May sound complicated to start but I assure you it starts much

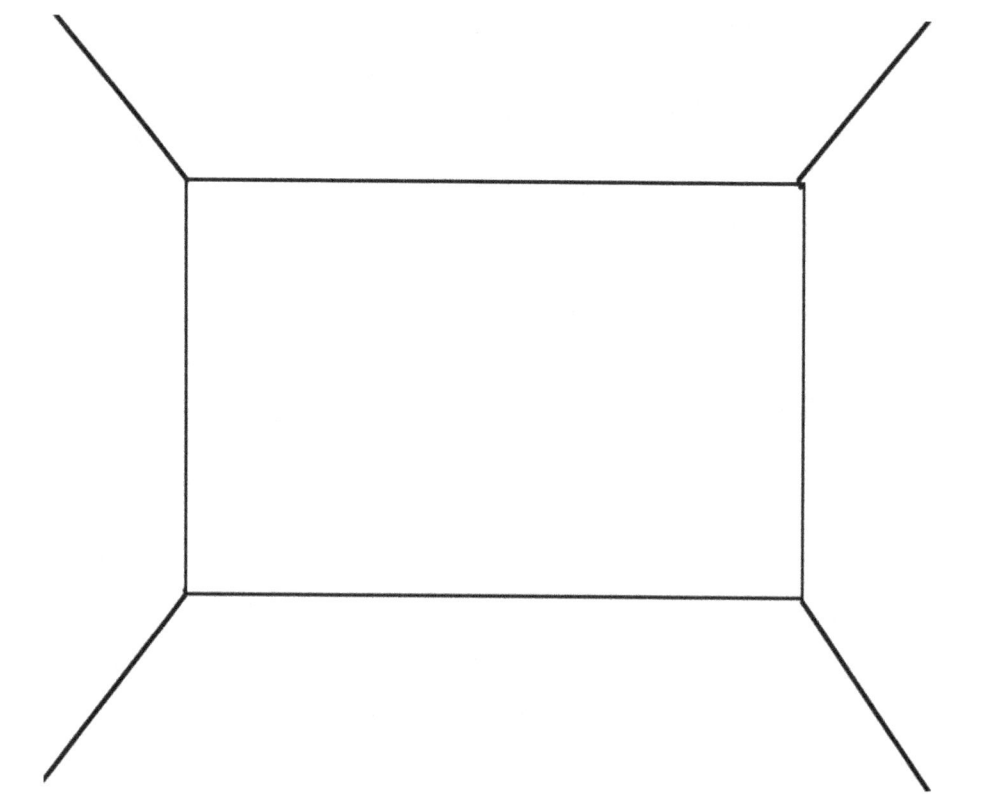

easier than that. For this first drawing we want to focus on learning the line work properly and knowing how to handle the actual concept of the drawing.

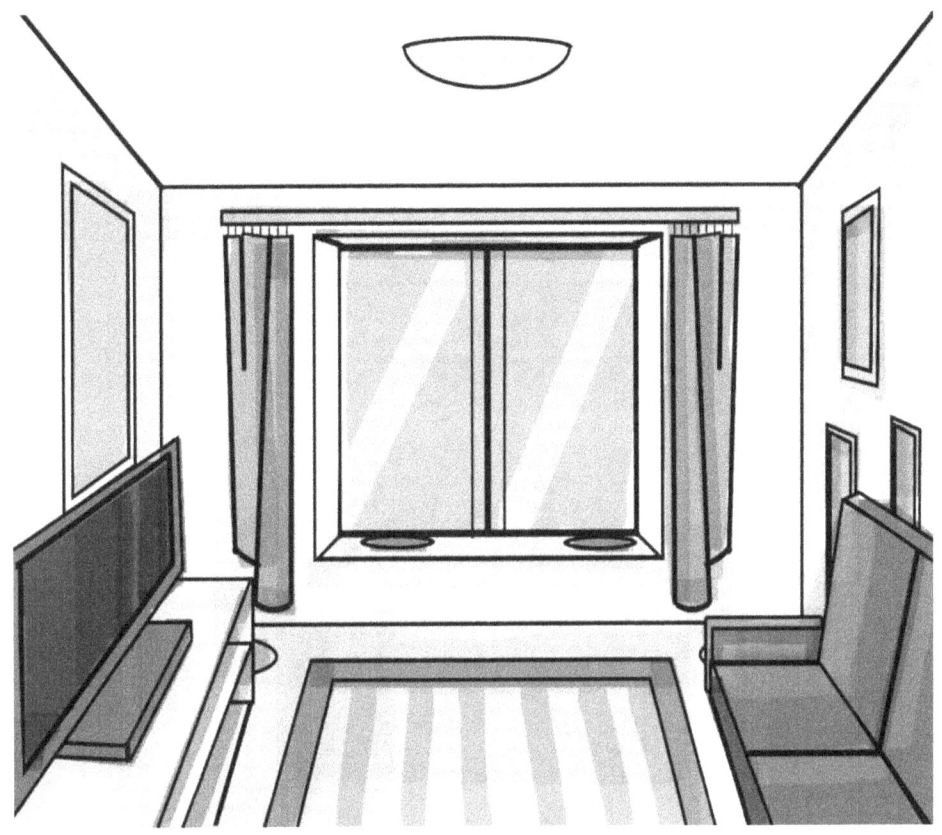

The photo on the left is the complete drawing, and the one on the right is the very first step! So as you can see there is a grandiose difference in what you start out with and what you are hoping to achieve. Don't let that discourage you but let it guide you. So lets get into it then. Follow that first photo on the upper right and get your lines drawn straight edge and perfect

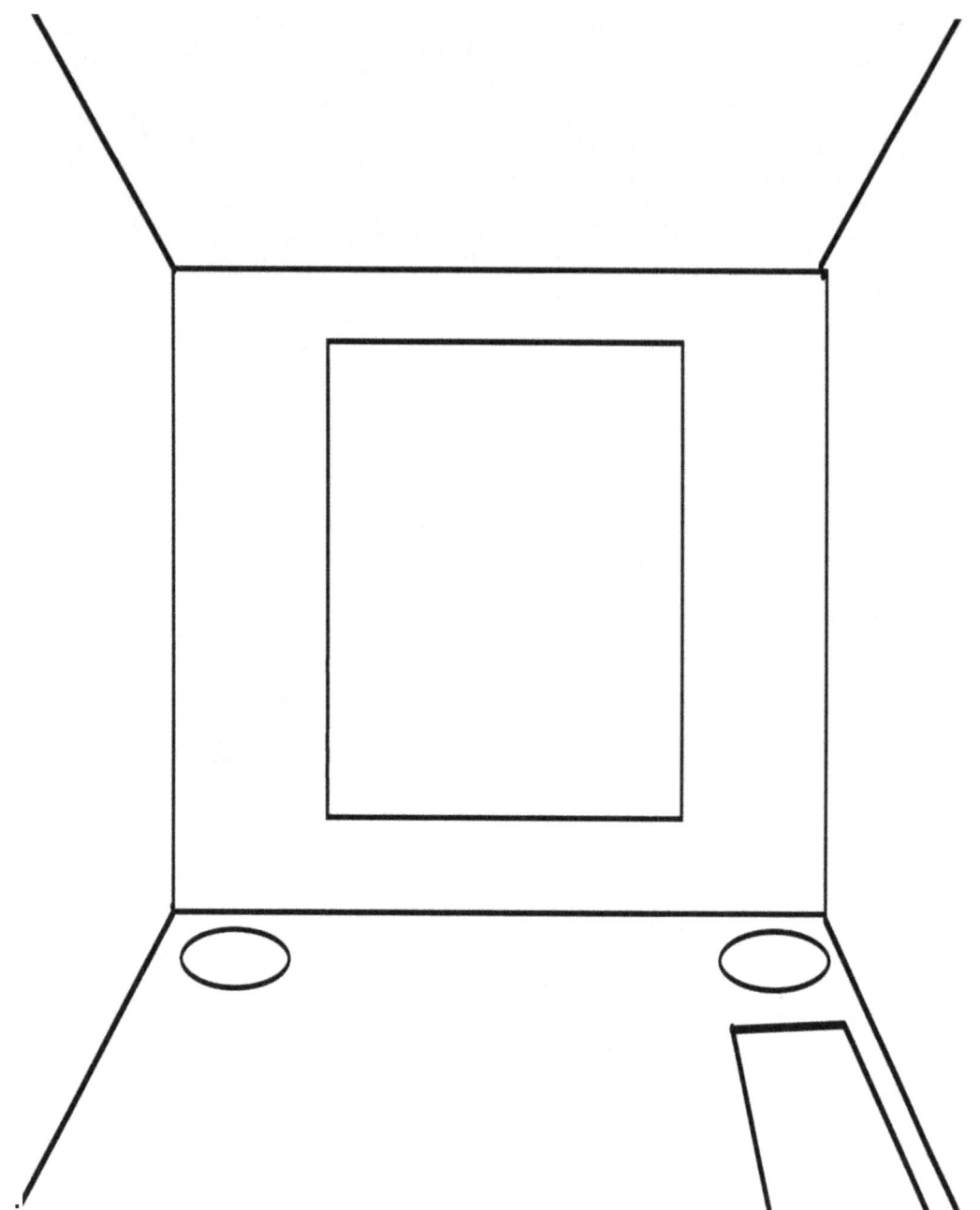

The next two steps are as seen above. So in the one on
the left you start adding in the beginnings of the couch on the bottom

left, and the window in the middle. As you can see it all starts out very basic looking. Nothing to be too intimidated by. In the photo on the right you can see that it adds the light on the ceiling and the crossbar for the curtains.

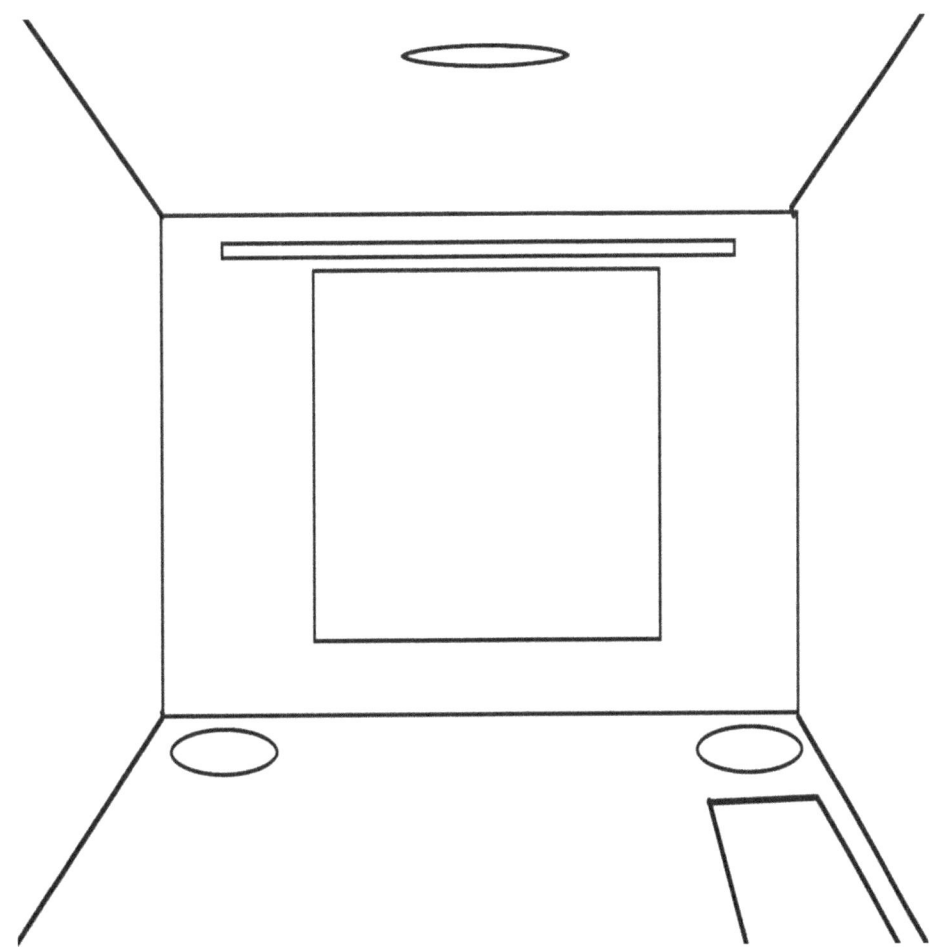

Now in these next two it starts to add more objects and also build on top of older ones with bolder lines. In the photo on the left it adds the pictures on the wall as well as the carpet. Then as you can see there are some thicker outlines on pre-existing objects.

The photo on the right adds upon more of the same with the window frame.

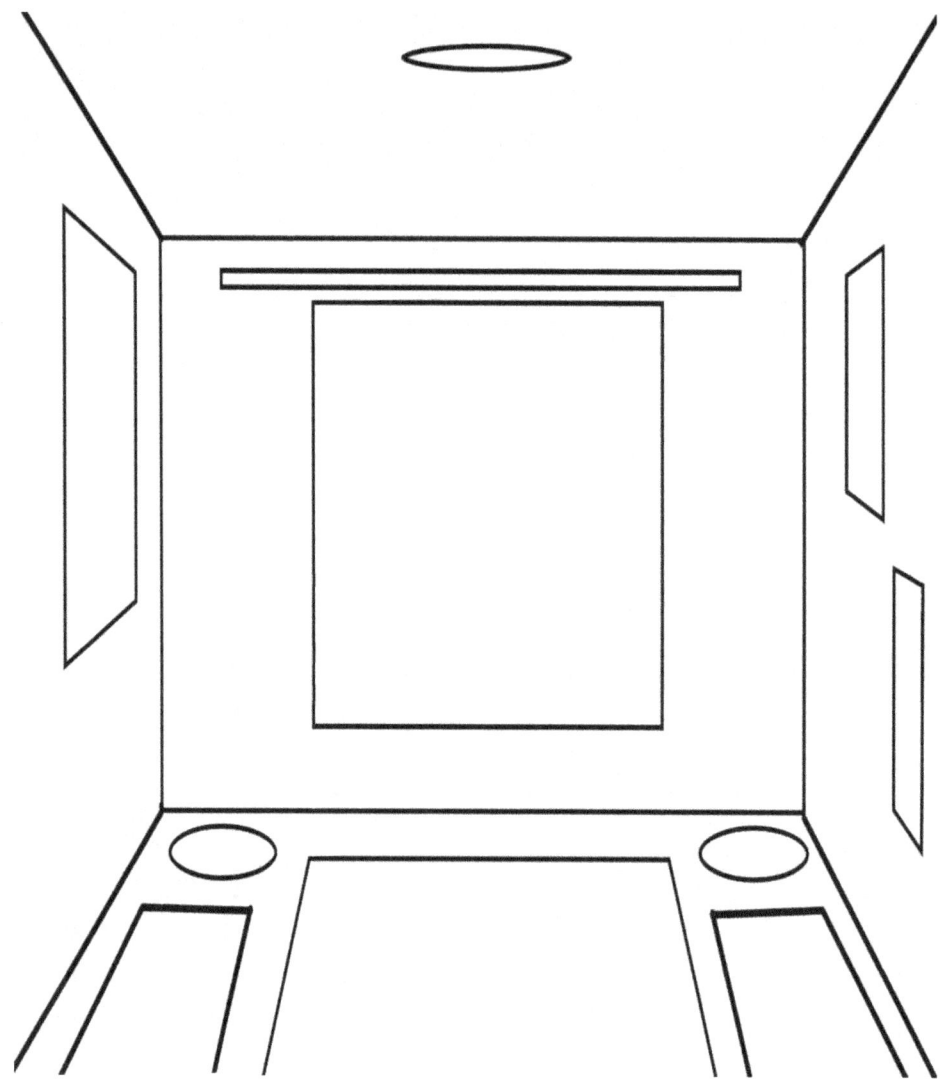

For the next two steps try not to get discouraged but they start ramping up the escalation of additions. In the first one you have more outlining for the photo frames and the window. In the next one we see the first addition of the curtains as well as a lot of detail in the initial production of them.

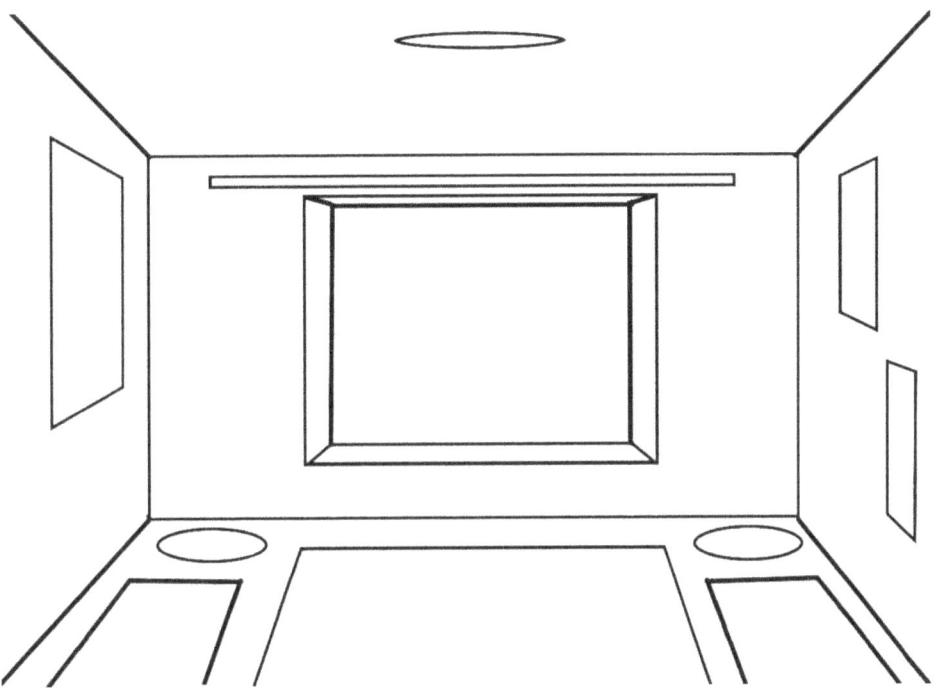

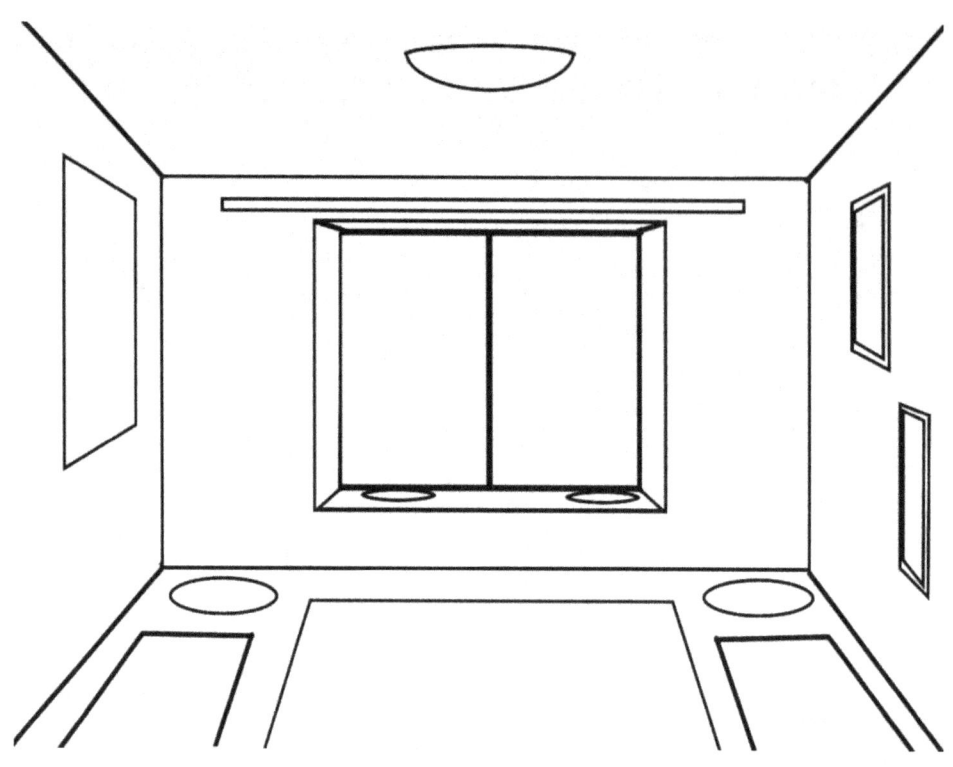

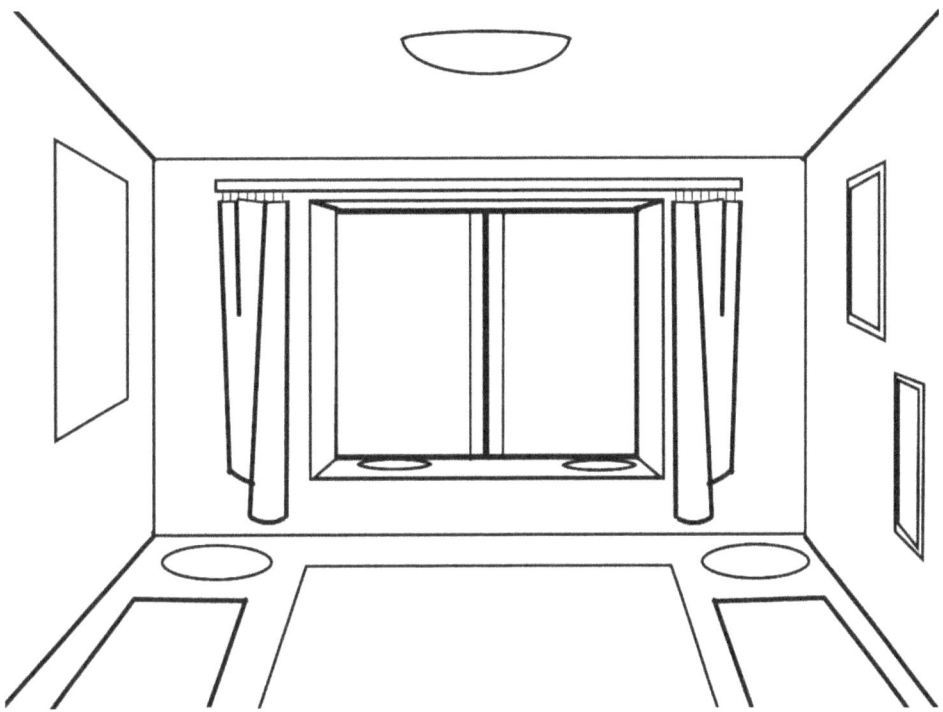

Now the next two are again a little more elaborate, but also more of the same type of idea. You're building on top of pre-existing objects. So keep that in mind as you start to add elements of the couch and the tv stand in the first step, and build even further upon them in the second. Also keep an eye on the picture frames and the carpet.

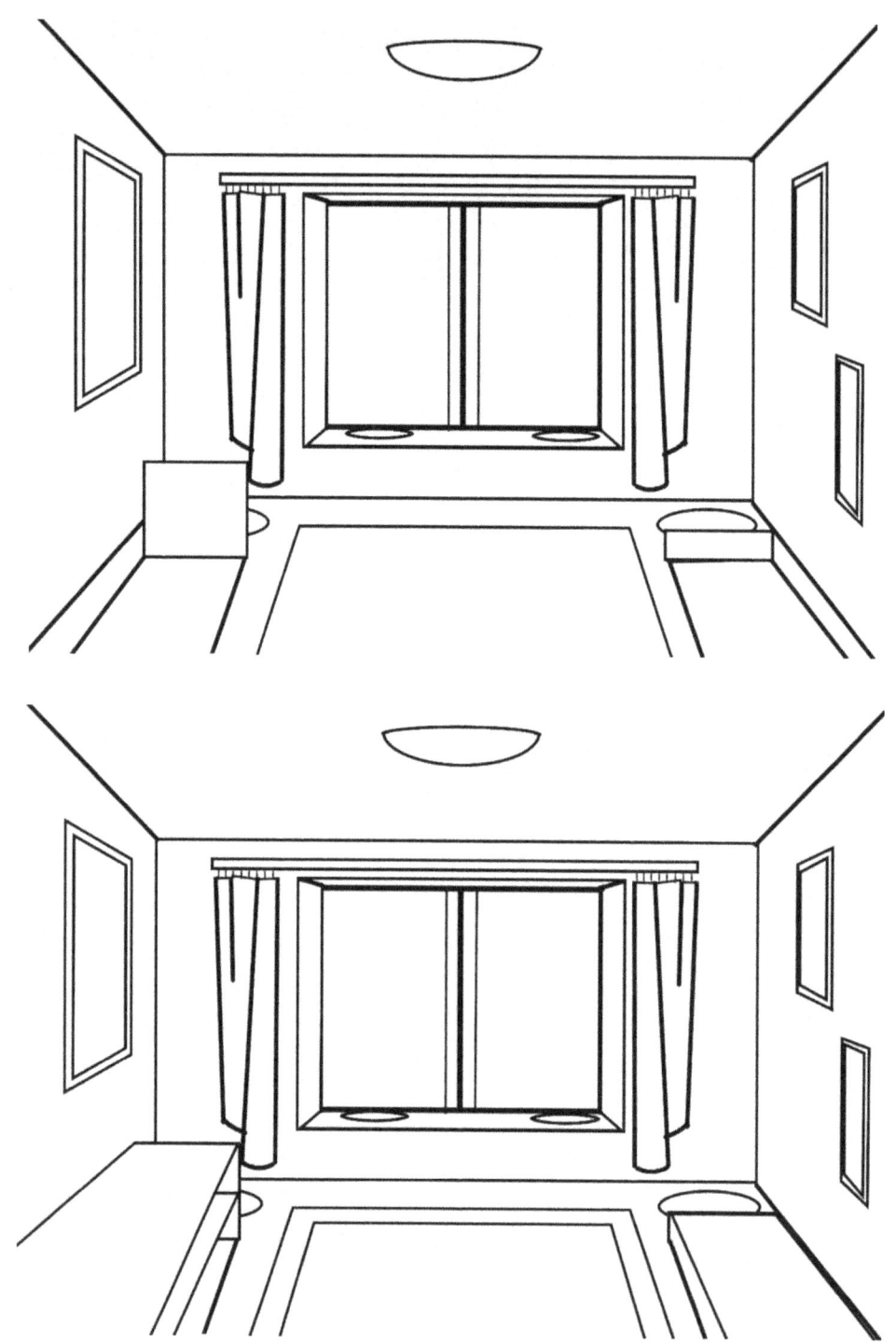

Keeping with the flow of your work, jump right into these next two which add even more detail to the preexisting items and build on the couch. The one on the right finishes off the sofa so.

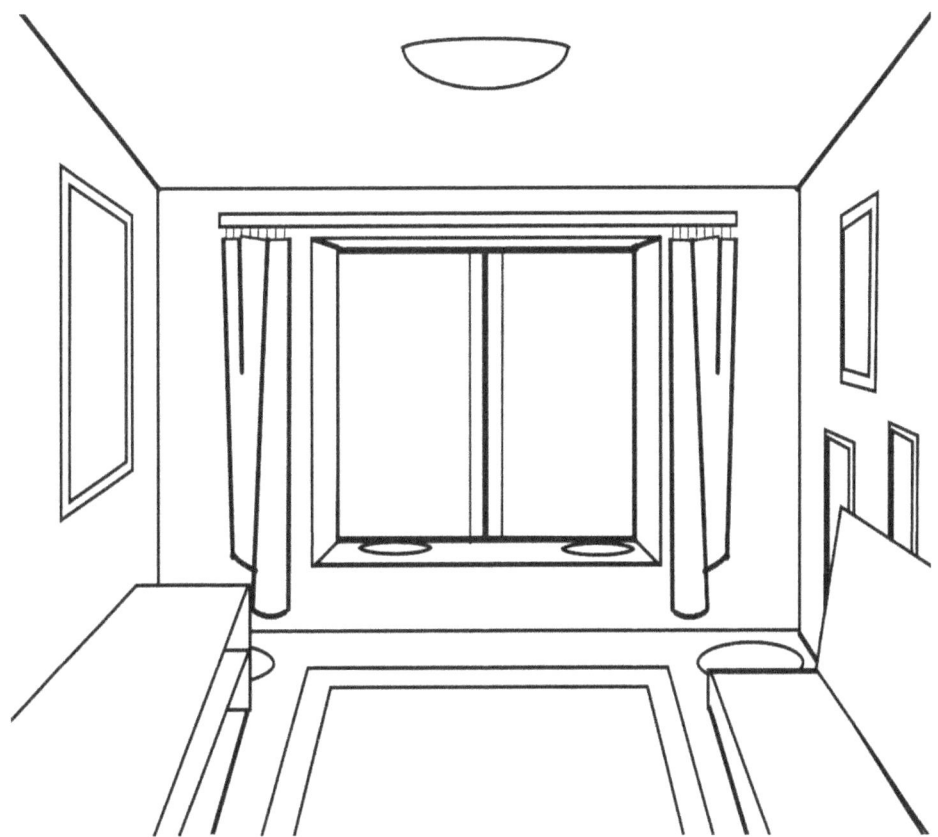

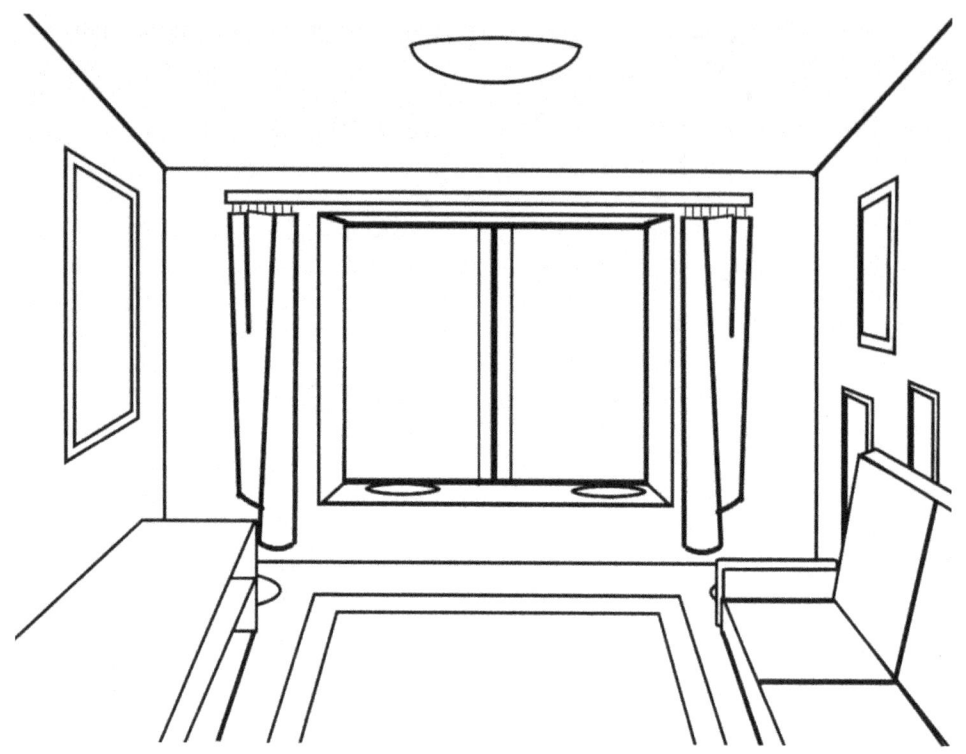

The main thing accomplished in these next two is building the television. Get to it and watch your bold lines!

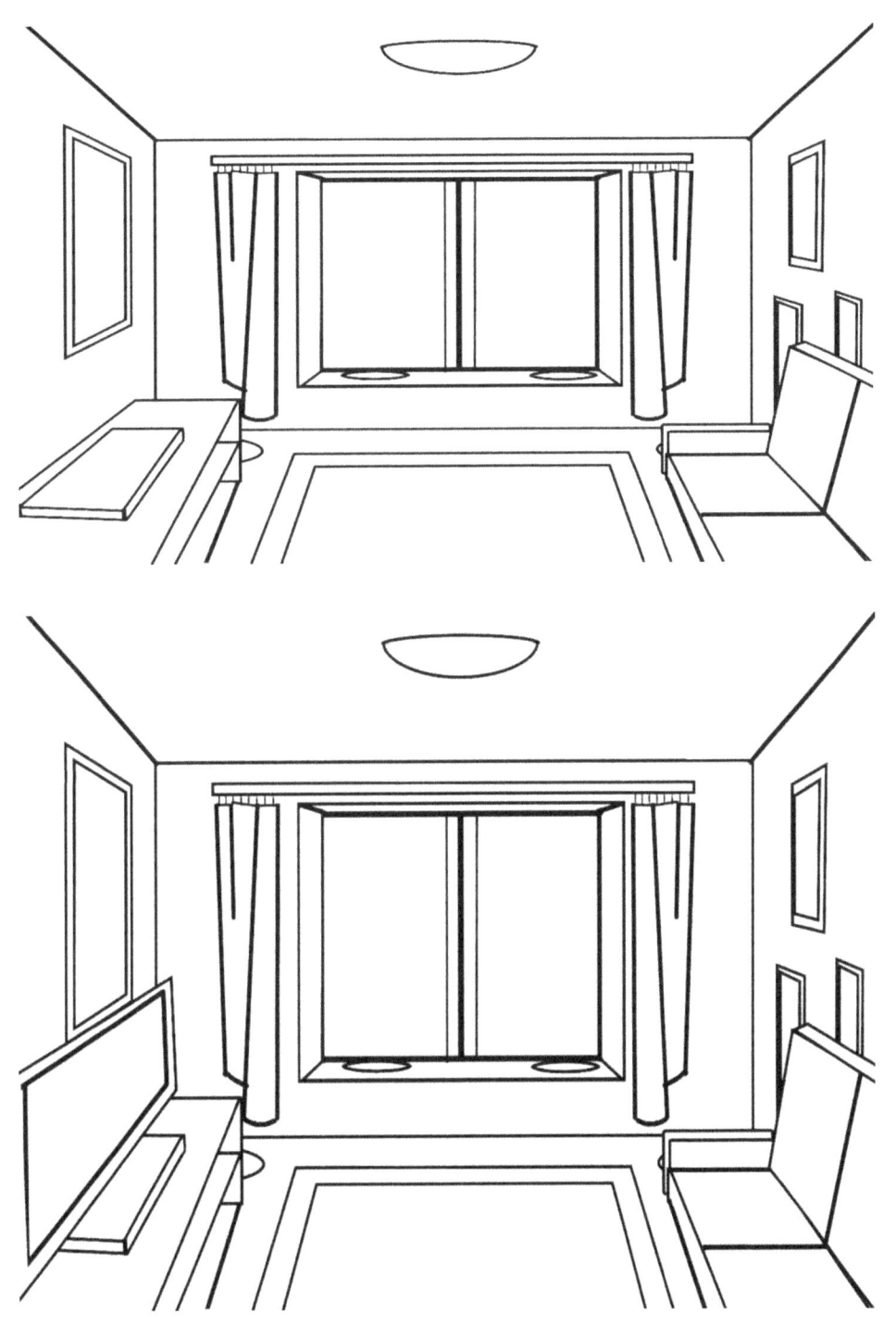

Now we arrive at the shading! The line work is finished and you have your room. So now we move on to actually fleshing out the detail that you already added. Follow the steps below with as much accuracy as you can exert, and you'll see the finished product take shape before your eyes.

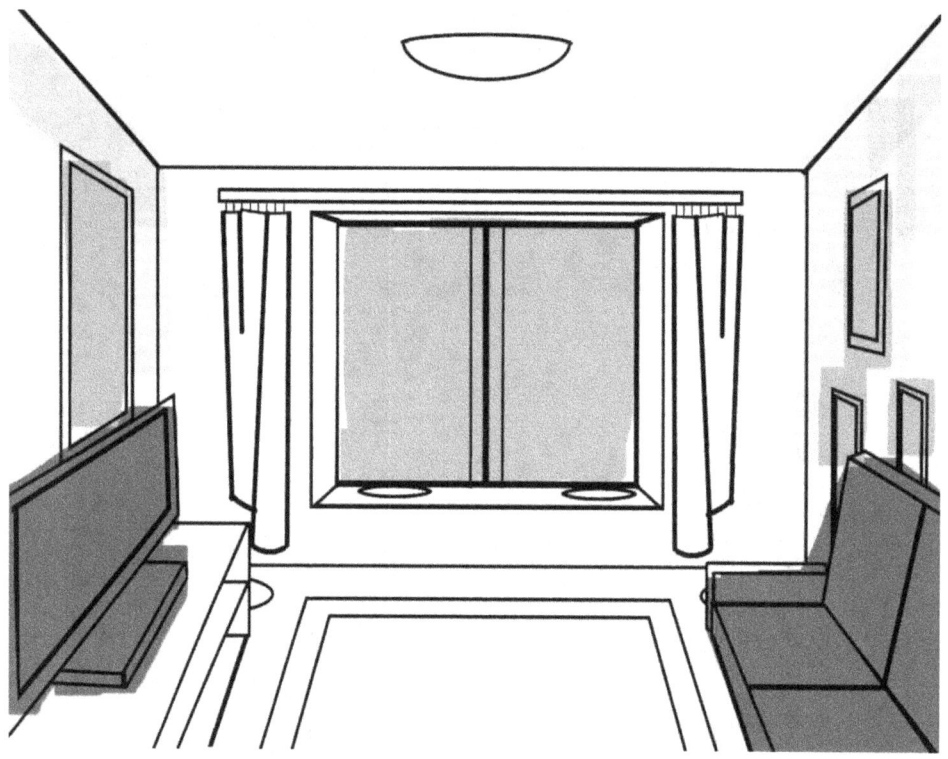

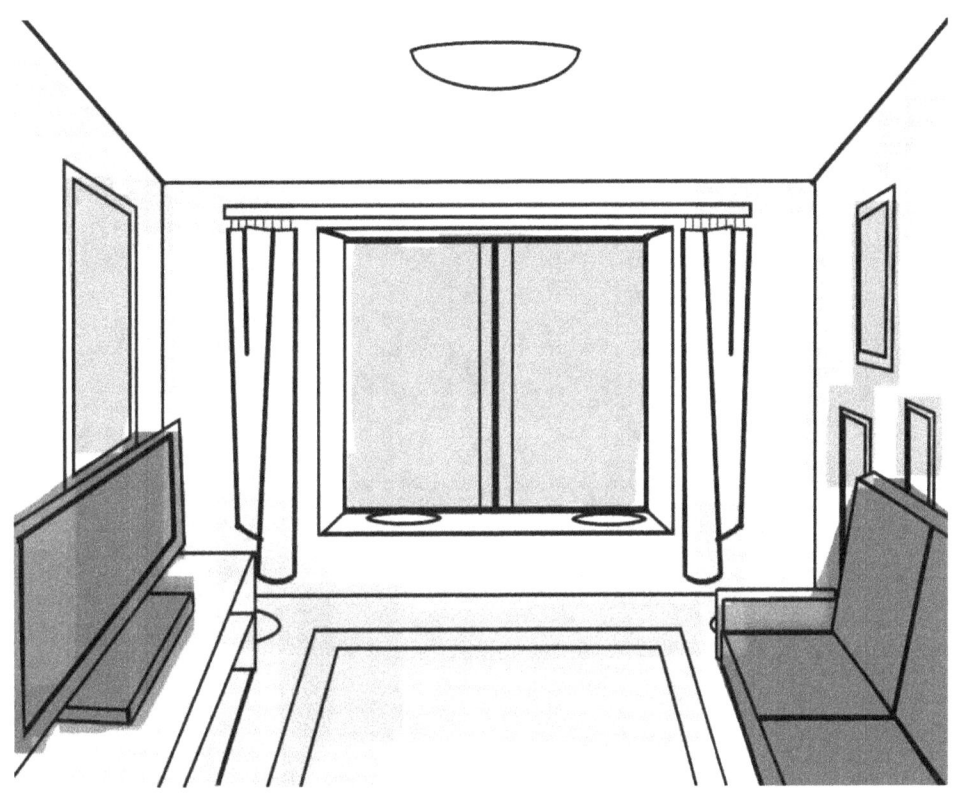

This next level of shading adds even more detail and continues to give the image that polished look. You are almost completely finished. So persist and get that developed look.

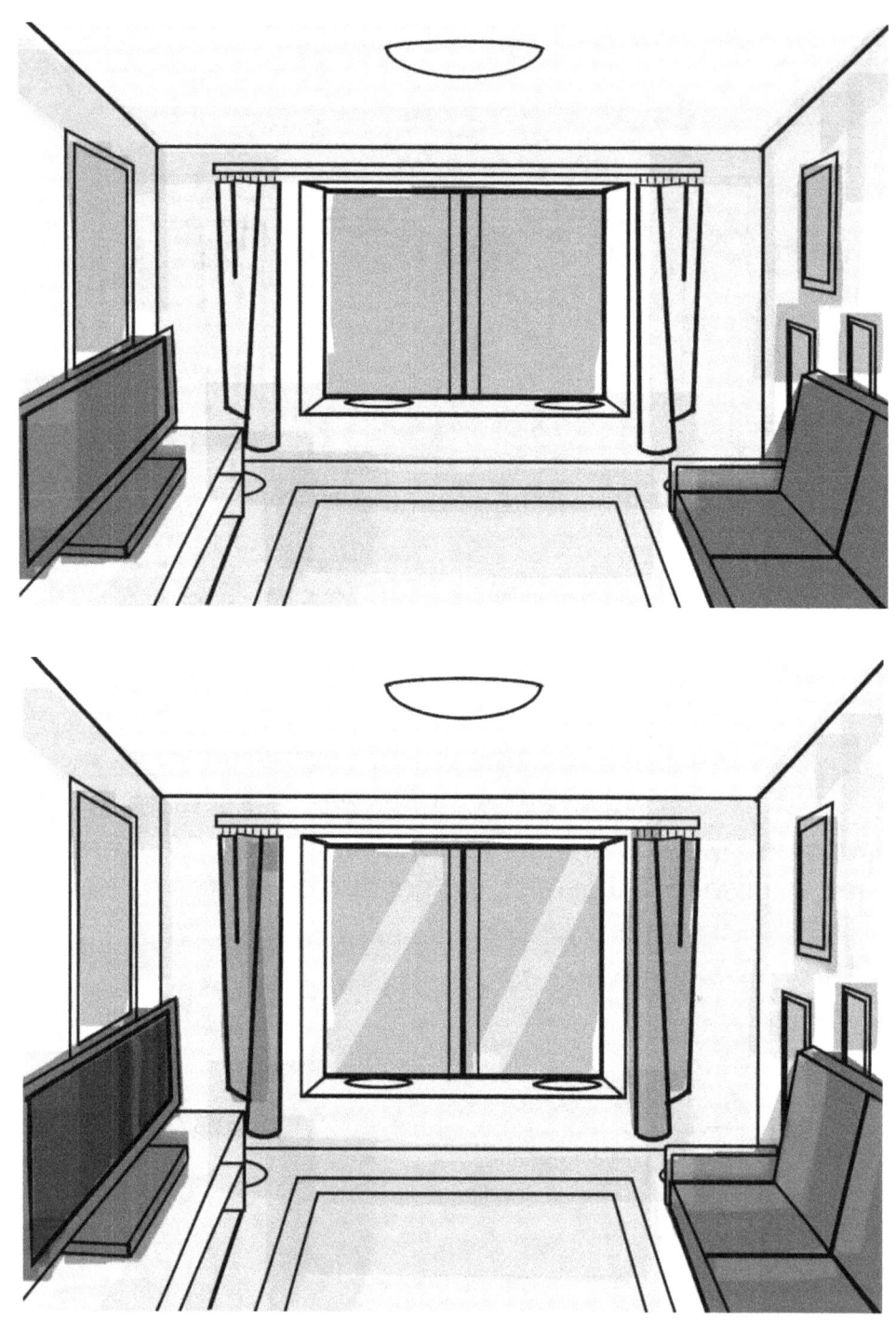

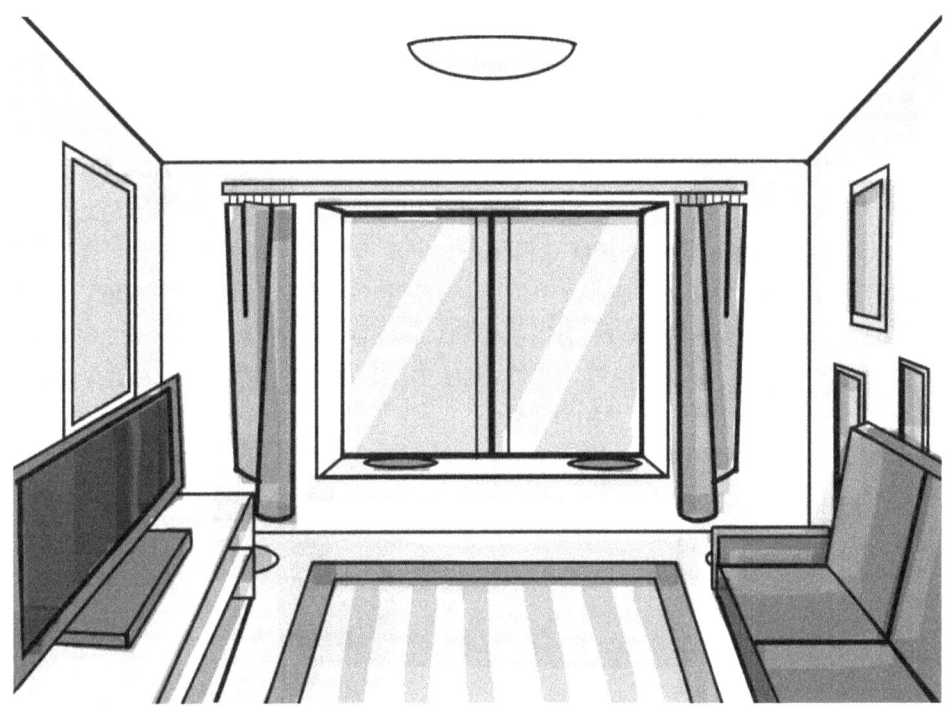

There we go! Your final image should look like the one here on the right! Congratulations on completing your very first perspective drawing. Keep reading and get started on the second one, there's a long road ahead and you're just beginning.

Second Perspective Drawing: Hallway Look Through

For this next drawing there is a much larger focus on the lighting during the shading phase. As you'll notice in the image below on the left there is a much larger amount of heavier shading than in the last drawing we did. Don't despair. It will all become clear to you as we go. So start with the first step on the right, and as before get those straight hard edged lines done.

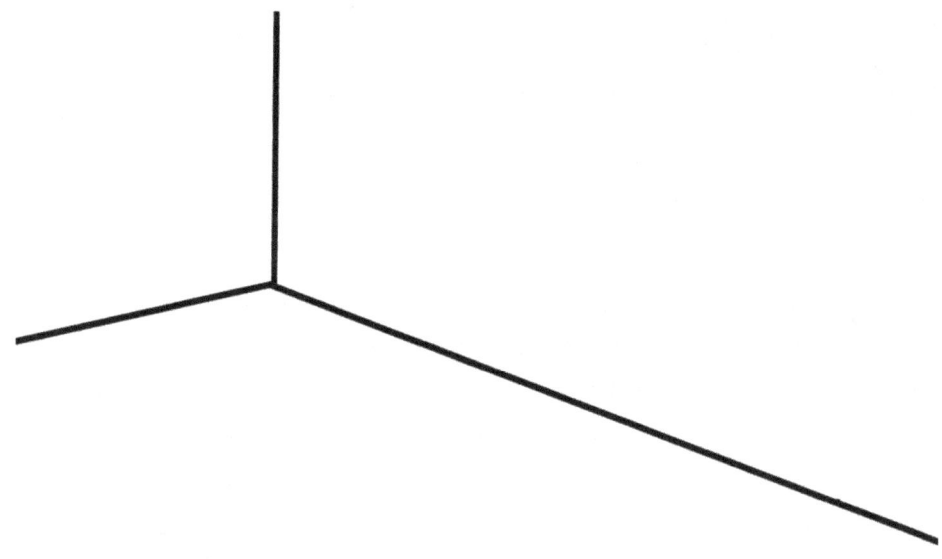

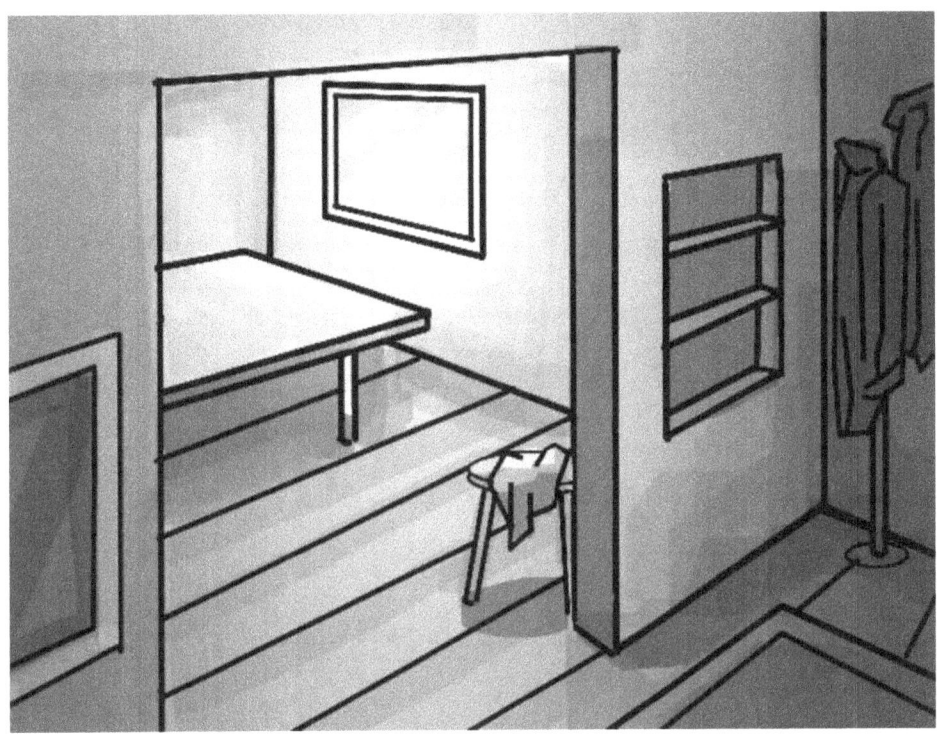

Moving in to the next step you already are required to erase sections of previous lines to make room for new ones. Do as you see in the drawing on the left and then follow procedure again in the next step on the right. This creates the basic foundation of the image.

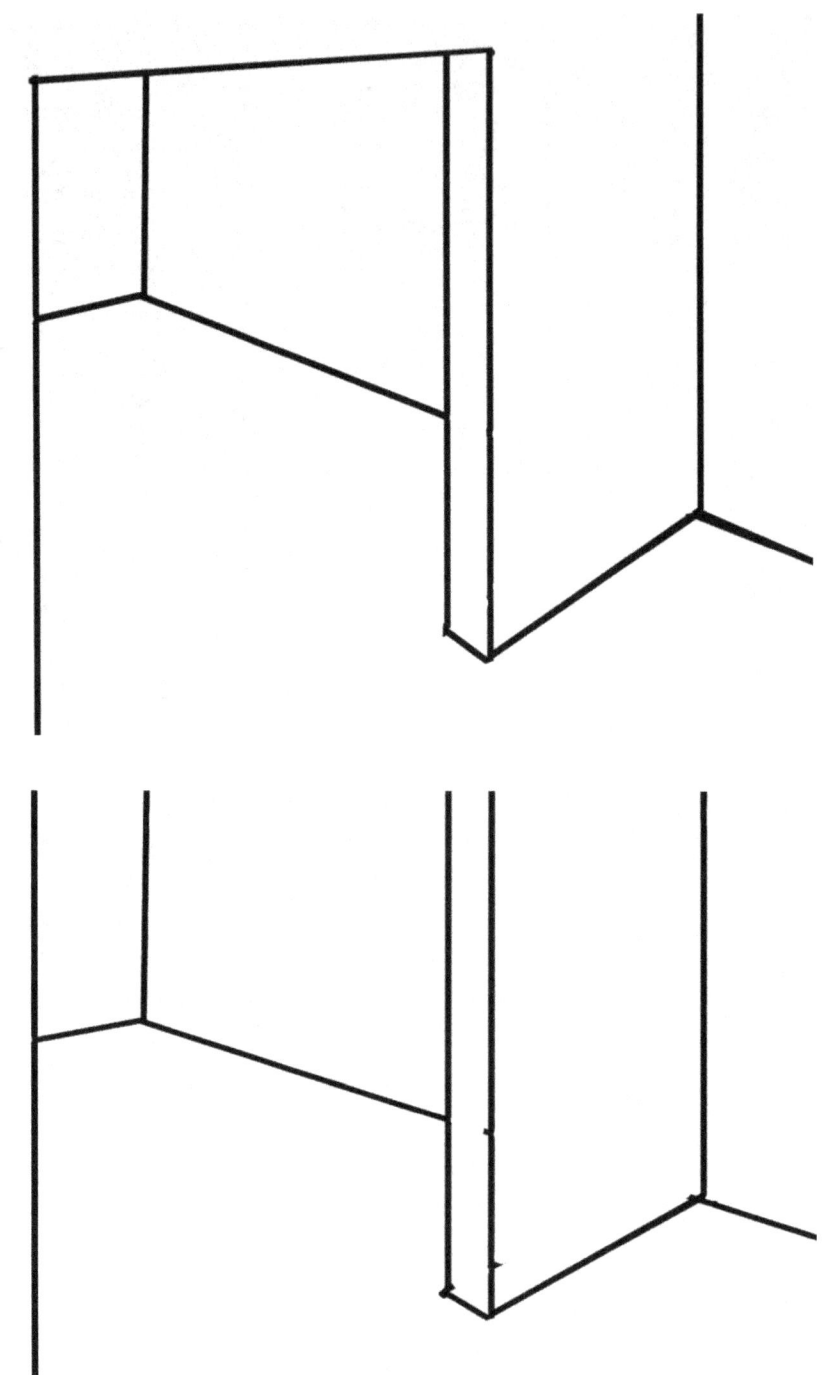

Next steps below, on the next page, are slightly different than the last two. In the first one you're focusing on starting the coat rack. Then in the next one you create the shelf in the wall and the carpet on the floor. Setting the stage for the finished product.

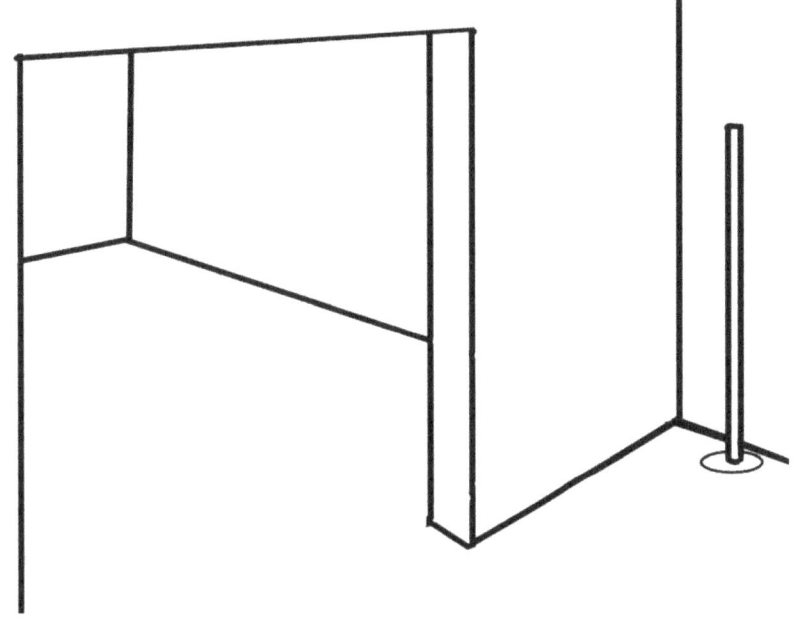

The next steps are for creating more of the actual furniture that occupies the space. In the first step it's the table for focus. Then in the step after that we craft the stool and the window. Fairly basic steps but integral to the finished product.

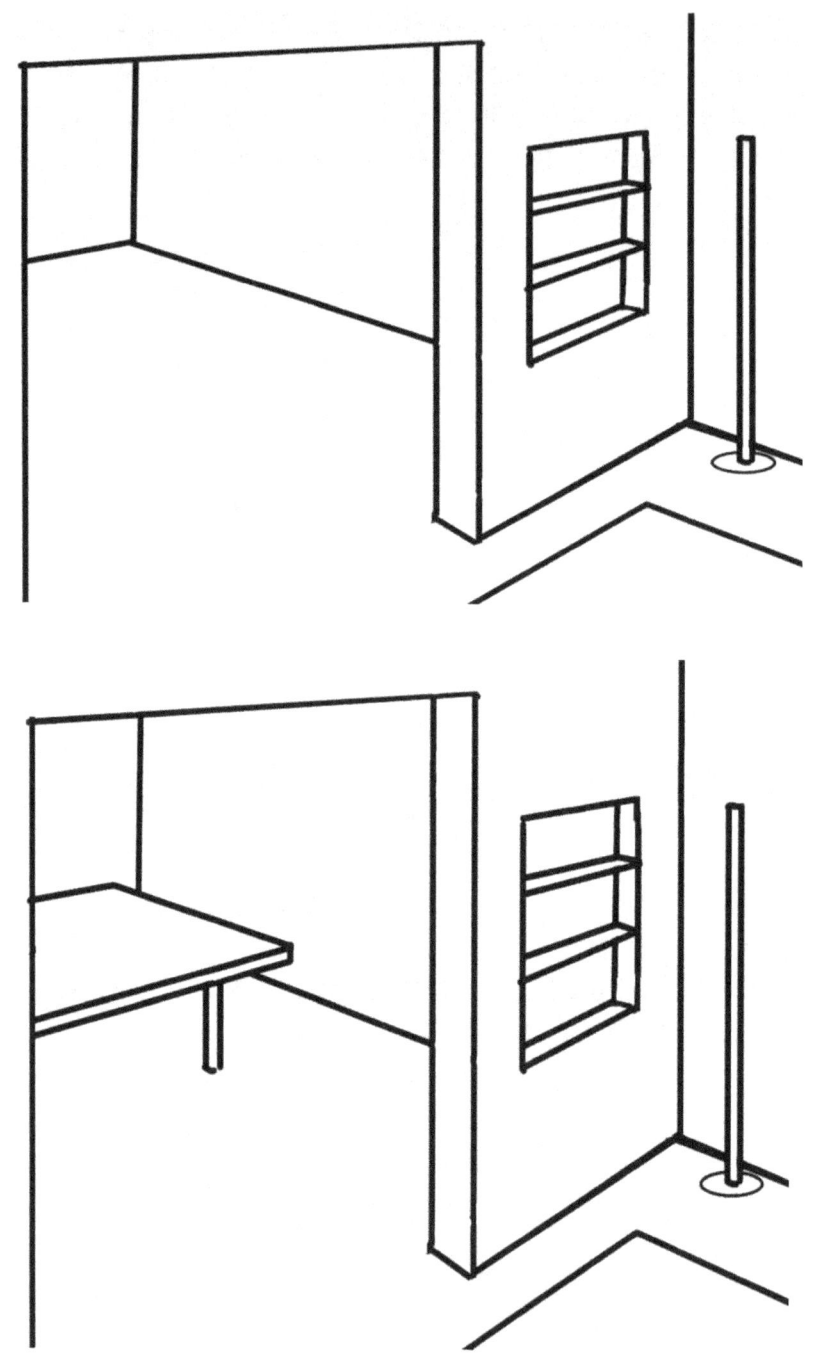

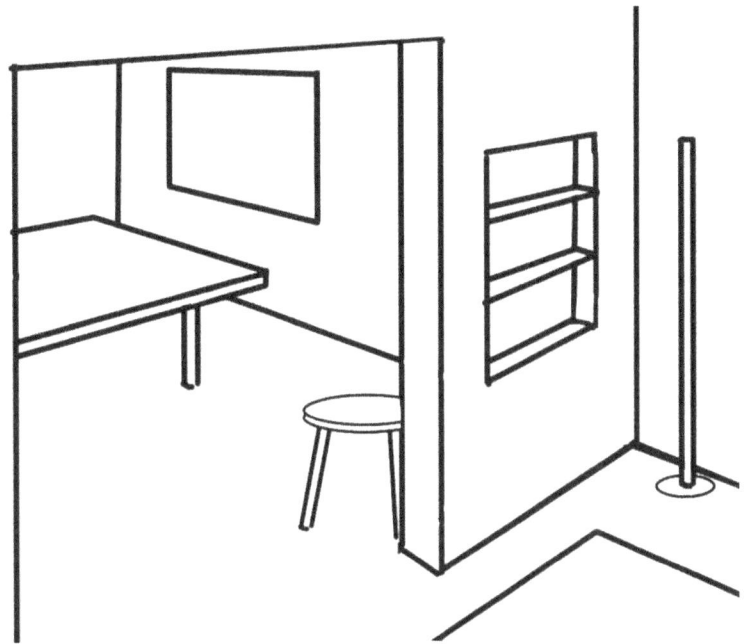

Now comes the slightly more elaborate steps. Doing the lining on the floorboards and the detail on the carpet and the photo frame in the hall. DOn't forget about the coat on the rack in the hallway and you'll nail these next two steps without flaw. Pay attention to the hard edges and don't sacrifice any design.

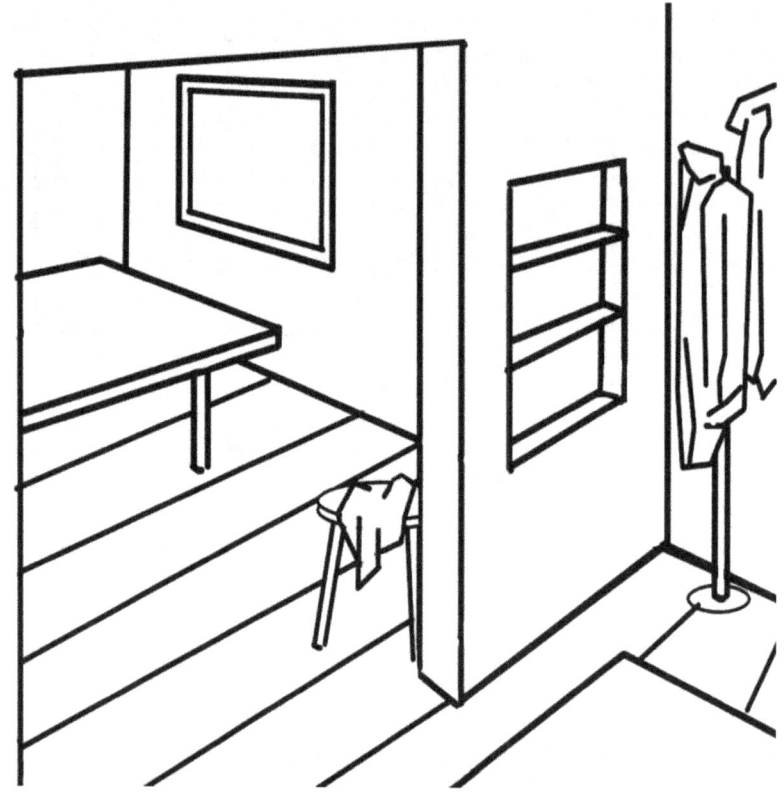

Now we embark on the most important aspect of this specific perspective drawing. The shading! As you'll notice below it starts dark right away and then moves into the lighter territories afterwards. So follow suit and make sure you're following the images for accuracy. The best bet would be to keep track of where the shading overlaps and where its at it most thin.

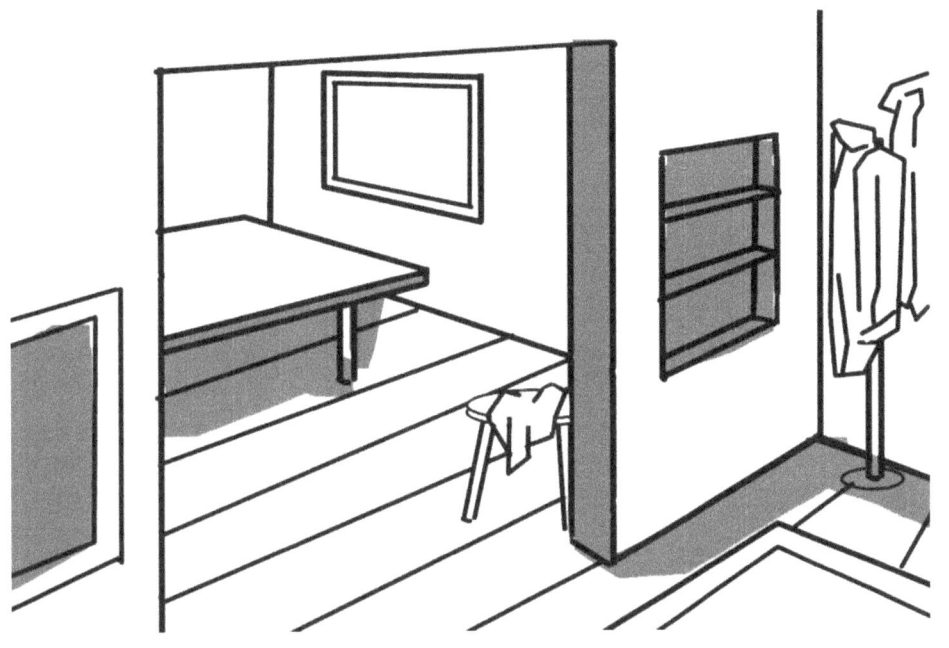

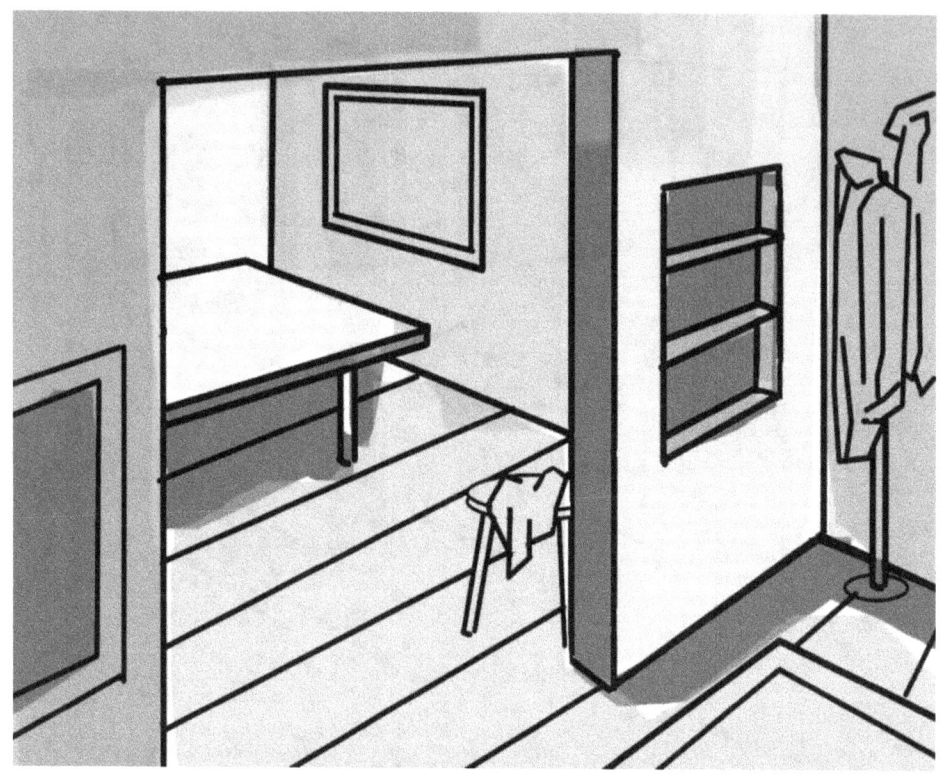

The final two steps are the most shading heavy yet. You'll see a major increase in darker patches of shading as well as an emphasis of dark in the hallway. Follow the differences and you'll have a perfect looking perspective image! In ones like these you need to watch out for the difference in the light and dark shading. This helps develop stronger abilities when detecting your own perspective image.

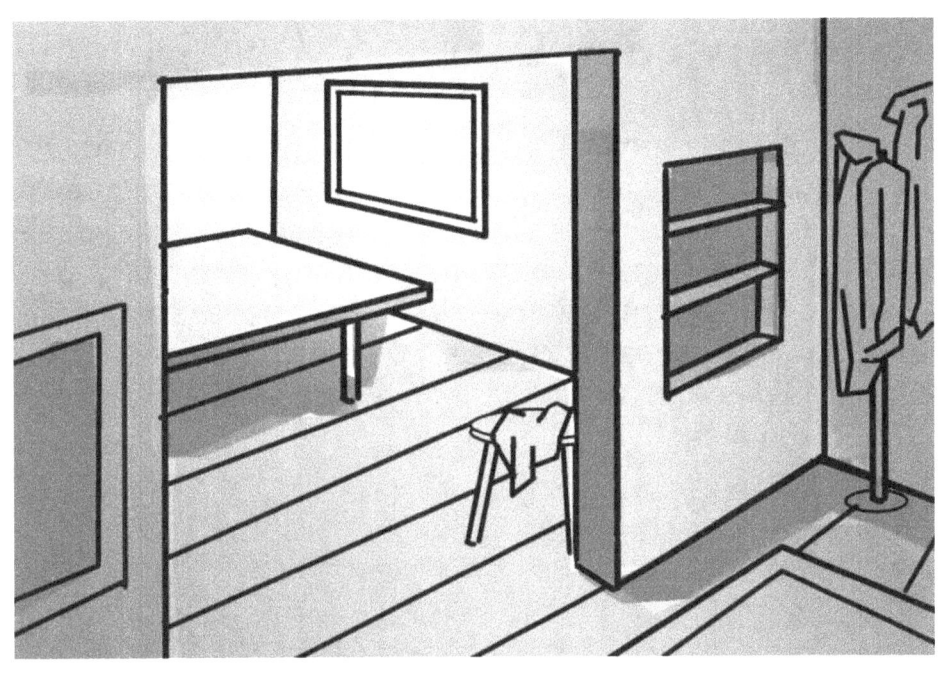

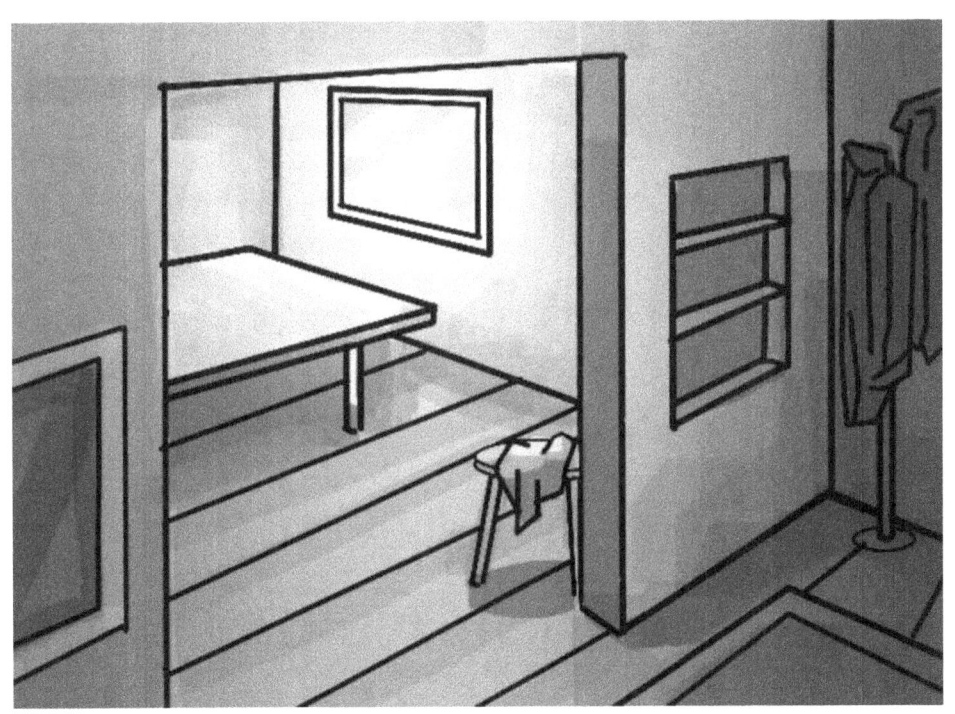

Third Perspective Drawing: Loft Hideaway

This next drawing utilizes more shapes that we haven't had much experience with as of yet. Most specifically curved shapes and circles. As you can see in the first image below there is also an emphasis on the shading as in the last drawing we did. If you look at the image on the right you see that there is a vast difference between the two images, of course. What you should keep in mind is the visible lines that inevitably require changes. Make your lines hard edged and straight and jump right in.

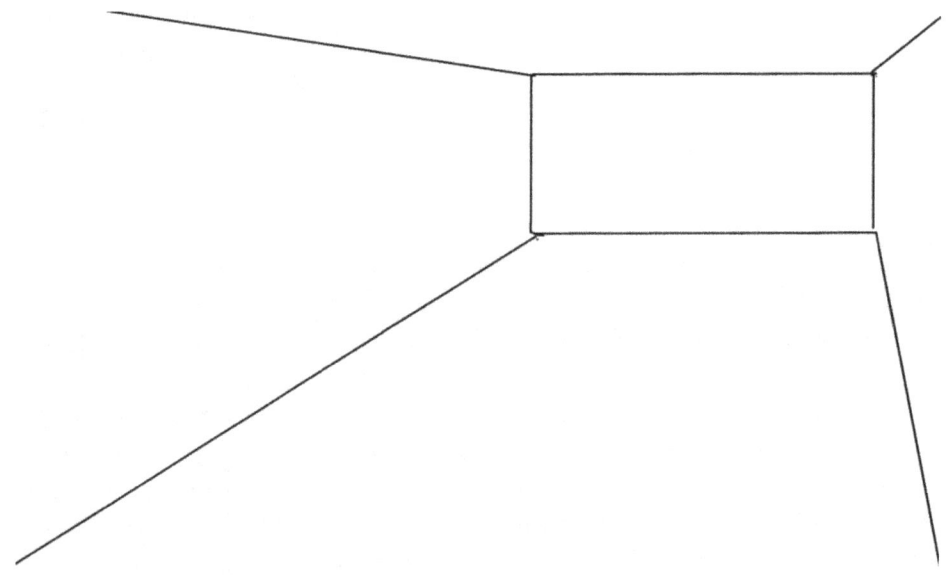

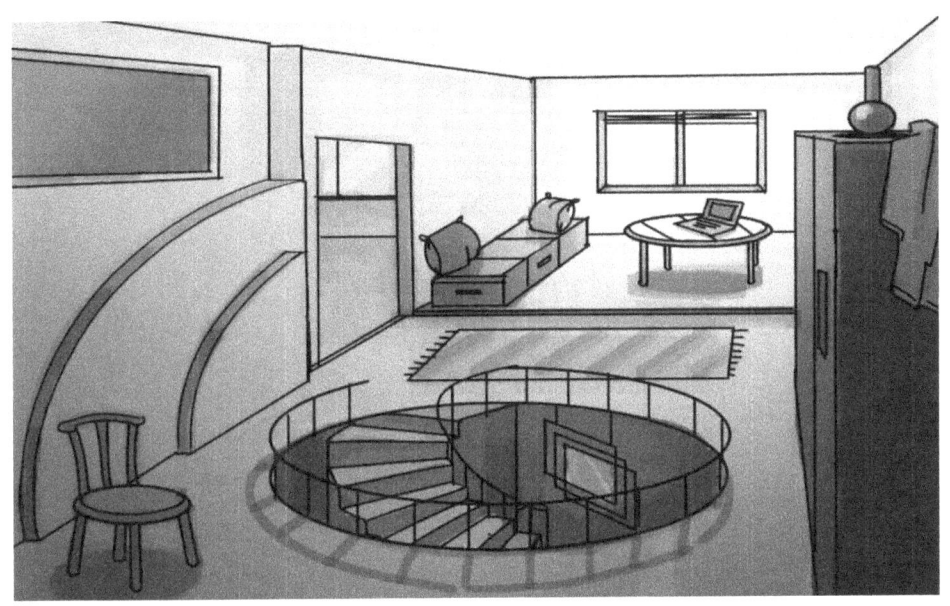

The next two steps require manipulation of the preexisting lines like we learned in the last drawing. The first step adds a doorway and the bookshelves and cabinets. The second one adds in the fancy architecture that you see in the first drawing. Another instance of paying attention to your line-work.

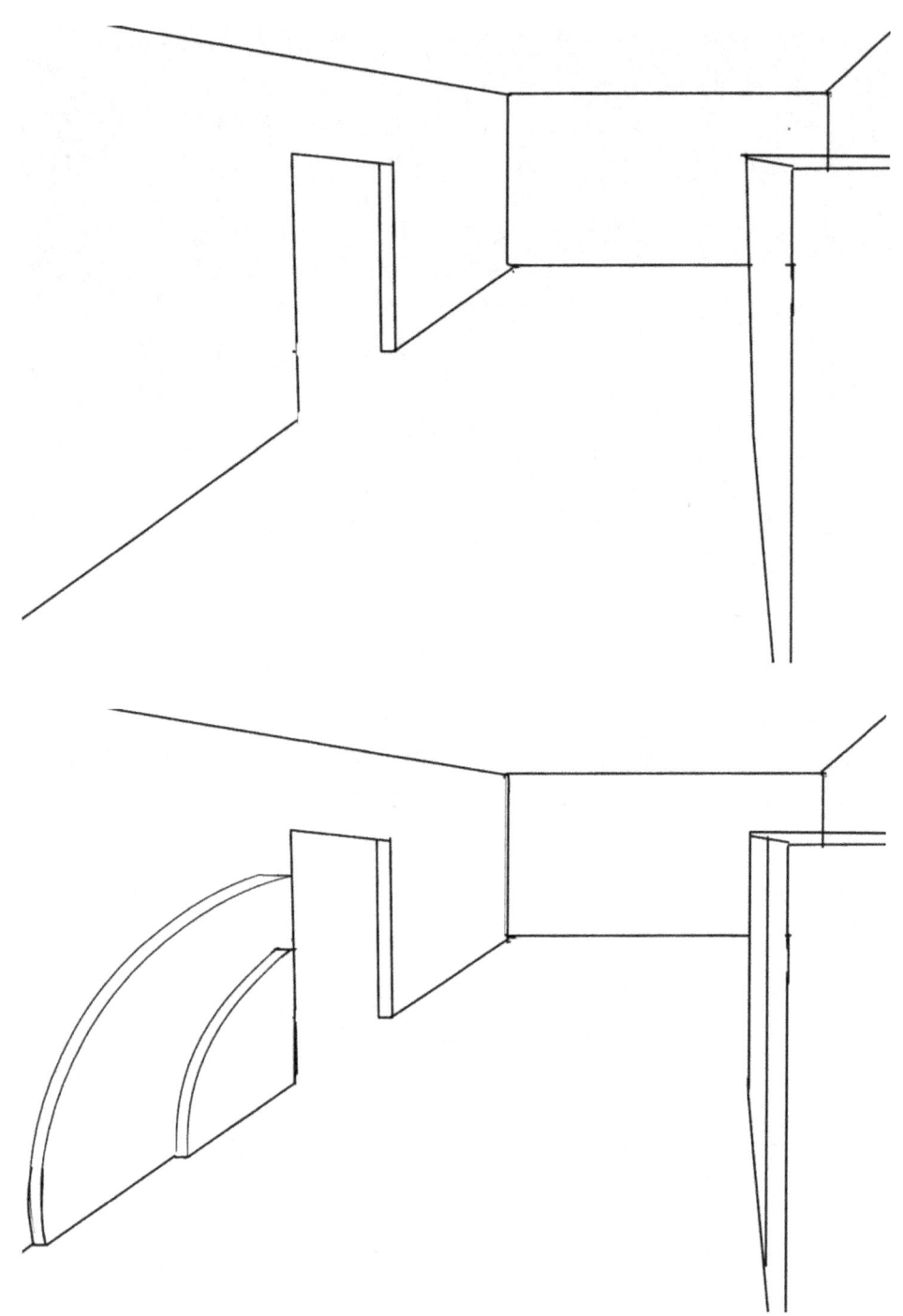

For the next two steps we focus on adding items and structure to the environment of the drawing. The most important addition is probably going to be the lines for the window and the step up into the back room of the loft, so keep an eye on the intricate details and push through these next two steps.

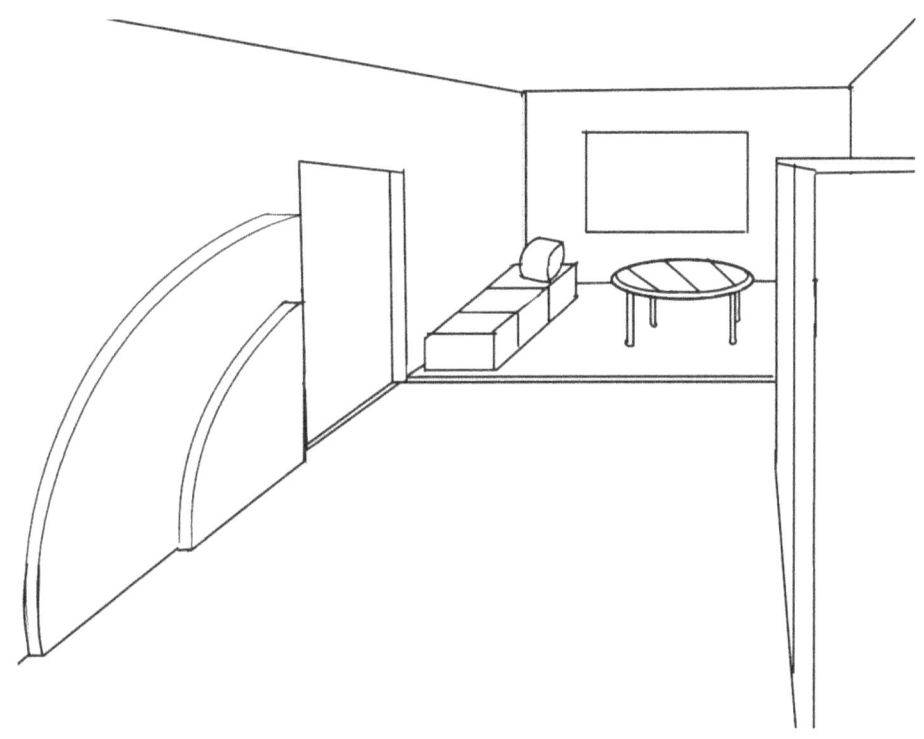

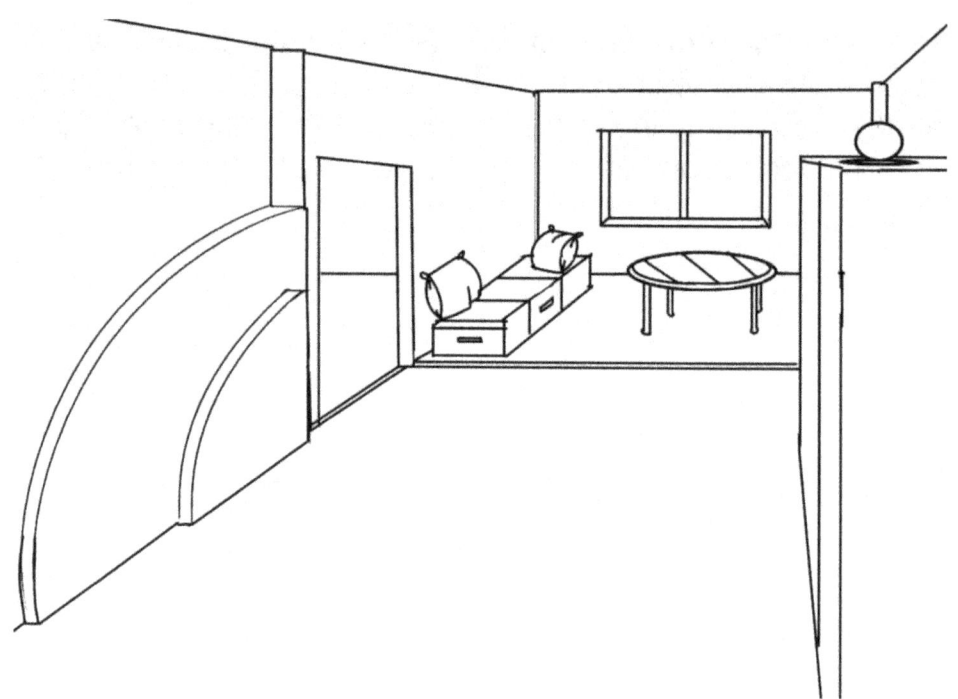

Moving on to the next set of steps you'll see that is what you literally will be starting on. The steps. Sketching in this round staircase may seem somewhat tricky at first, but its all about angles and the initial circle and two curved lines. Once you nail those its smooth sailing.

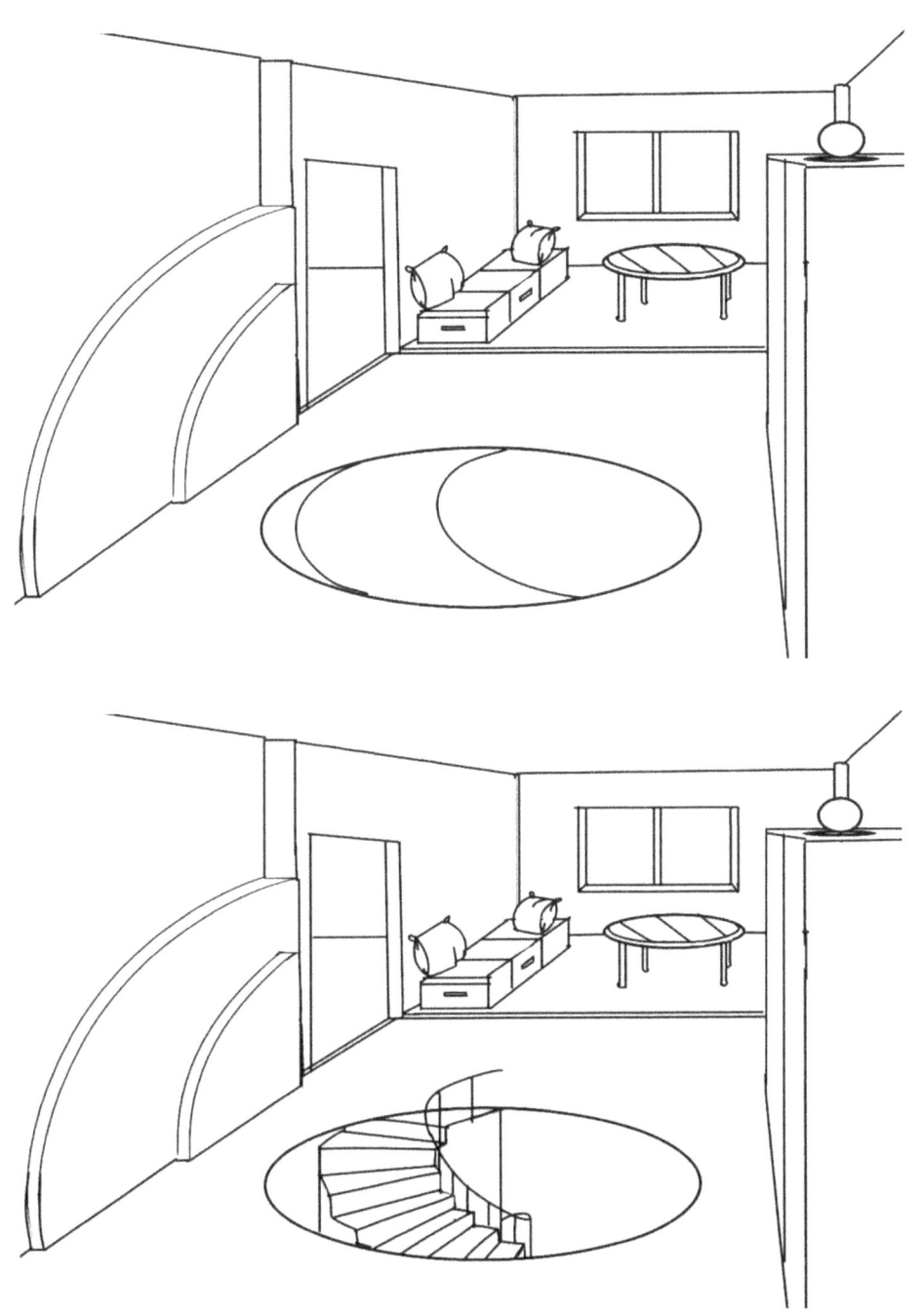

These next couple steps focus on several additions of items as well as detail on the staircase. Pay attention to your lining on the curves and look out for any small additions you might miss.

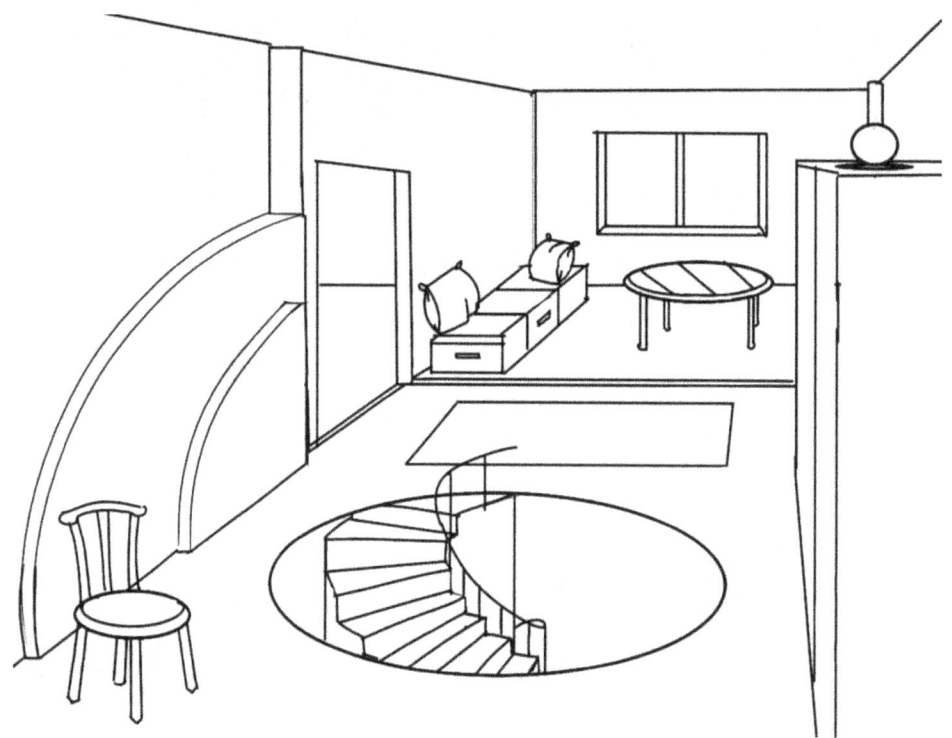

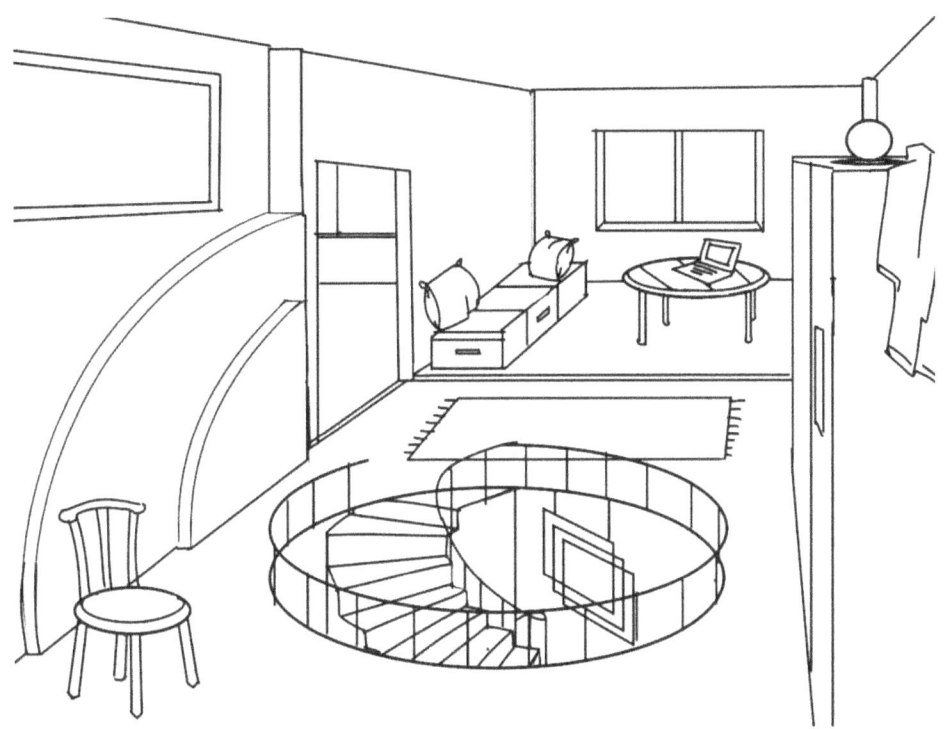

Paying attention to the image on the left first, you'll notice that it adds aa few final little delicate touches to the image before the shading starts. Then in regards to the shading you can see that it too starts heavy and dark like the last image.

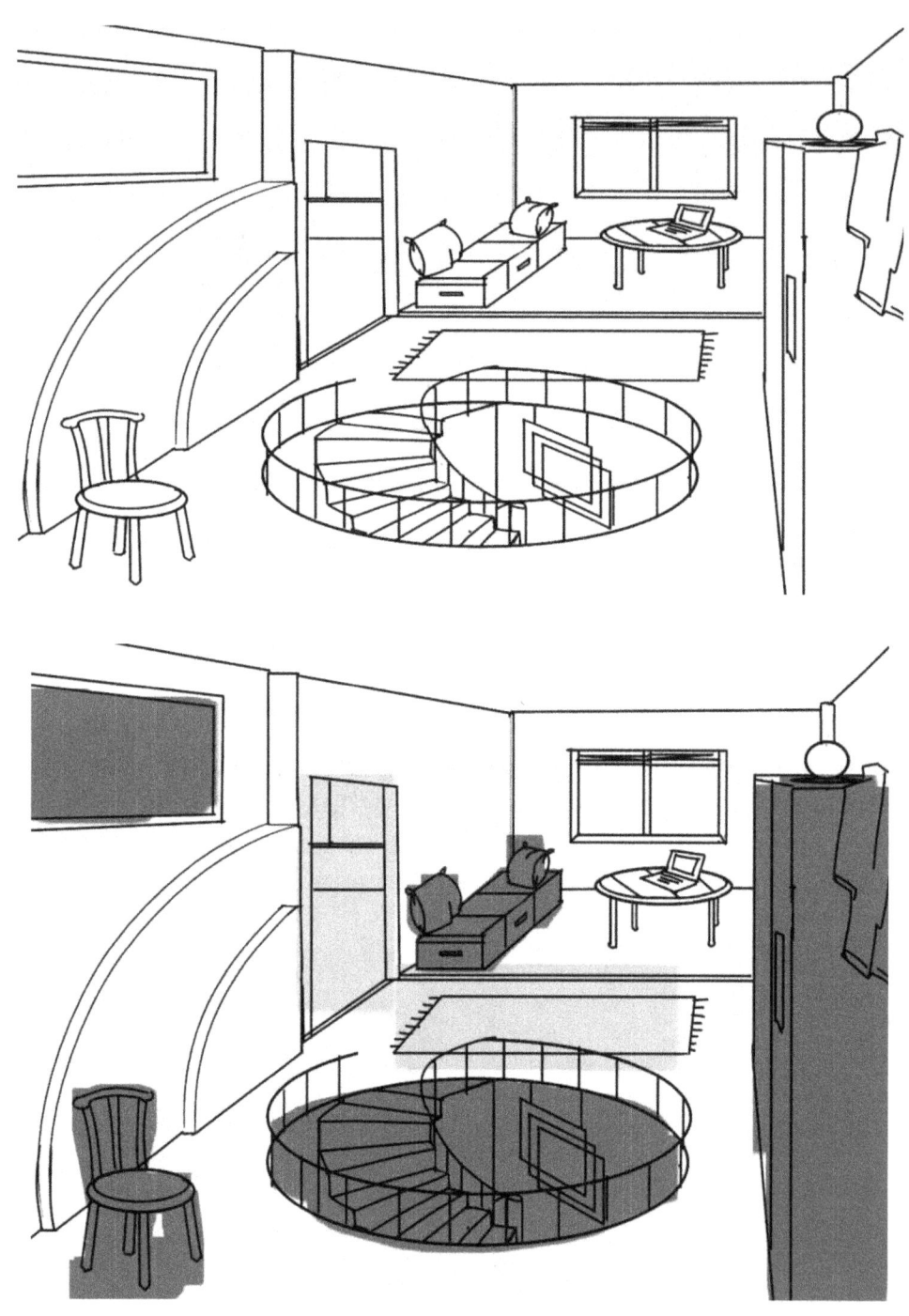

Continue the shading by adding the lighter areas and blending them in with the darker ones until you have a nice even grouping of shades. Which will really accentuate the lighting patterns.

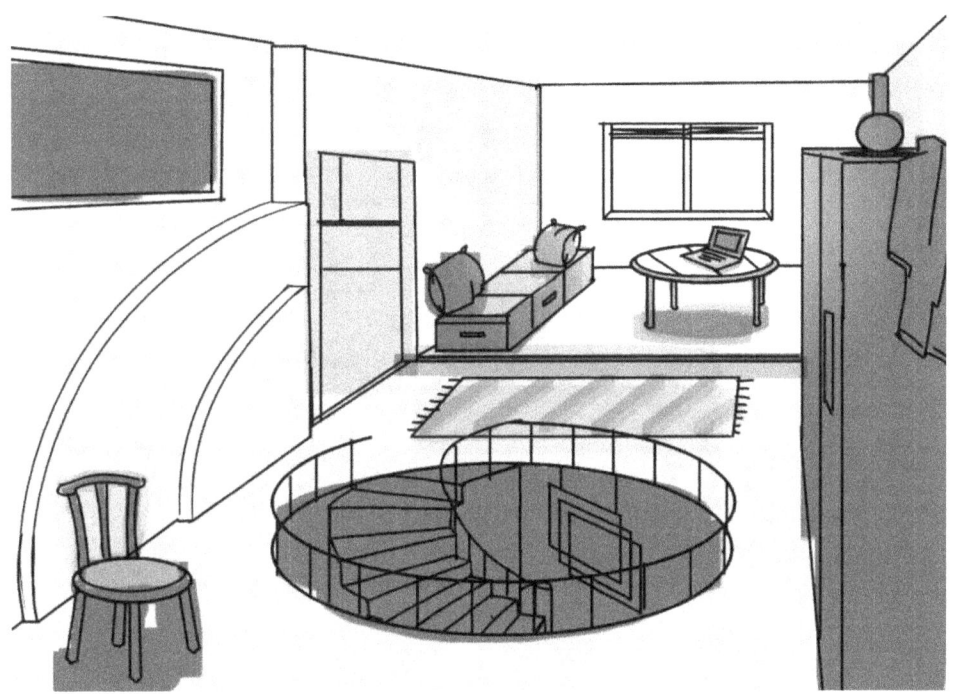

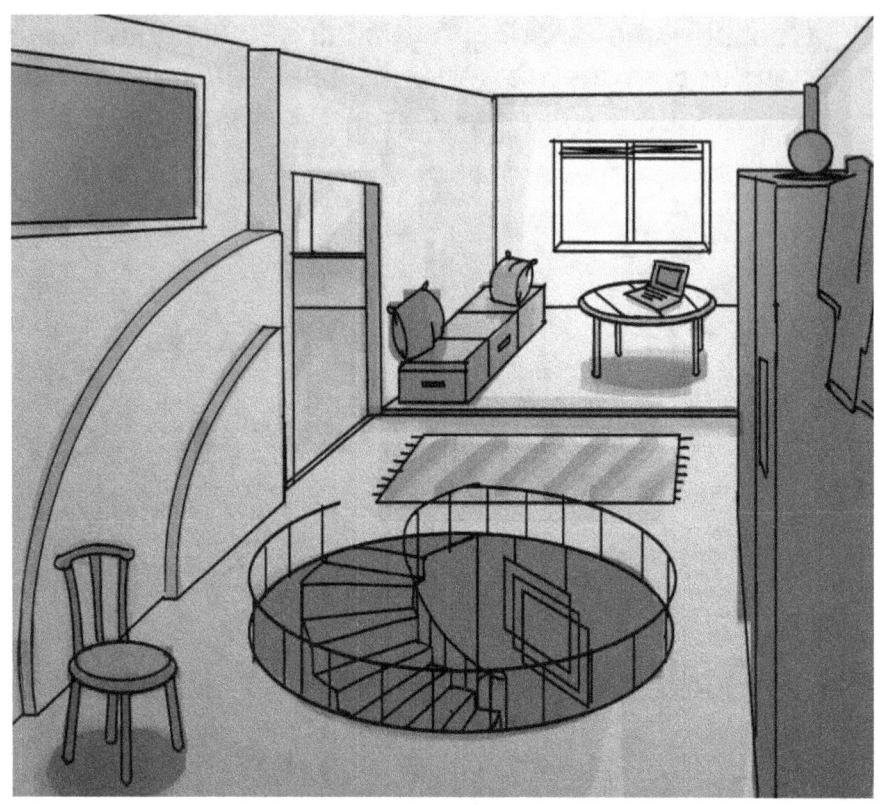

The final steps are a lot like the last two, finish up the blending in the first image on the left, and then it's the final serious details that make it a complete image. Adding the highlights and final focus features to the staircase and the carpet. Then you'll have completed another perspective drawing! These are flying by eh?

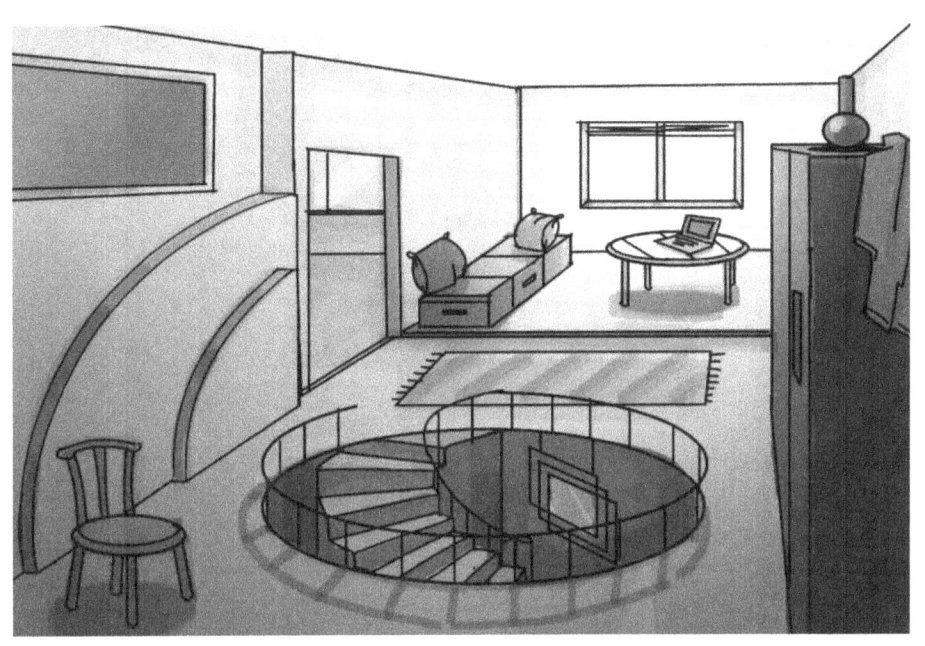

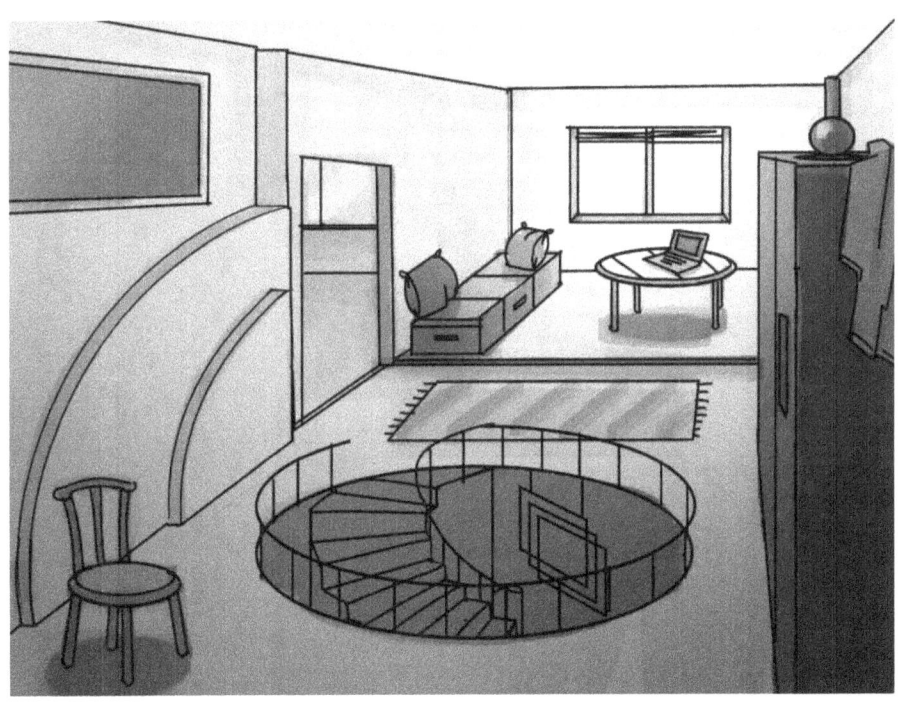

Fourth Perspective Drawing: Exterior Building

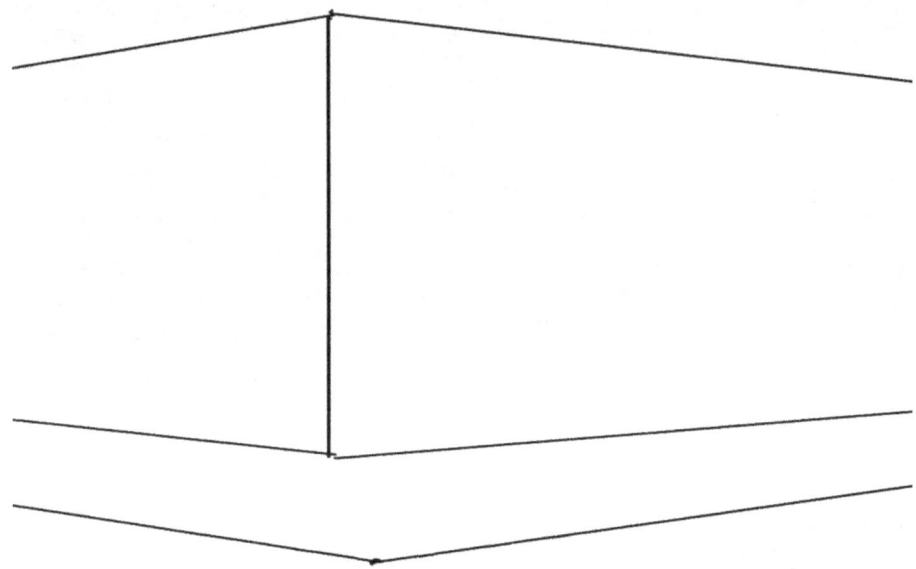

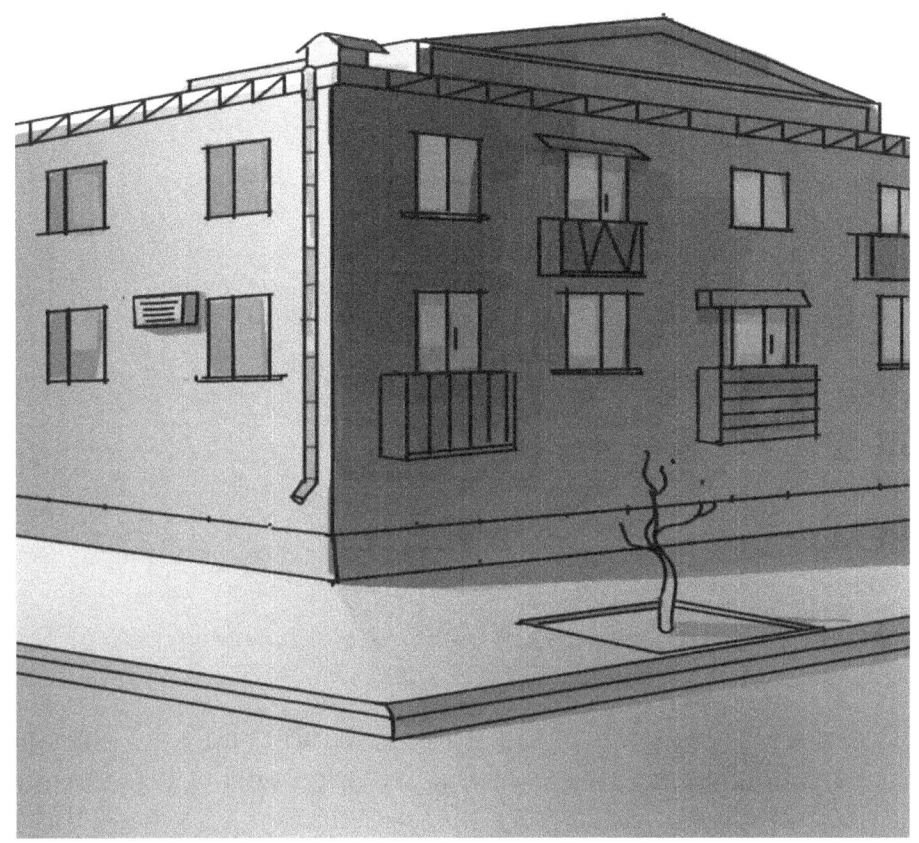

Here we are, on drawing number four, at long last. This is another huge step in a different direction for us. This time were doing an outdoors shot of a building. An exterior building wall. As you can see there's another huge focus on the shading and the lighting. This time, however, you'll notice that we're going in the opposite direction with the perspective. Follow the first step there on the right and let's get into this one.

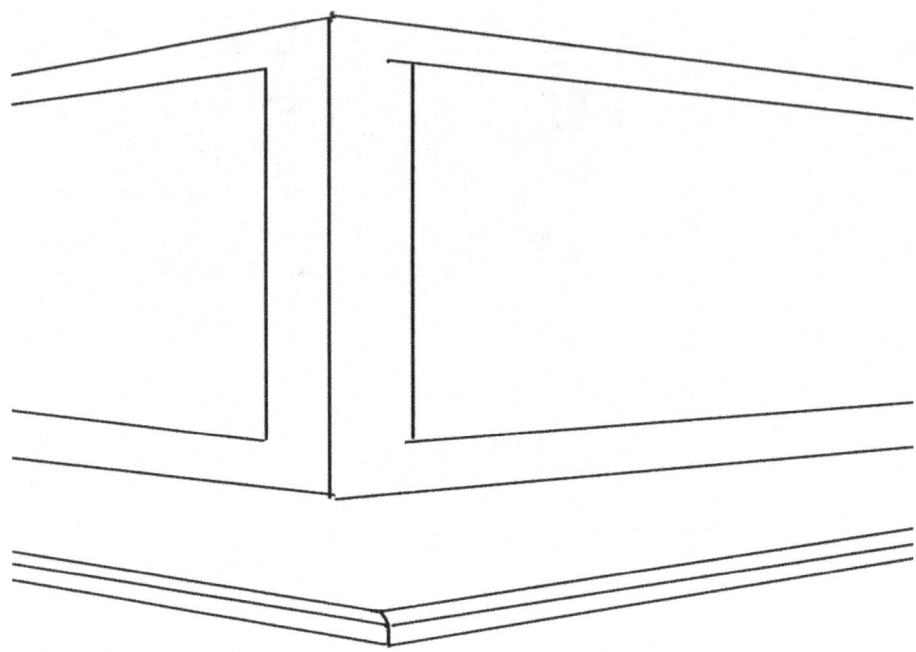

Then once the main lines are drawn in, you can start adding more of the basic foundation of the exterior wall. You can see the start of the windows as well as the addition of layers to the street corner.

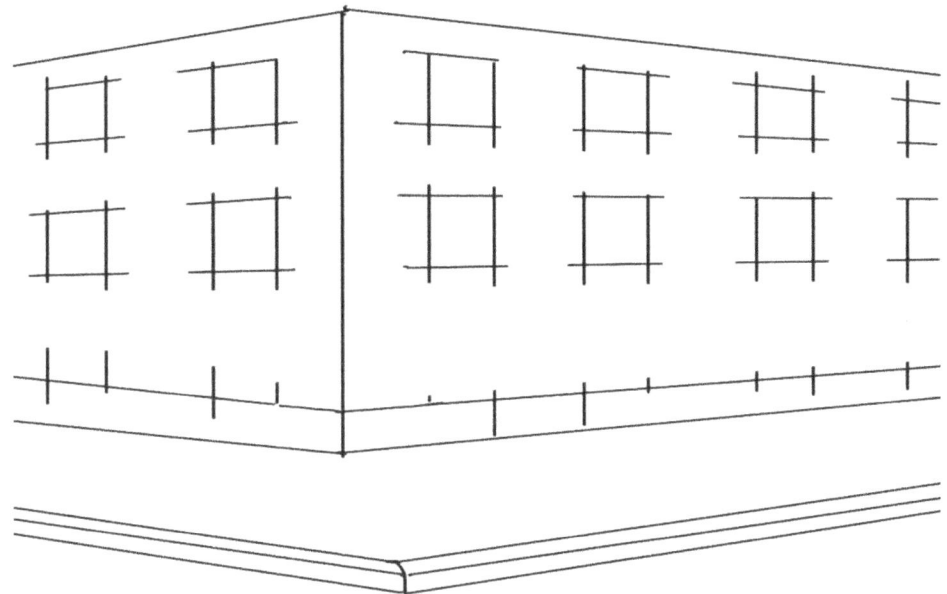

Then we move on to highlighting the windows and then adding in the rooftop. This is a meticulous part of the drawing as there are many smaller lines that need paying attention to, double check your work against these drawings so you know you're acing it.

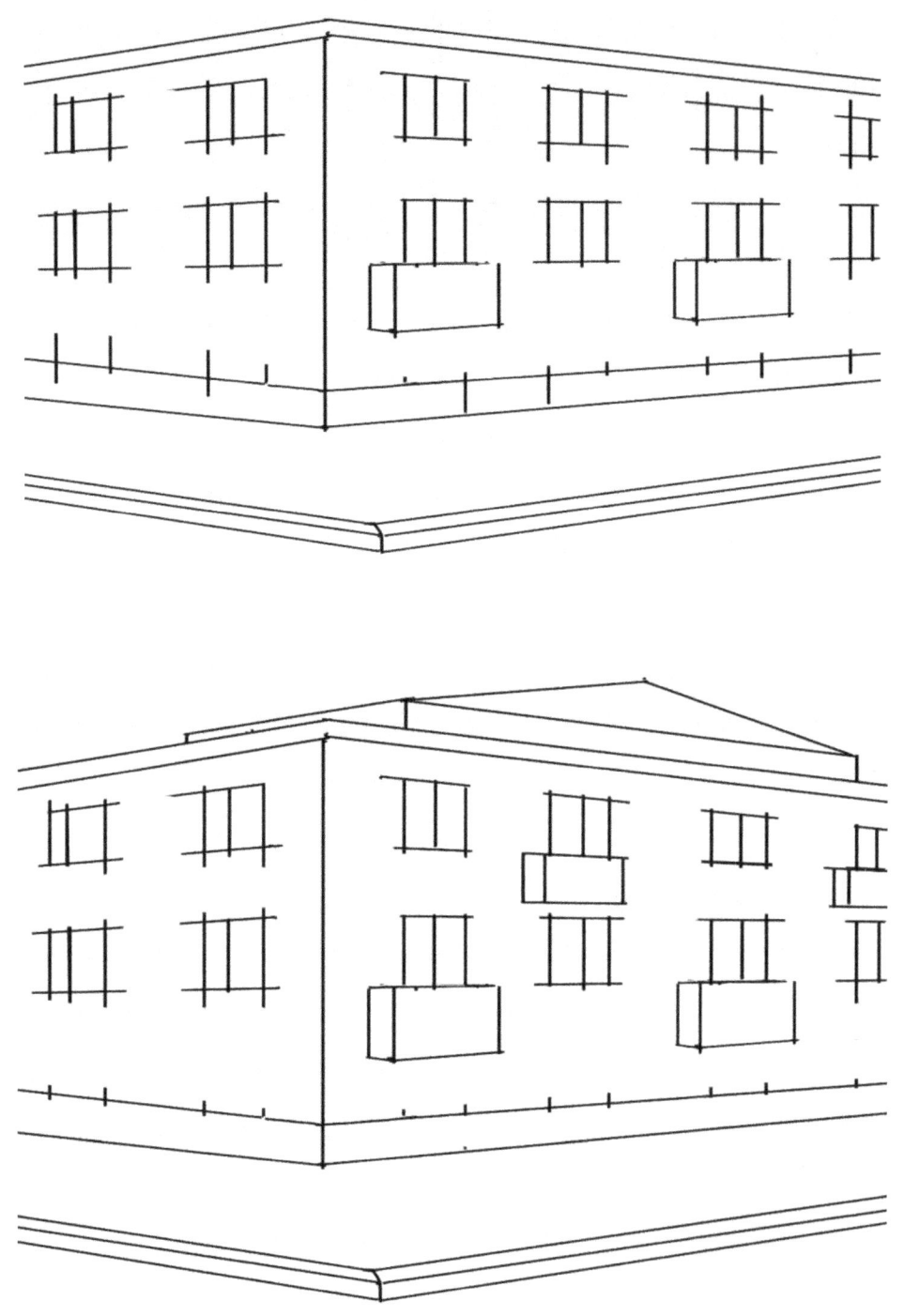

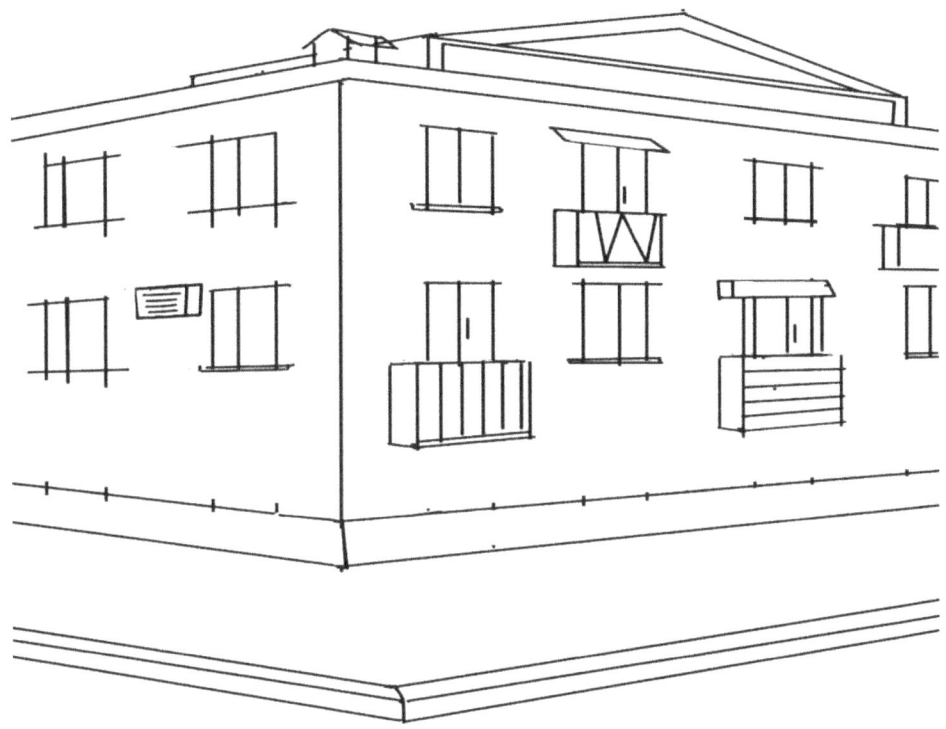

Next is a lot more detail on and around the windows. Small patios are added in as well as exterior additions to the building itself. Then in the image on the right there's a tree with a plot of land added in.

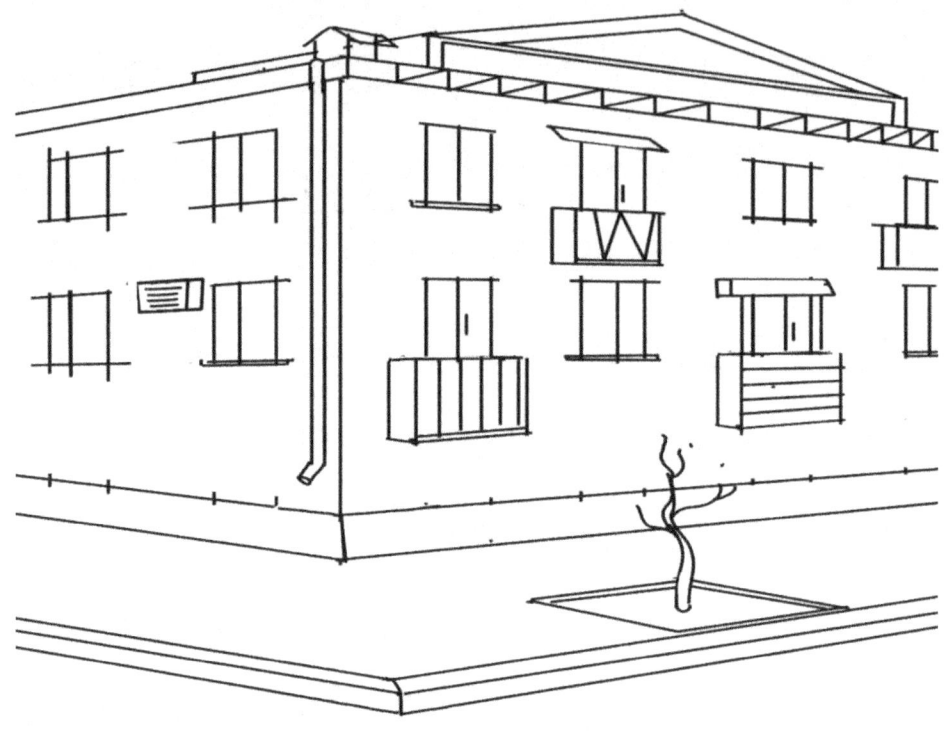

This next step is a subtle one. There are very few changes to be made besides very small basic adjustments. Keep your eyes open for that. Then the next step is the first bit of progress on shading. You start dark to begin and then the next couple steps afterwards will elaborate on that.

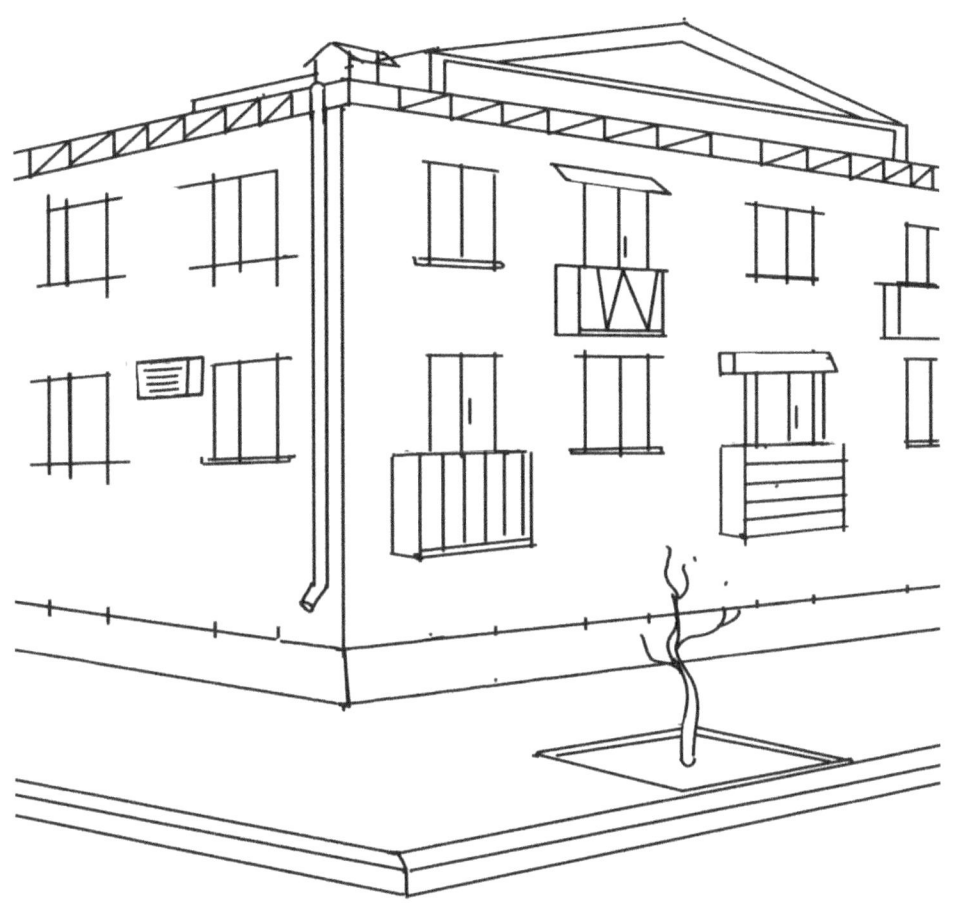

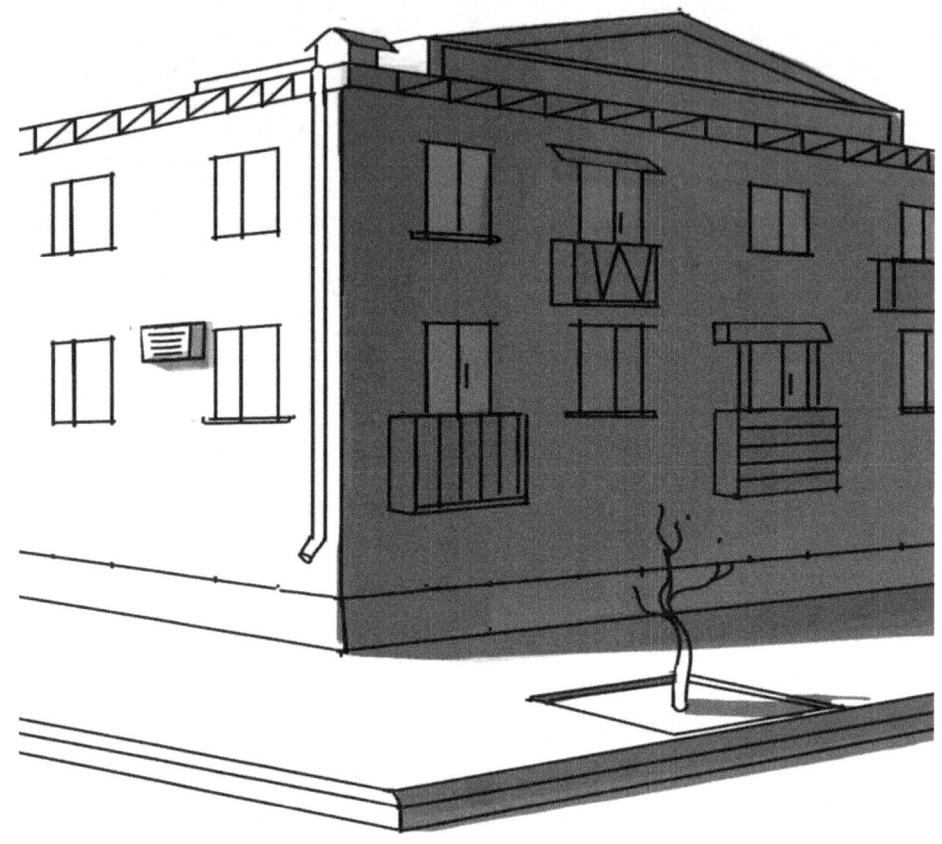

The next couple steps are more of the same as before. Shading is the main focal point now. As you can see the first image is the step for getting those windows shaded lighter than the surrounding areas as well as adding some blending to the main building exterior wall. Then the step after that focuses more on the rest of the environment. Adding layers is important and what you should be paying the most attention too.

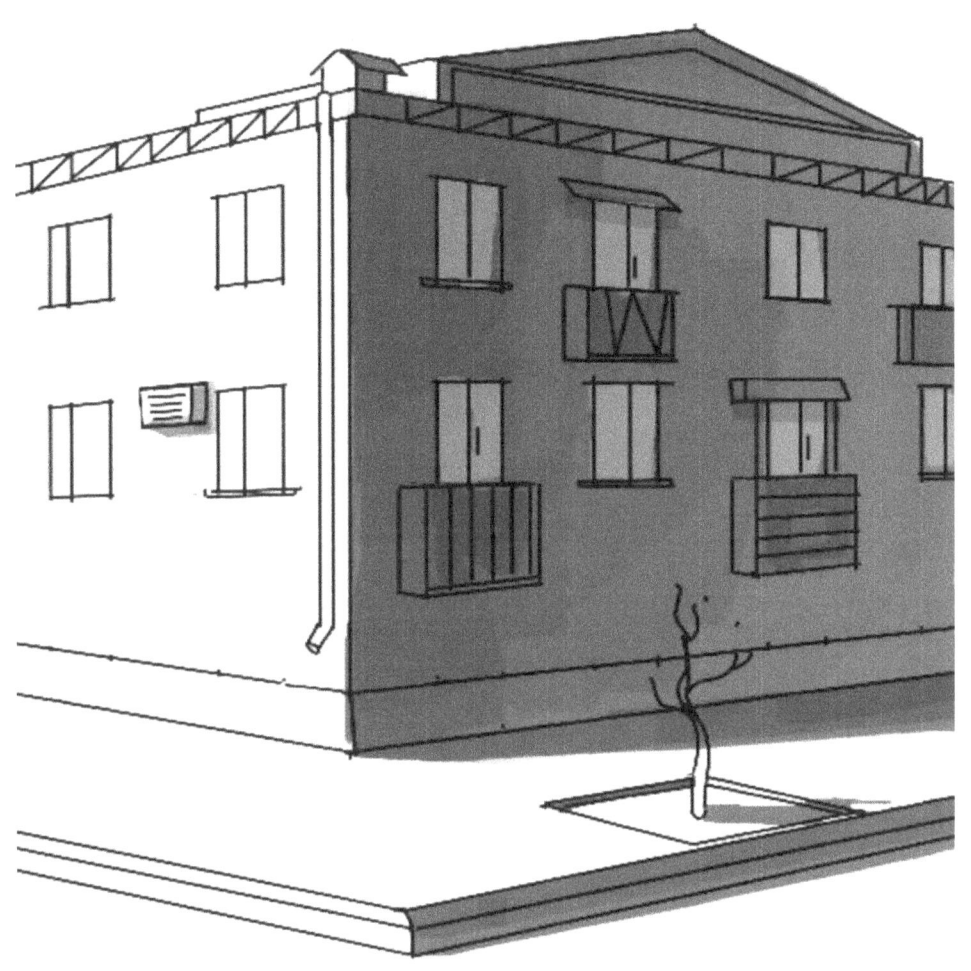

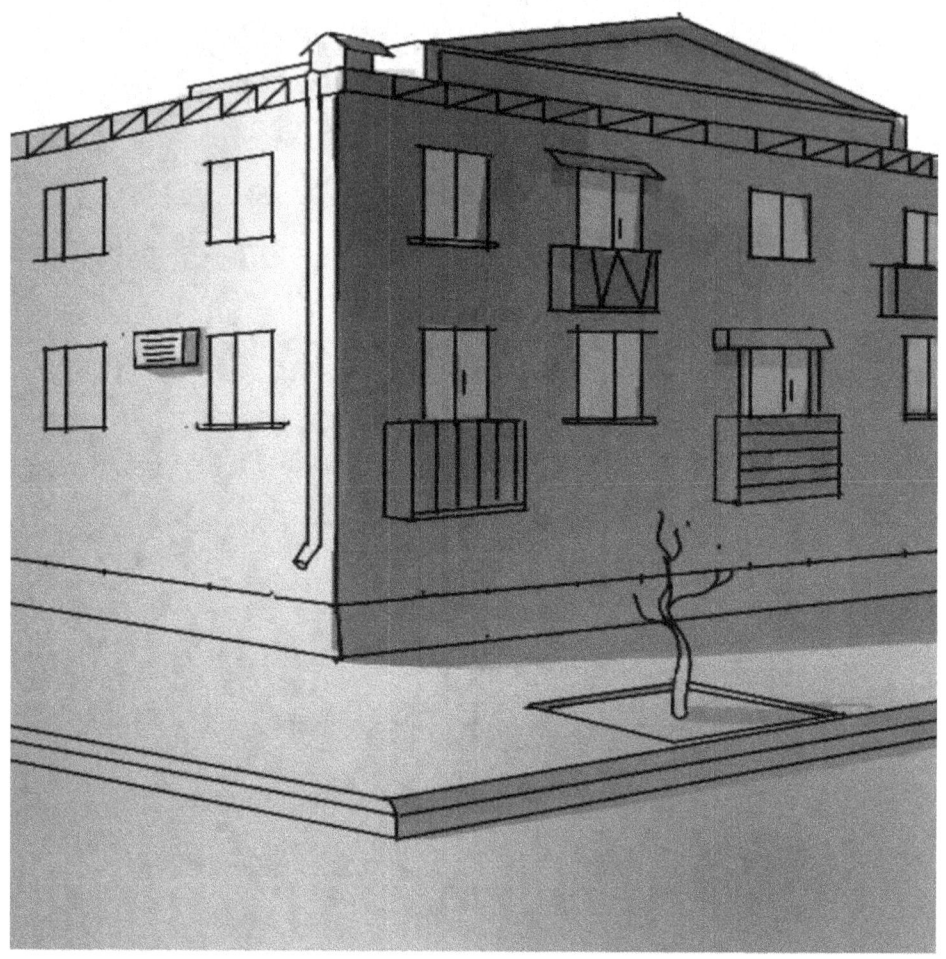

Last but not least are the final steps of shading for this specific project. As you can see there aren't huge differences between the two images but when given a closer look you'll see the subtle differences in shading and blending. So look closely and do your best to match them! Then your finished and on to the next one!

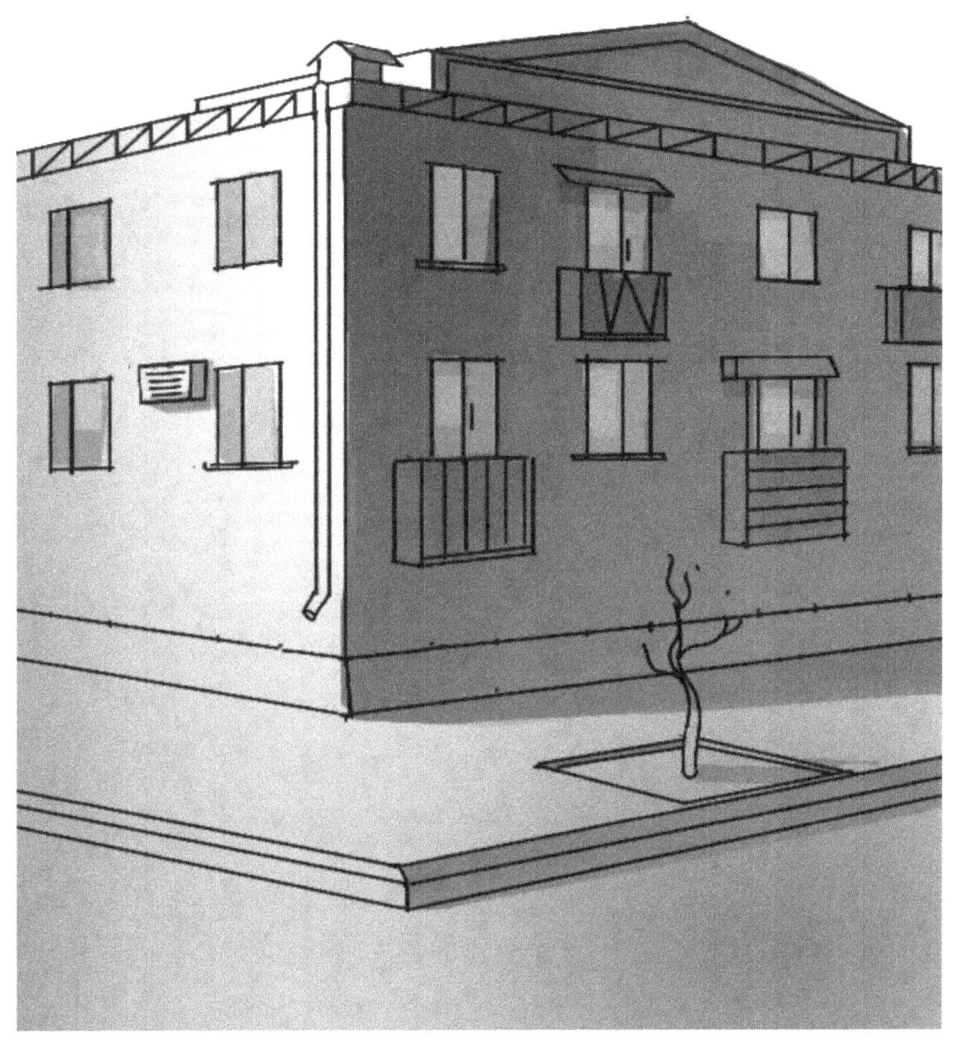

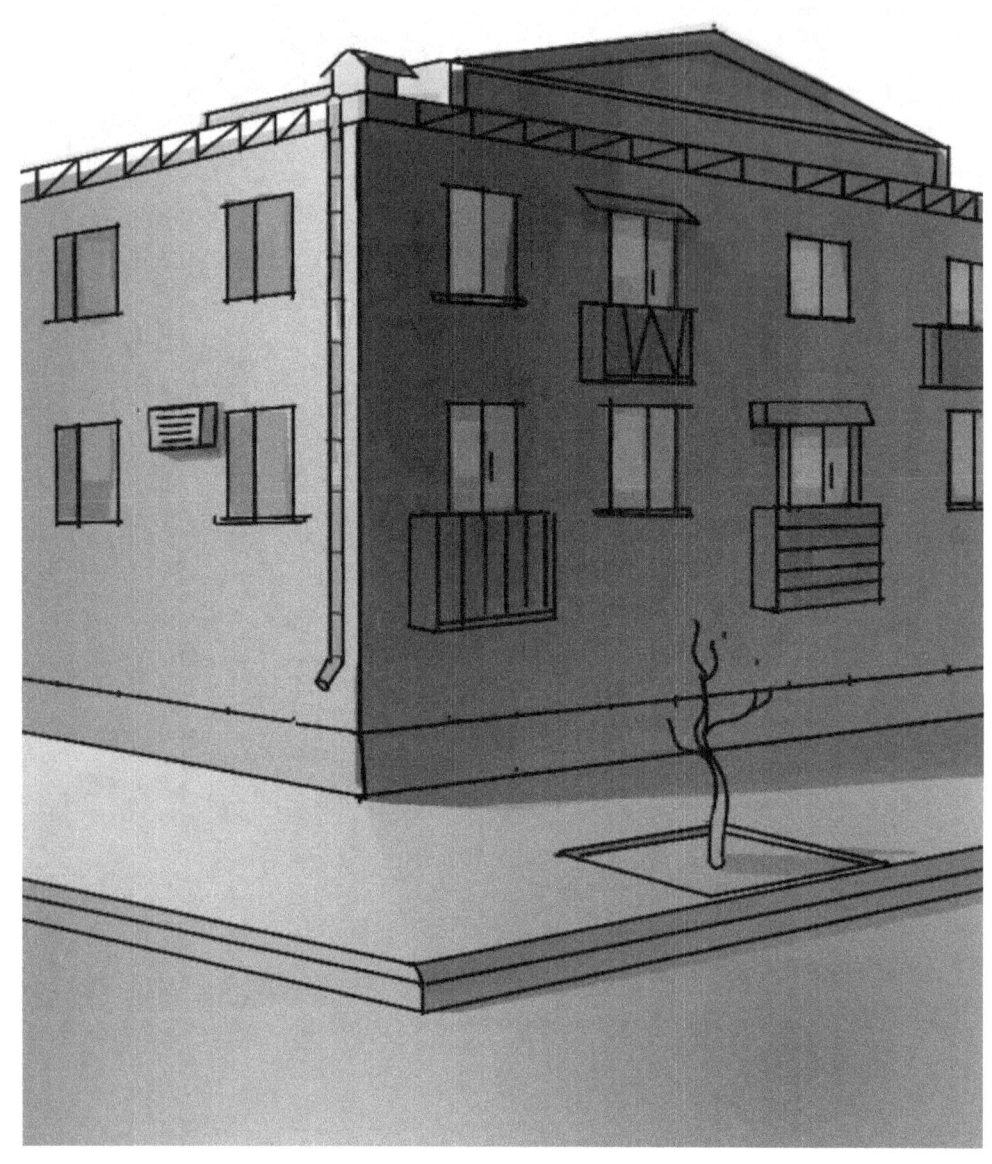

Fifth Perspective Drawing: Alleyway

This next one is another different style. This time you're dealing with a long distance and many perspectives along throughout the singular perspective of the image. Keeping everything in context may seem tricky but follow the steps and you'll see. The image on the left is the completed product, and the right is the humble beginnings. Start out with the lifework on the right and trust me it'll all make sense eventually.

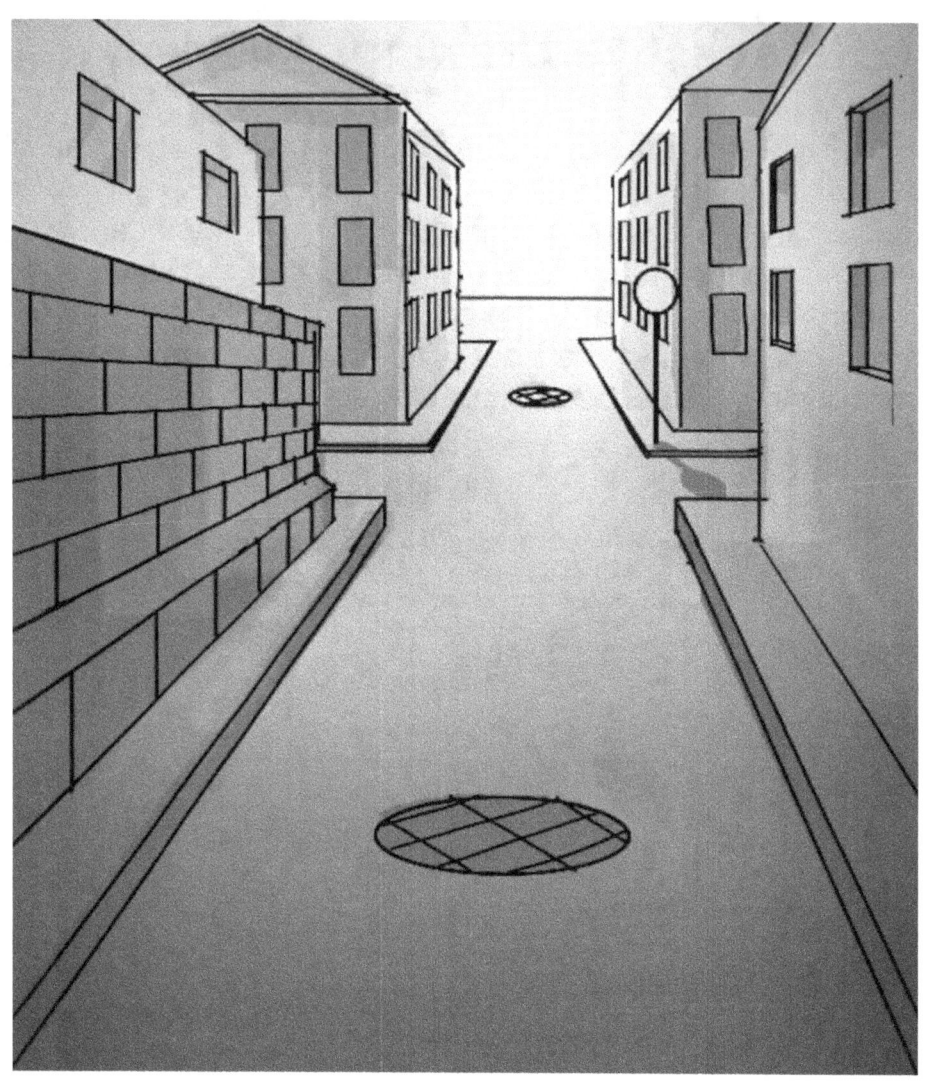

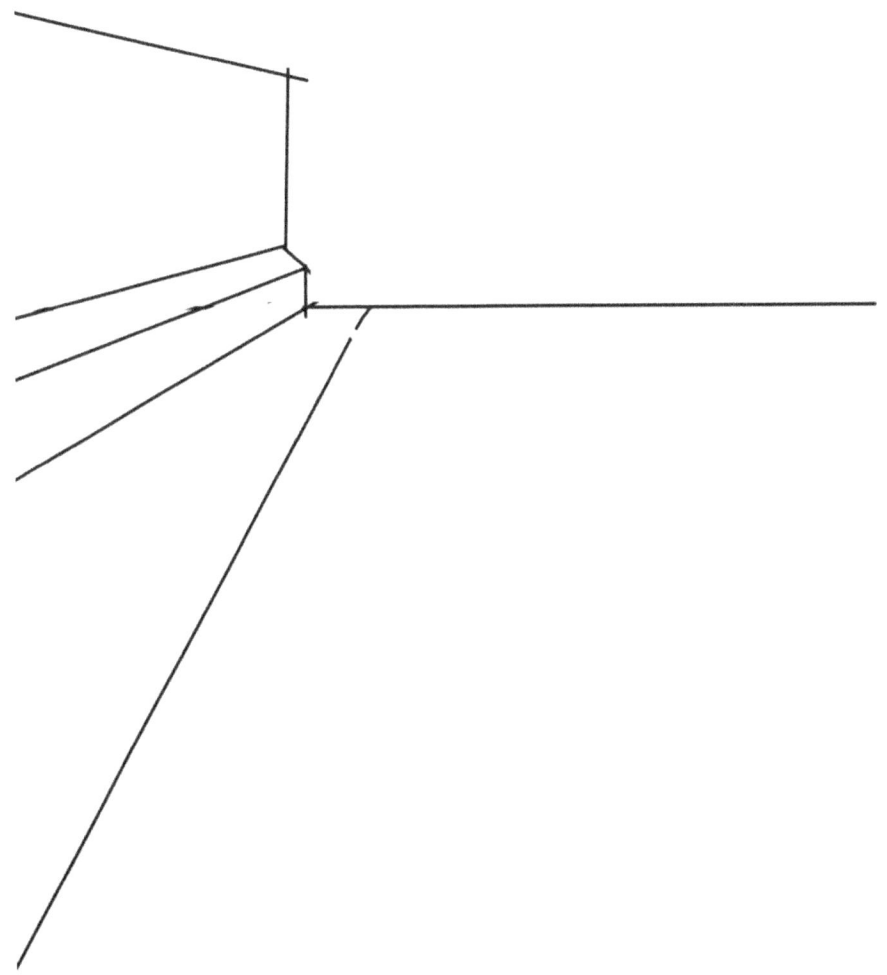

As you see the lines get even more involved and start to overlap in the second image. Again trust me it will all make sense. Just follow the line work and make sure you're using those straight edges. Watch the corners as well, just as a point of observation.

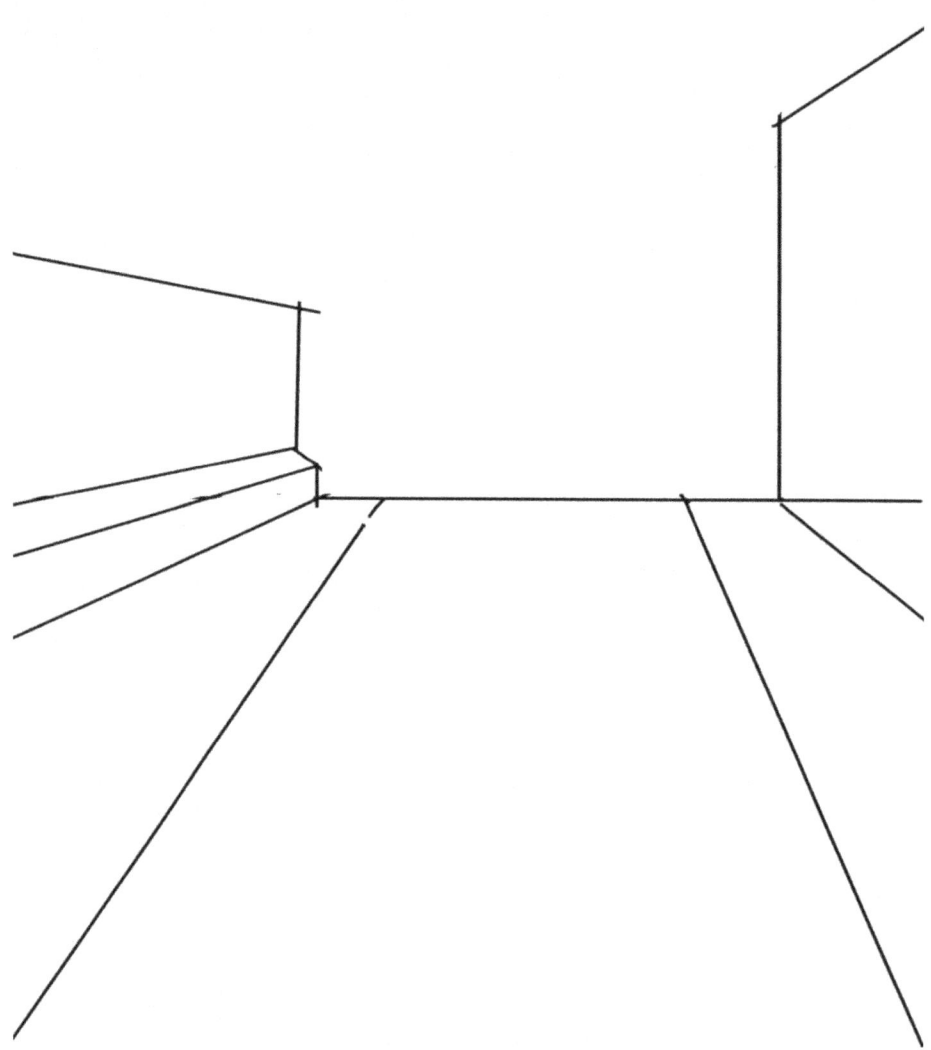

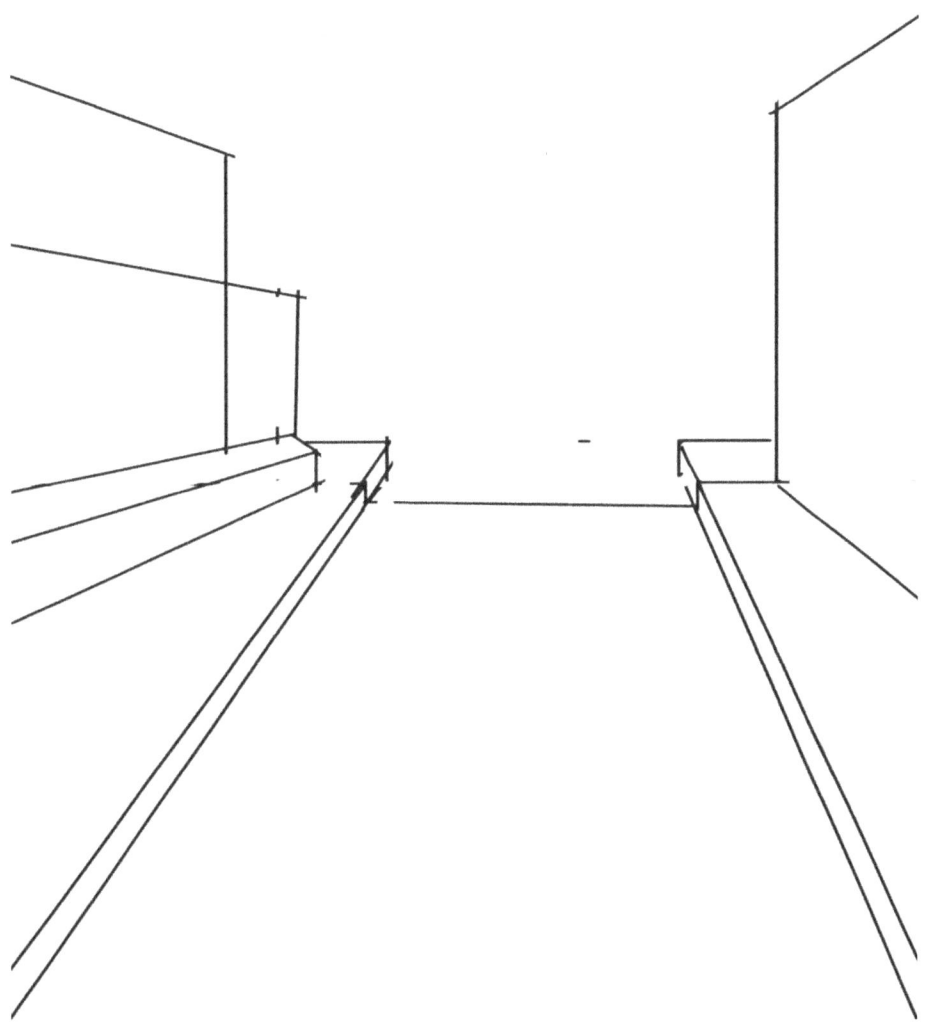

As the images get more developed and the line work becomes more pronounced you can see the alleyway slowly coming together. You can see the street starting to take shape as well as the buildings that give it the structure.

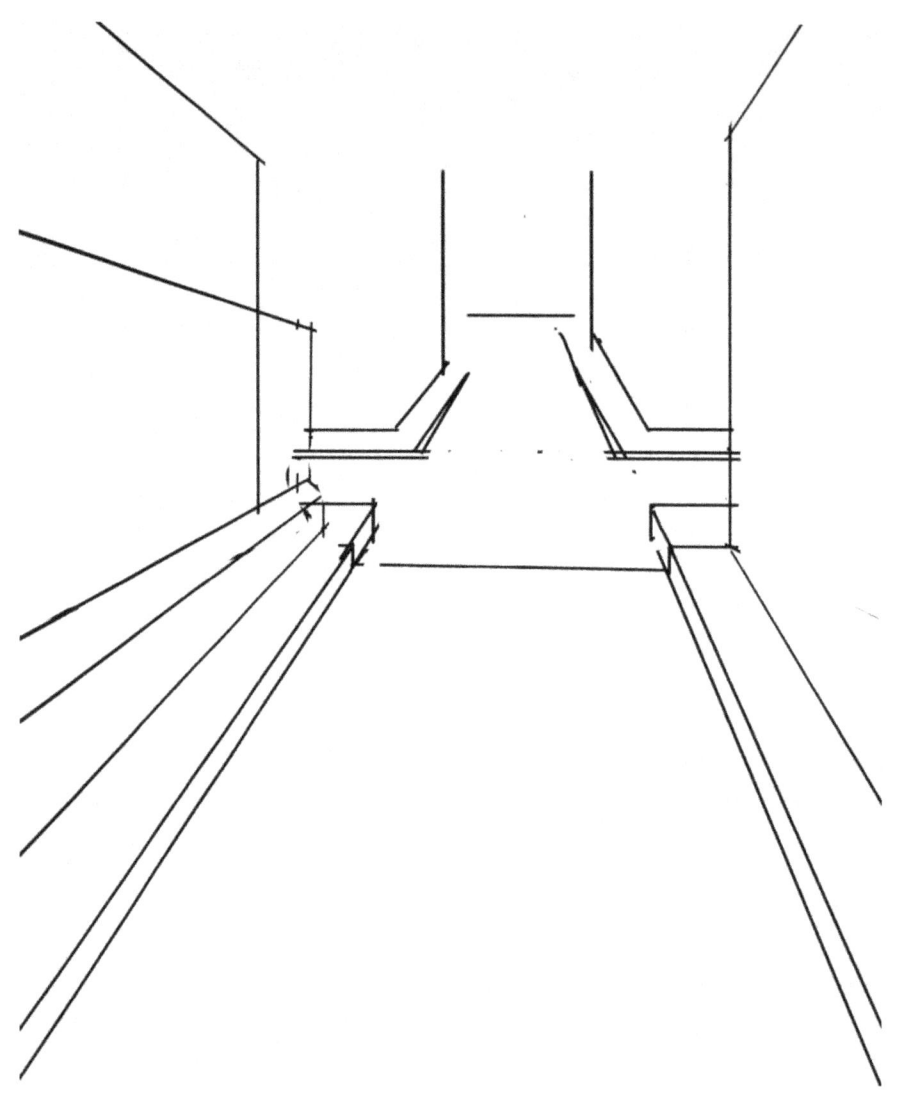

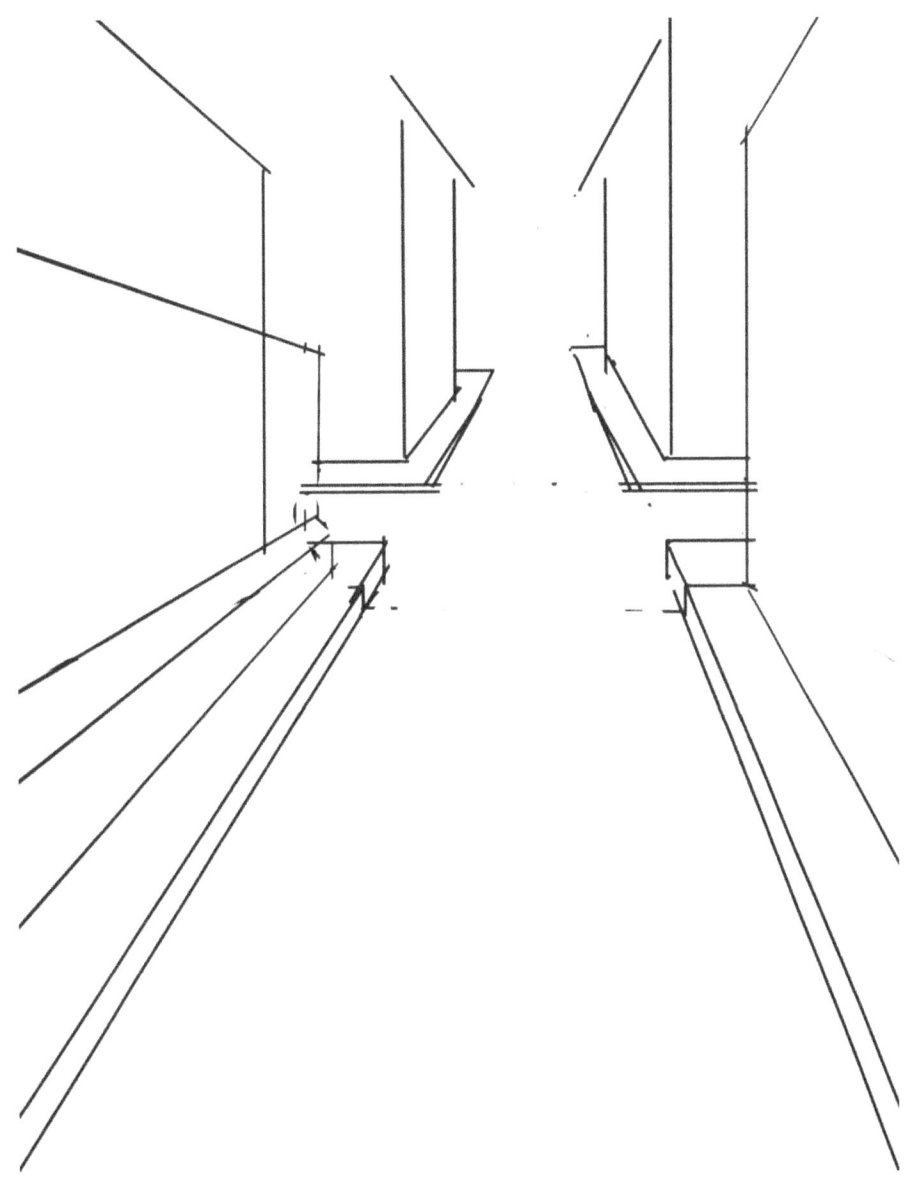

Now is an important part of the process. This is when you start really constructing the buildings. Adding the lines in for the brick work and windows is crucial and you'll want to constantly check your for against the images.

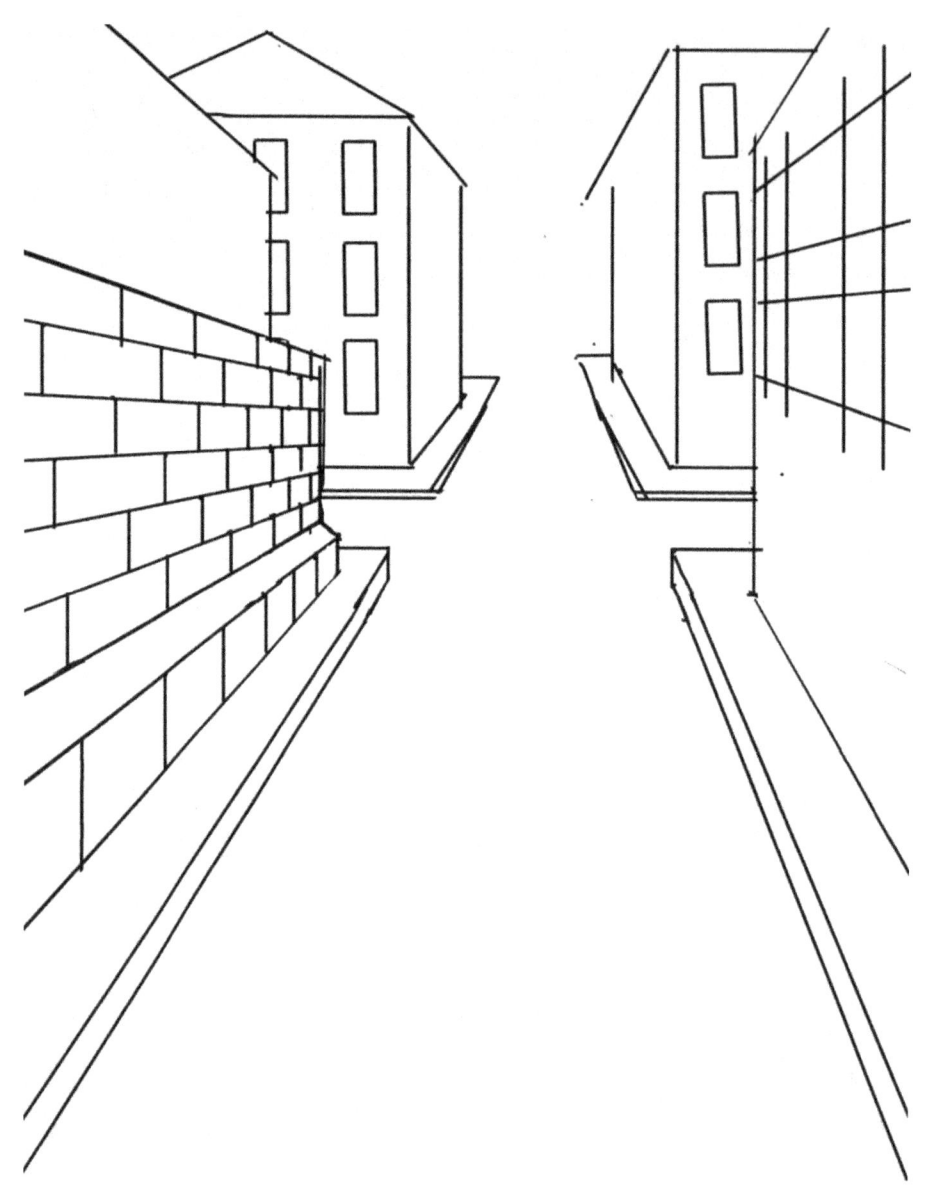

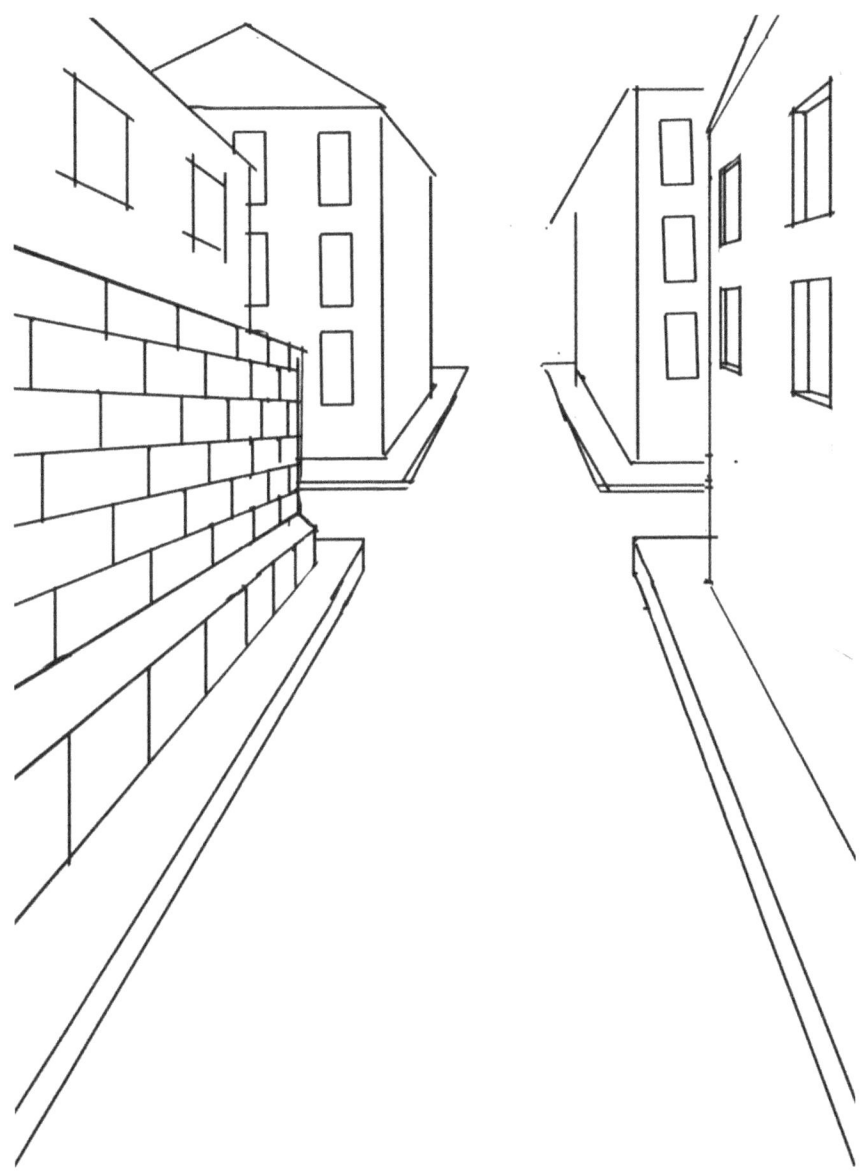

This is when we start fleshing out the rest of the buildings walls and the streets accents as well. Notice the manhole covers and the buildings in the distance.

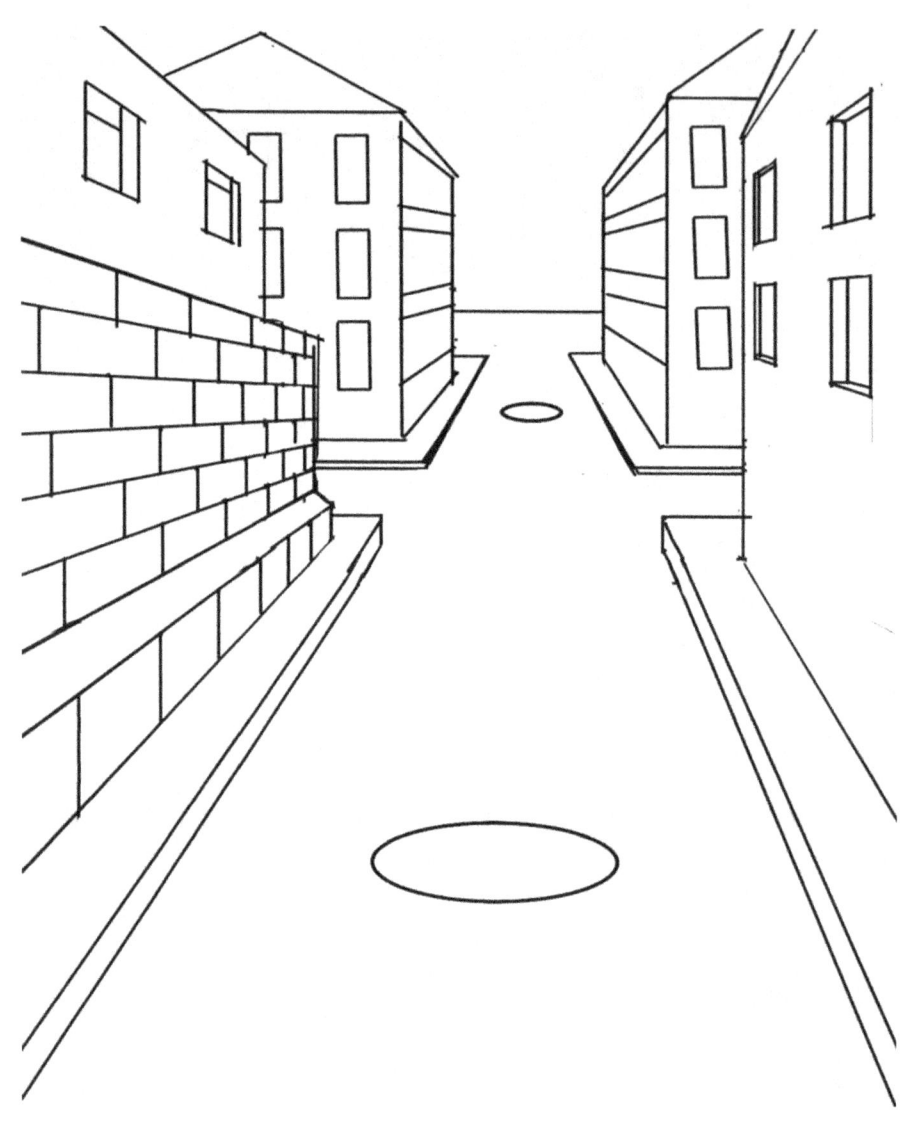

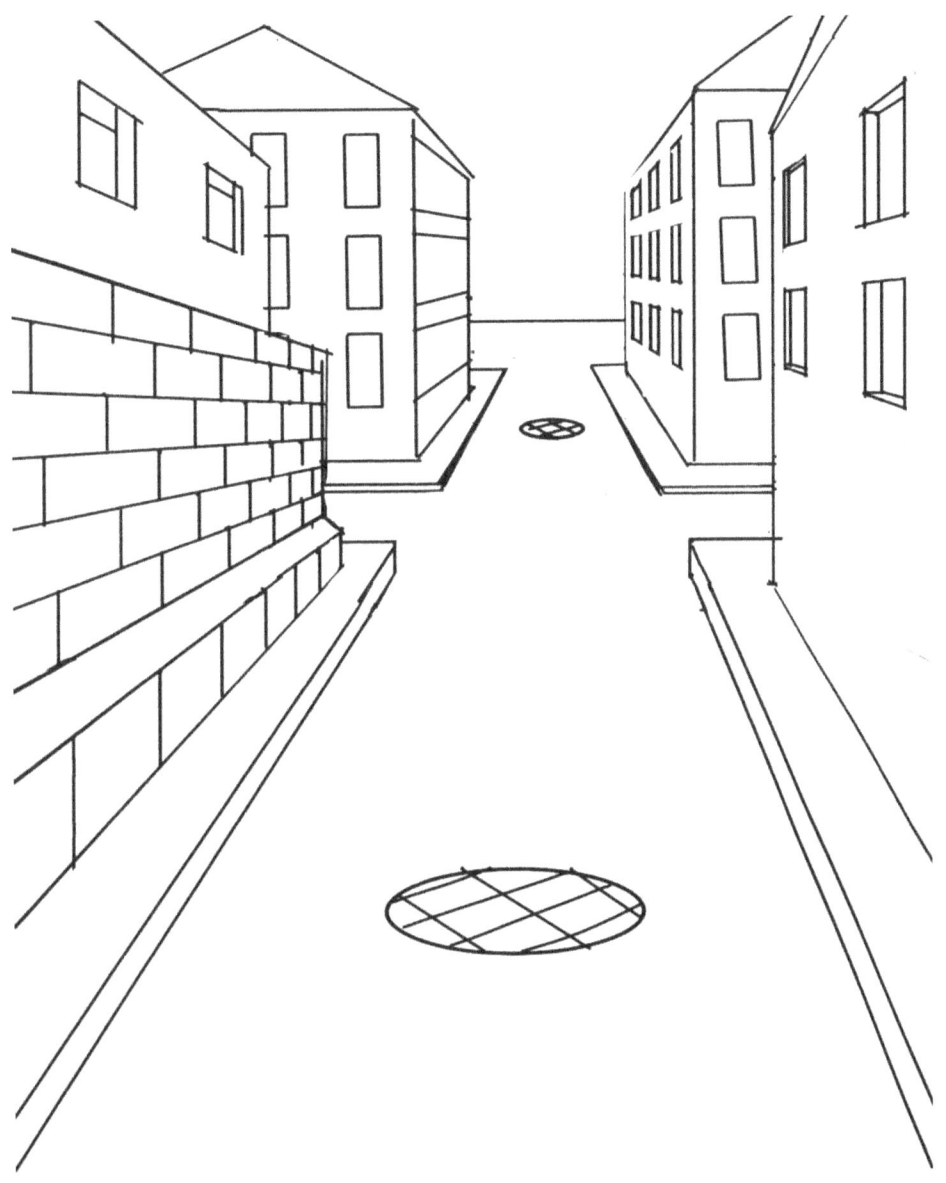

Like the last step its more fleshing out of the streets, this
time the addition of a street sign an then more elaboration on the
windows in the distant buildings wall.

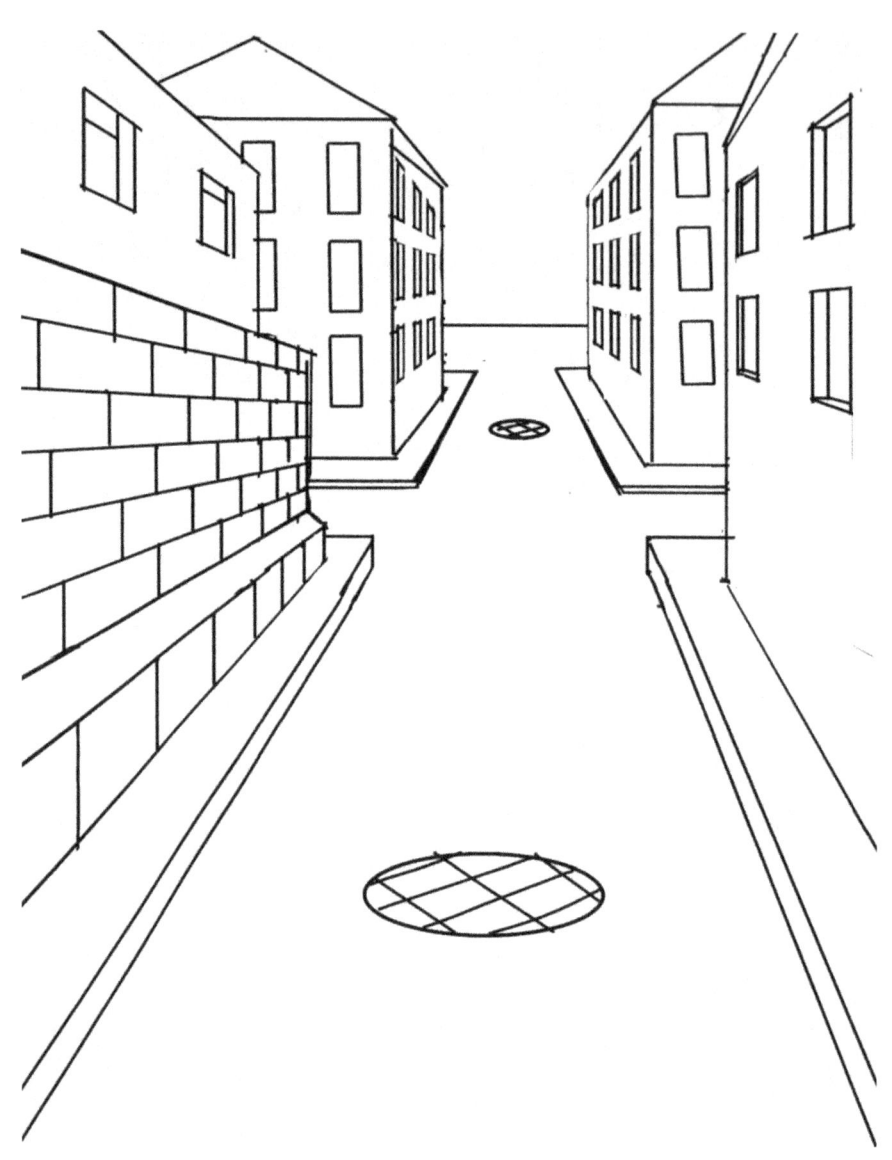

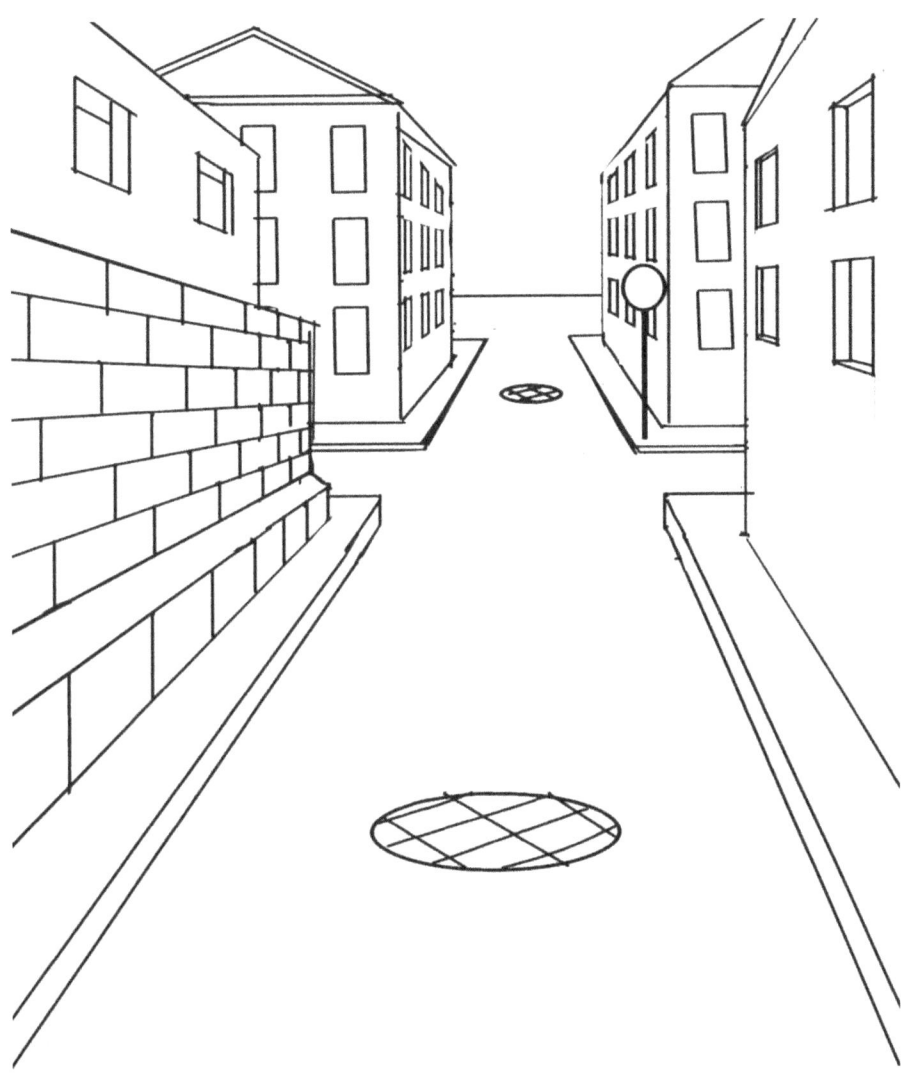

At long last we arrive at the shading phase. The light orientation plays a huge part in this one as you can see with the building faces and the street corners. Watch out for the blending along the street edges at the brick wall as well.

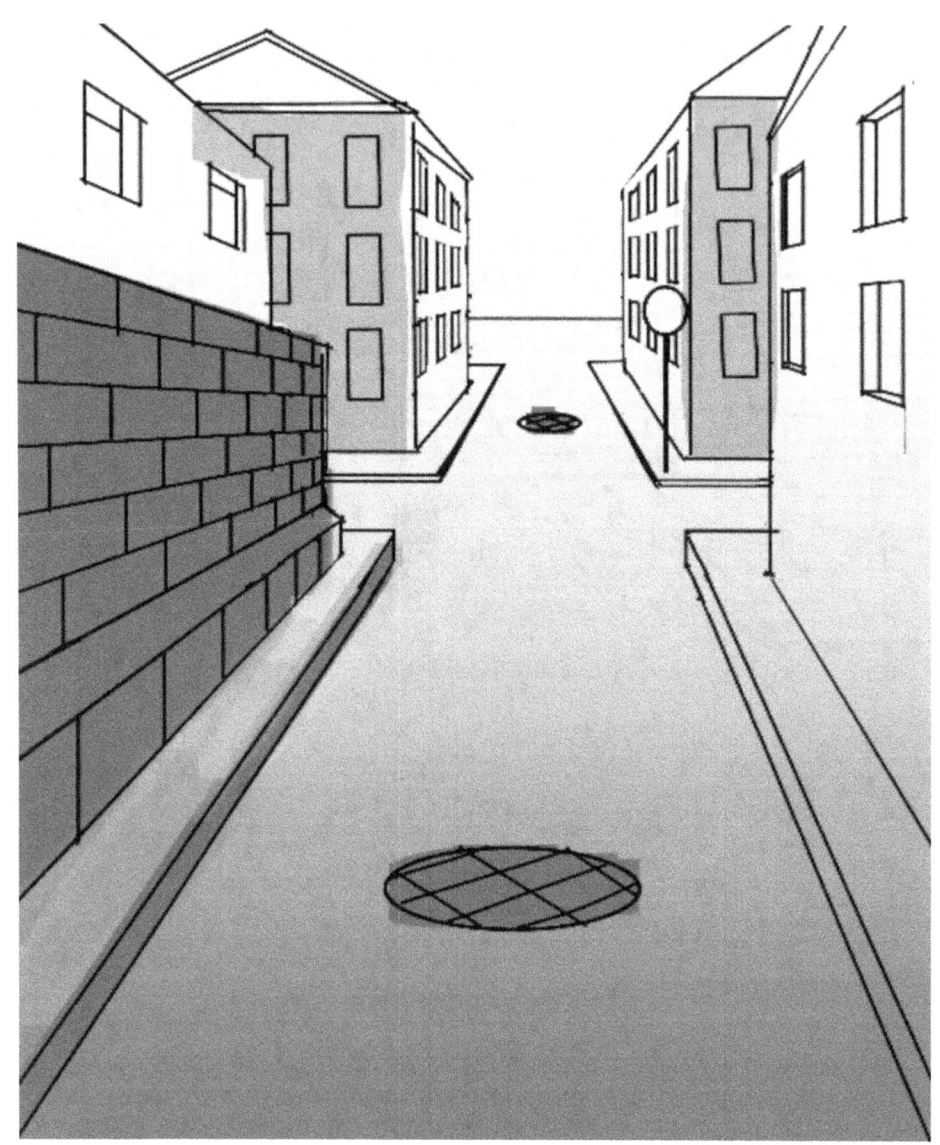

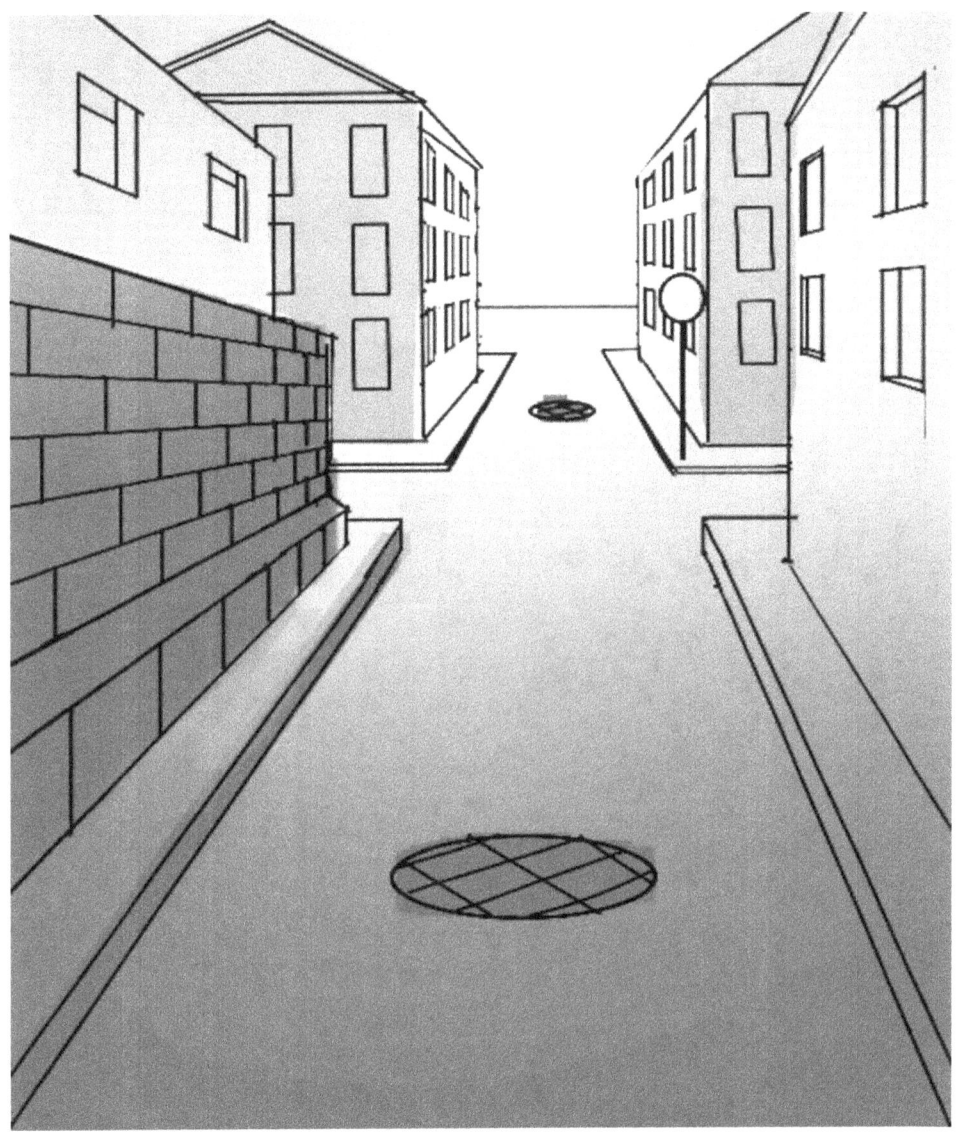

Blending is a critical aspect of the next couple steps, as you add more shading into the drawing you'll need to really blend it together to get that smooth look of light and dark meeting. As you can see below.

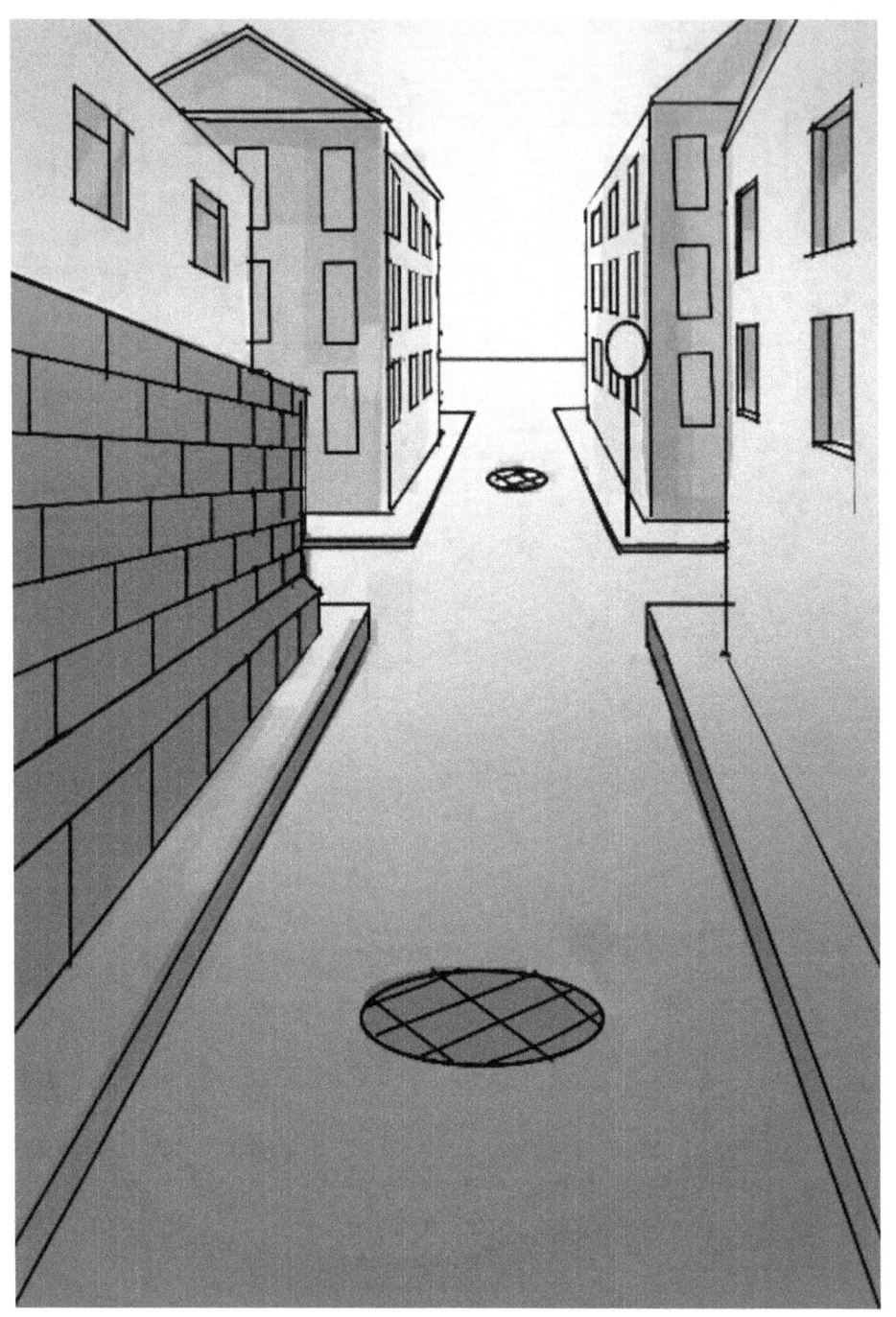

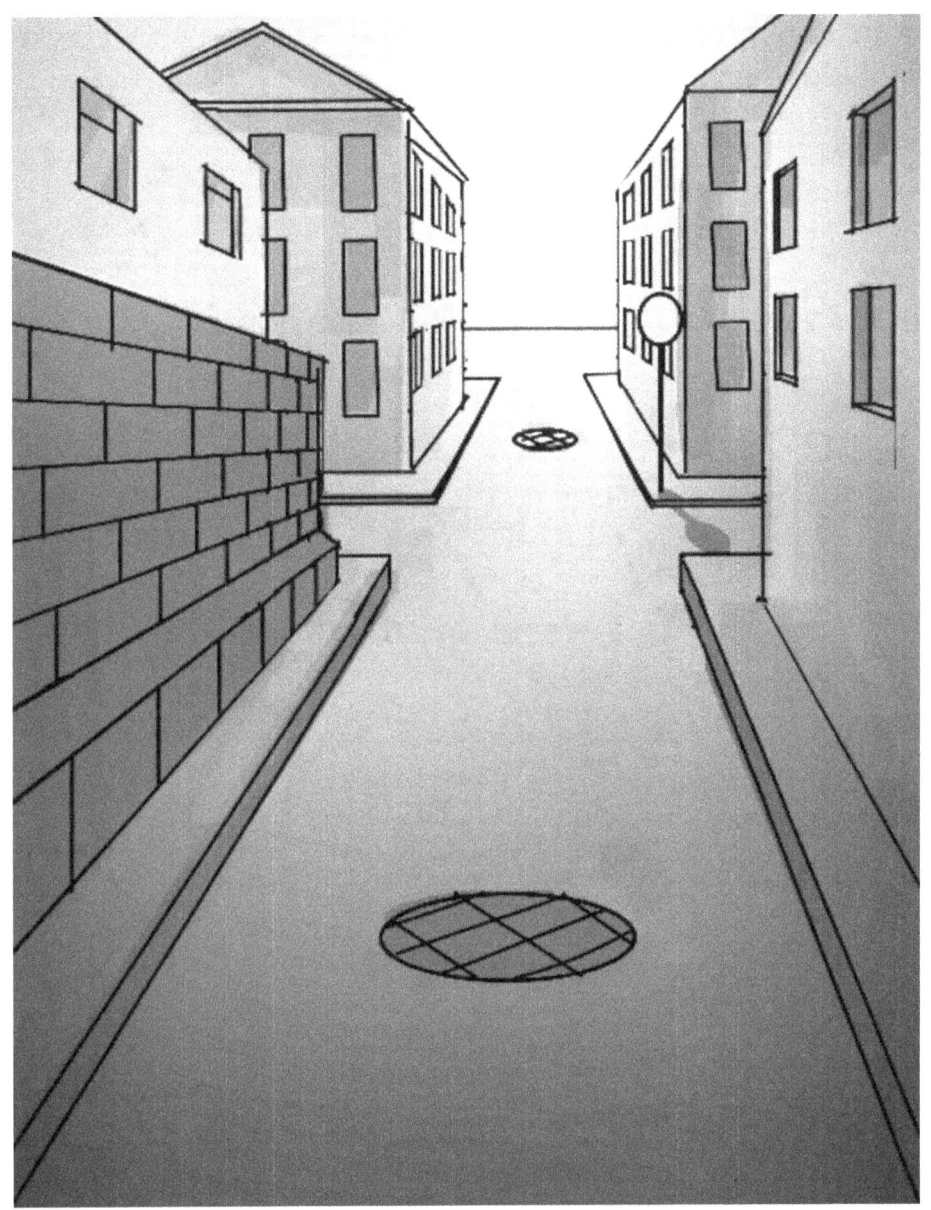

This is the final product here! As you can see its enlarged a little more than the others. That is to bring attention to all the minute details you may have missed. See the stop signs shadow, and the subtle gloss to the windows? Those are important details to notice in the moments and after. Good work on this challenging drawing! Move on to the next one.

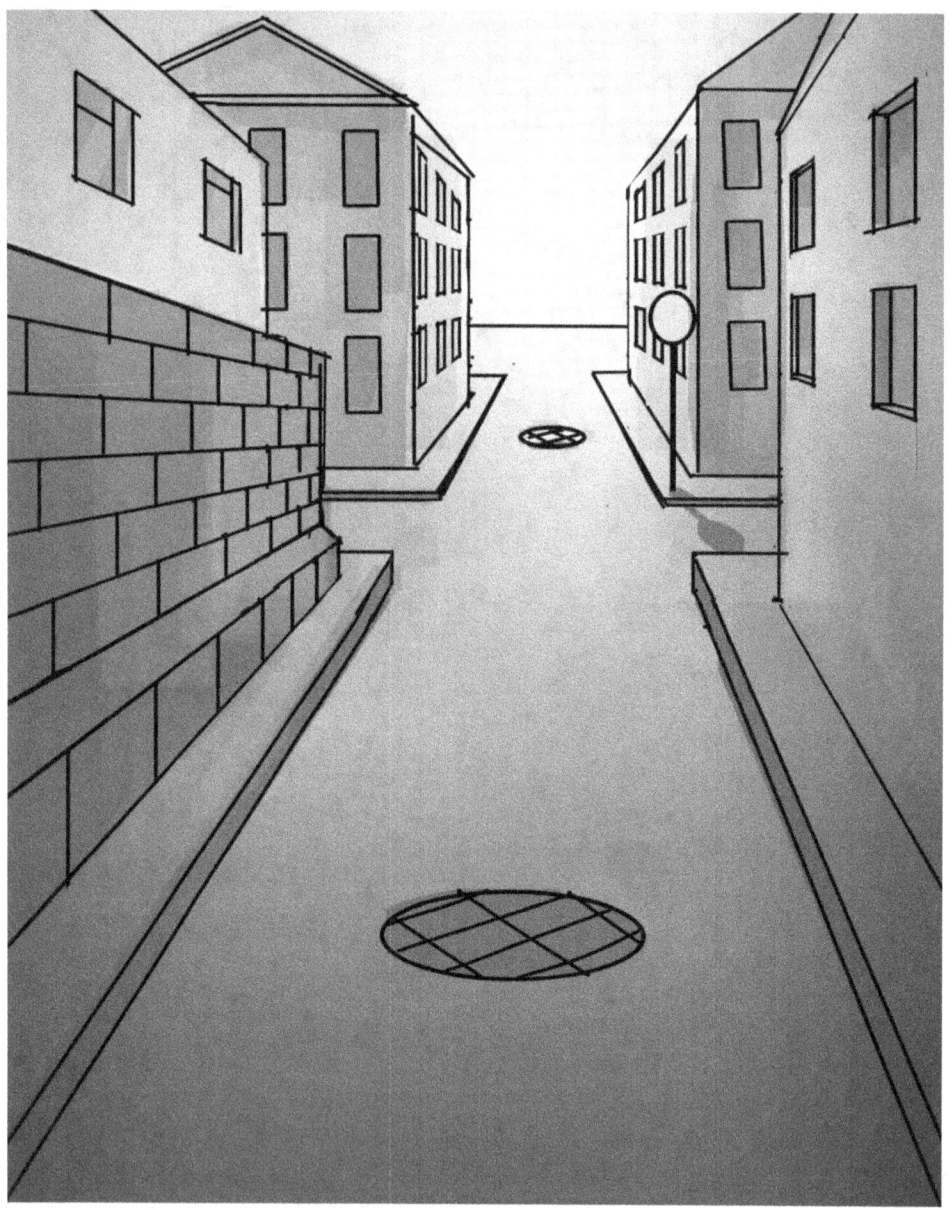

Sixth Perspective Drawing: Estate Overview

For this next one we're tackling another unique perspective. This time around its an aerial overview of a manor or estate. As you can see its a drastic change from the beginning image. This one is a very technical process that utilizes a lot of different line work, so don't be discouraged and do your best to pay attention to the difficult precision.

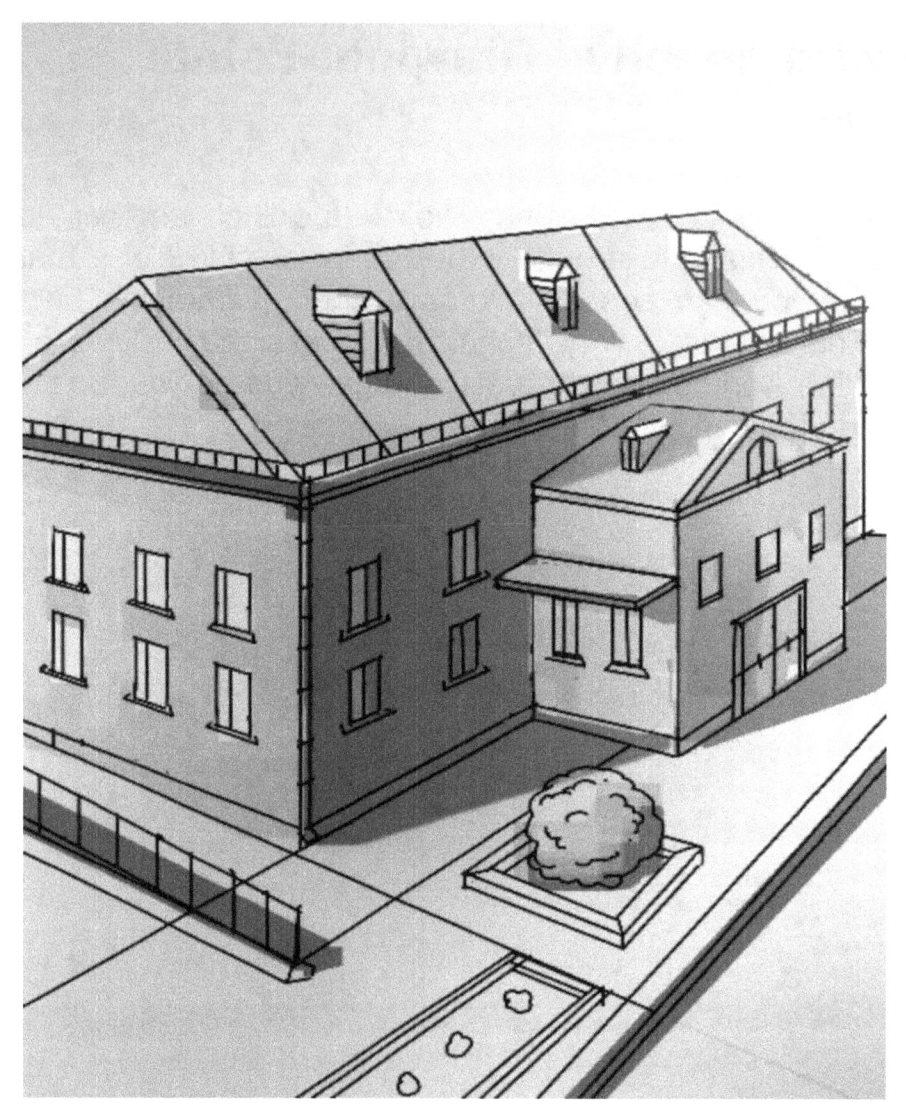

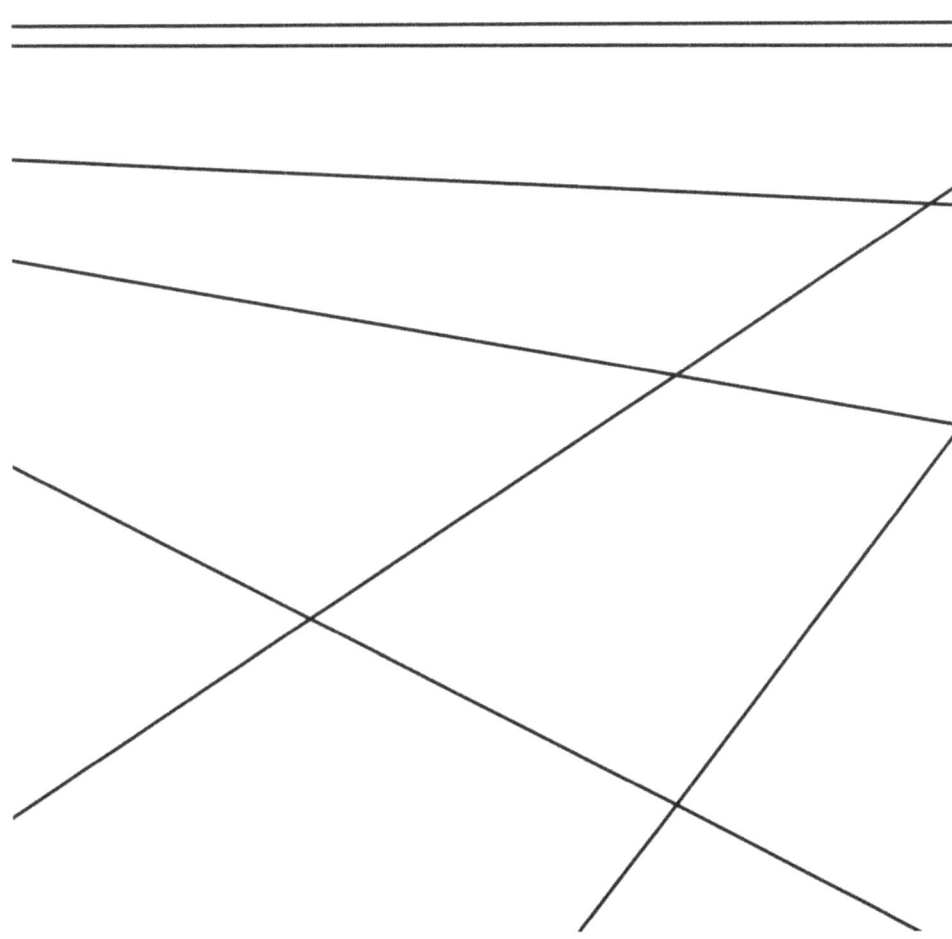

After dealing with the initial line work you need to add many more. Keep your hard edges and straight lines on point. There's an incredible amount of overlap here, which will all play into the structure of the estate. This is the most intricate project we've had so far. So keep on your lines and follow the next two steps.

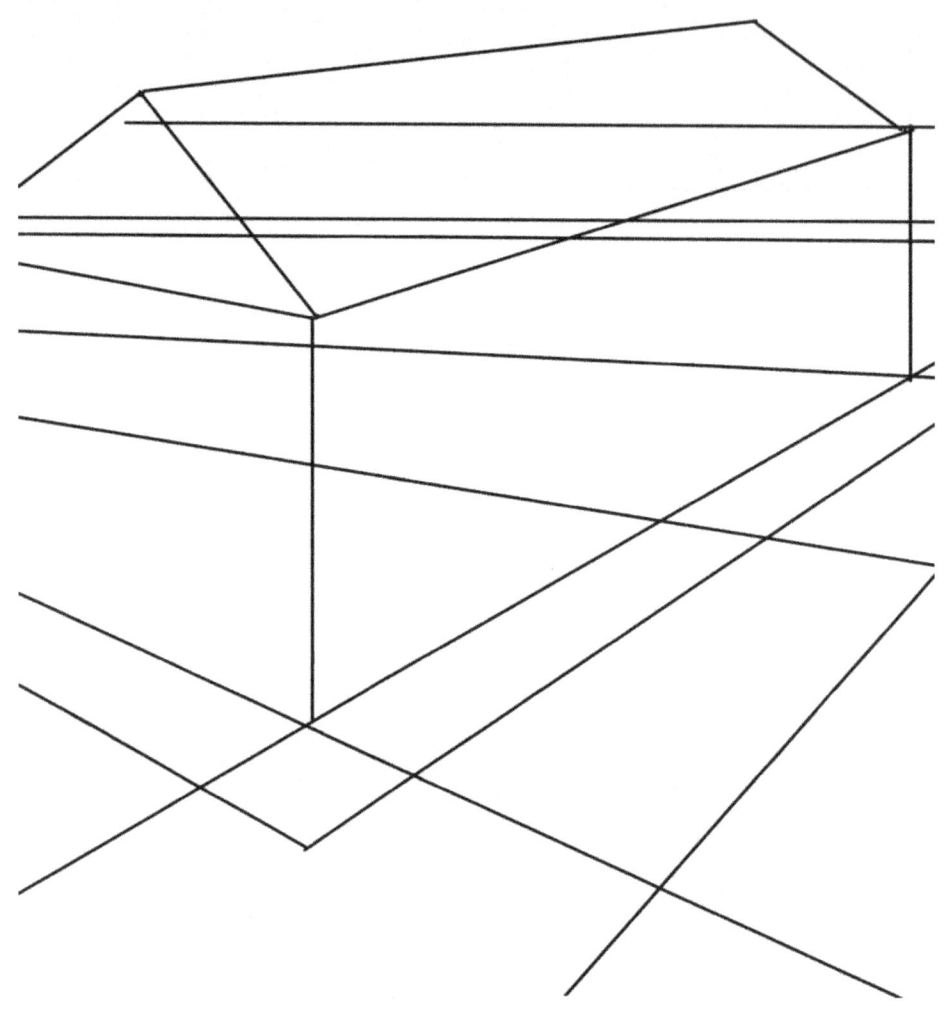

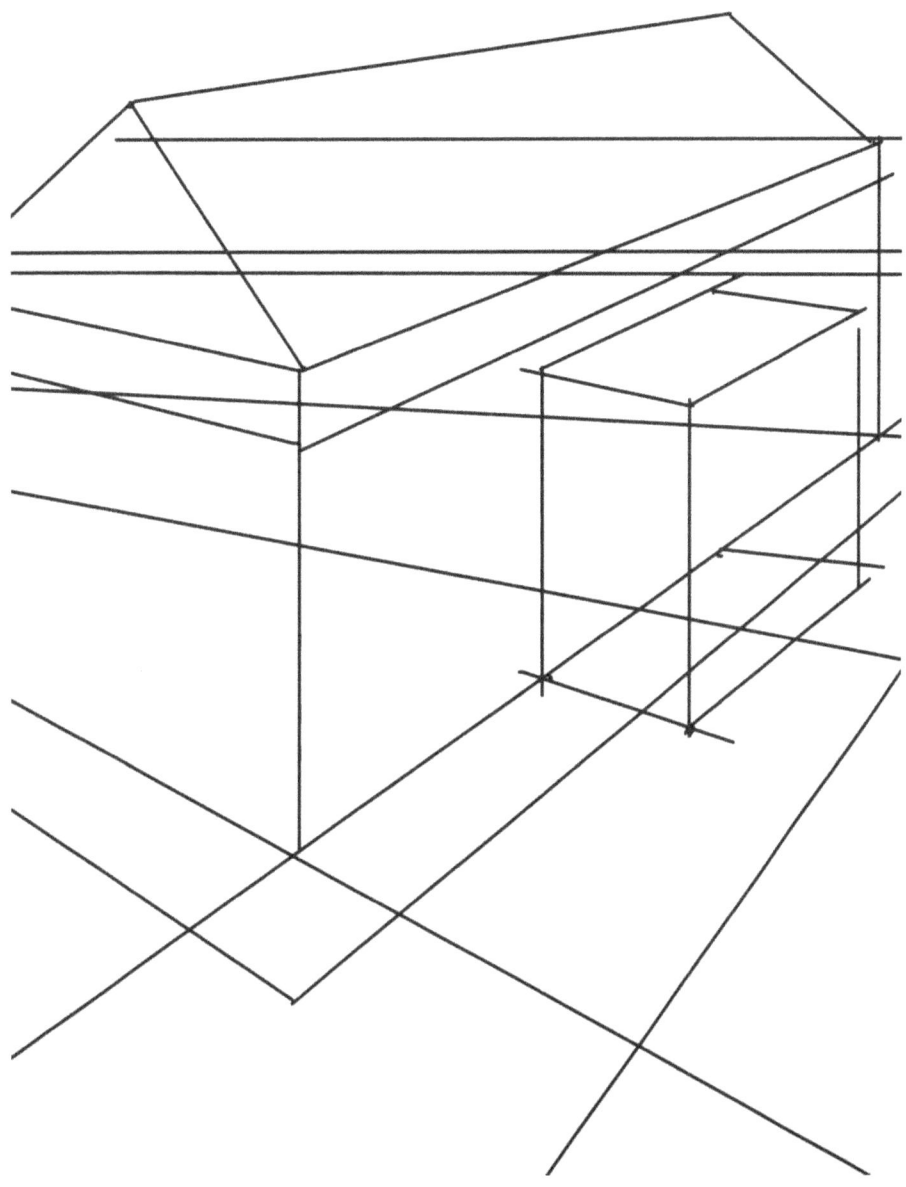

The next couple steps require considerable more overlap. The main lines through the estate will later dictate the windows and the other structural integrities of the building. As you see the roof is now being added in as well as the main windows on the front entrance of the estate. Pay close attention here as you have more lines coming in along the sides and the front.

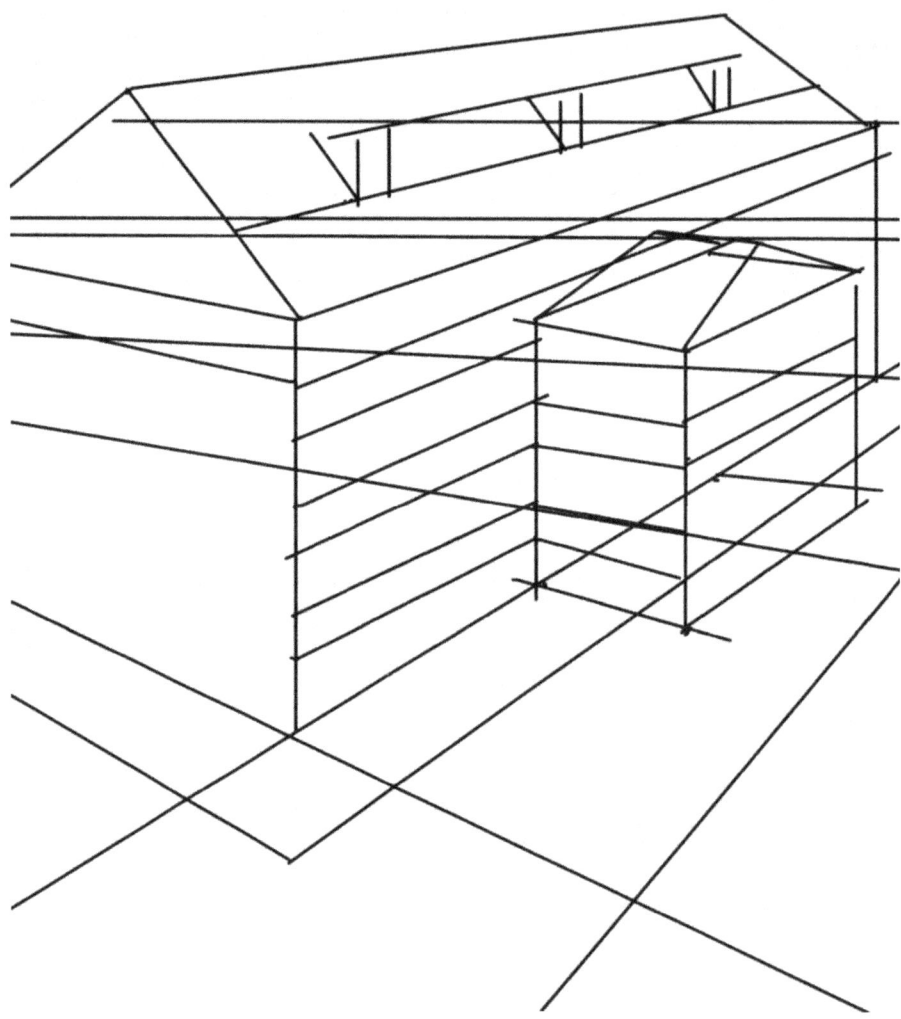

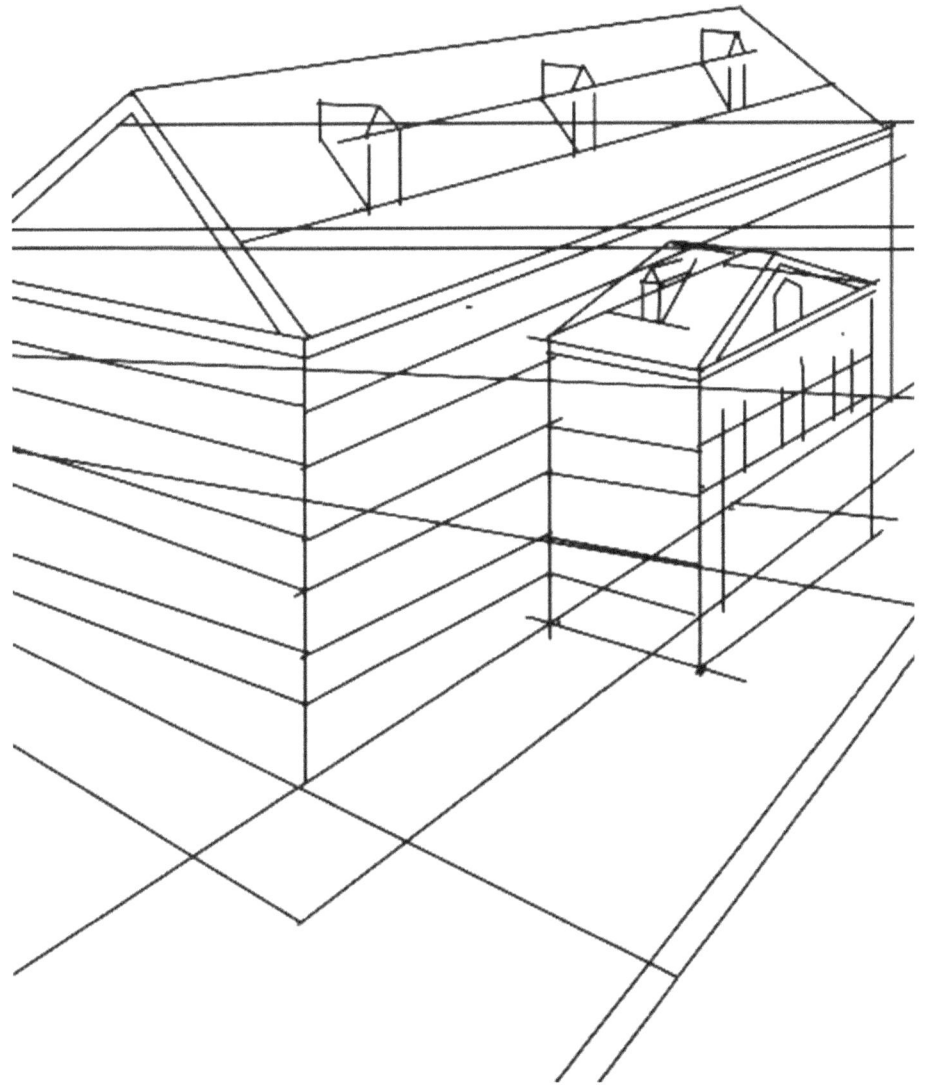

Here we see the development of the outside street and the main doors. Then we further add to the street with an outside planter and then more detail along the outer walls of the house.

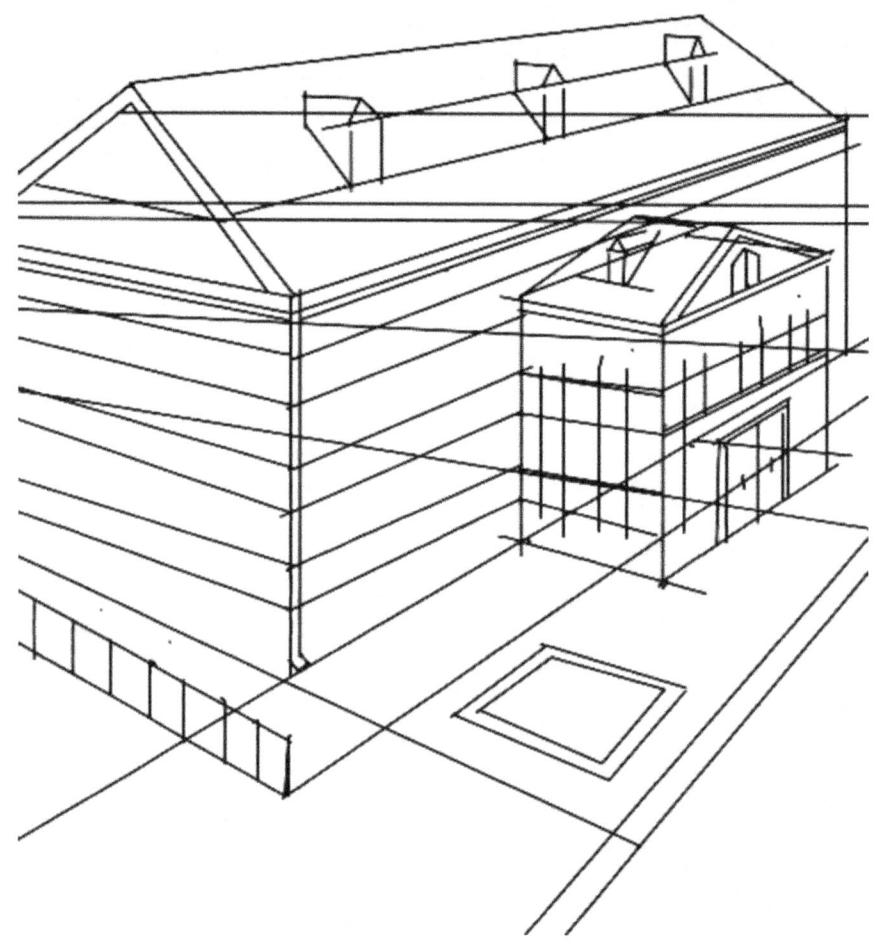

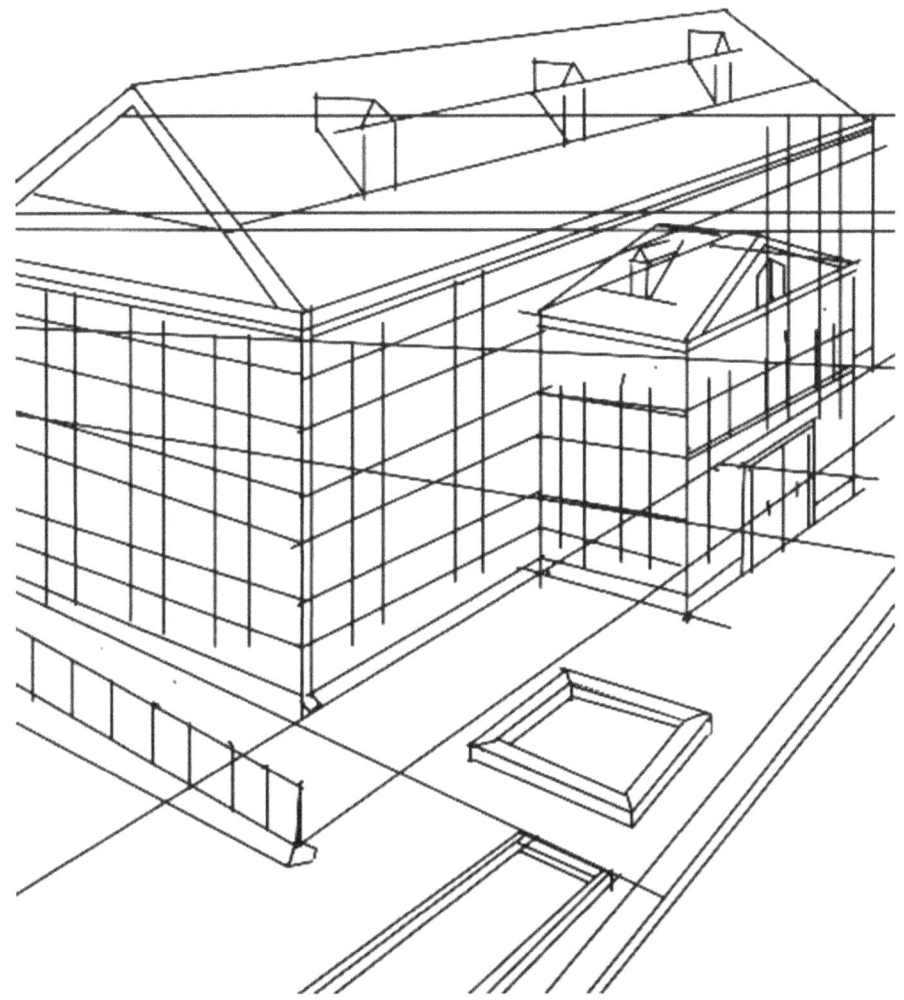

Here we see the removal of the lines through the roof, dictating the completion of its structure. Then we see more lines removed above the main entrance on the lower roof like structure.

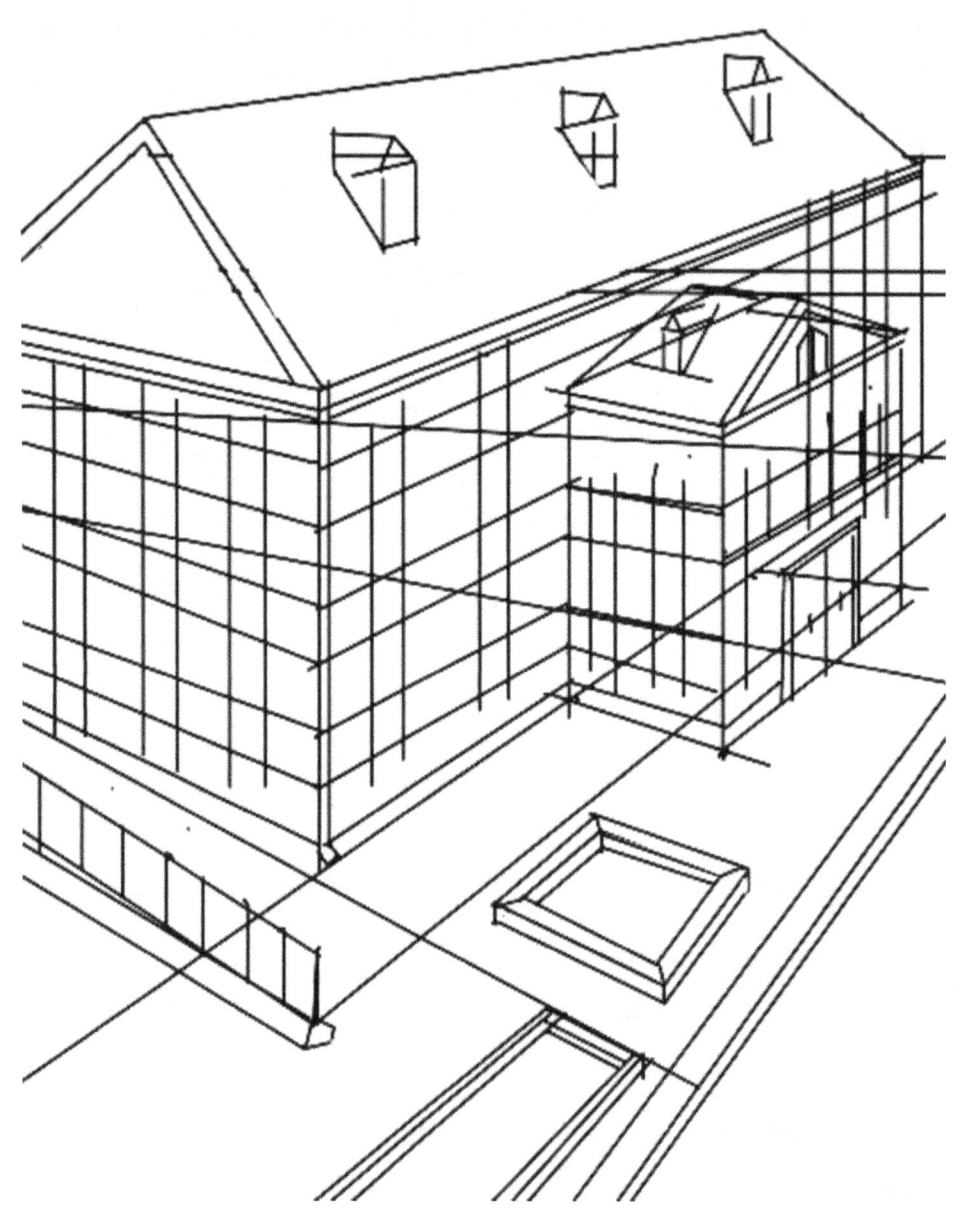

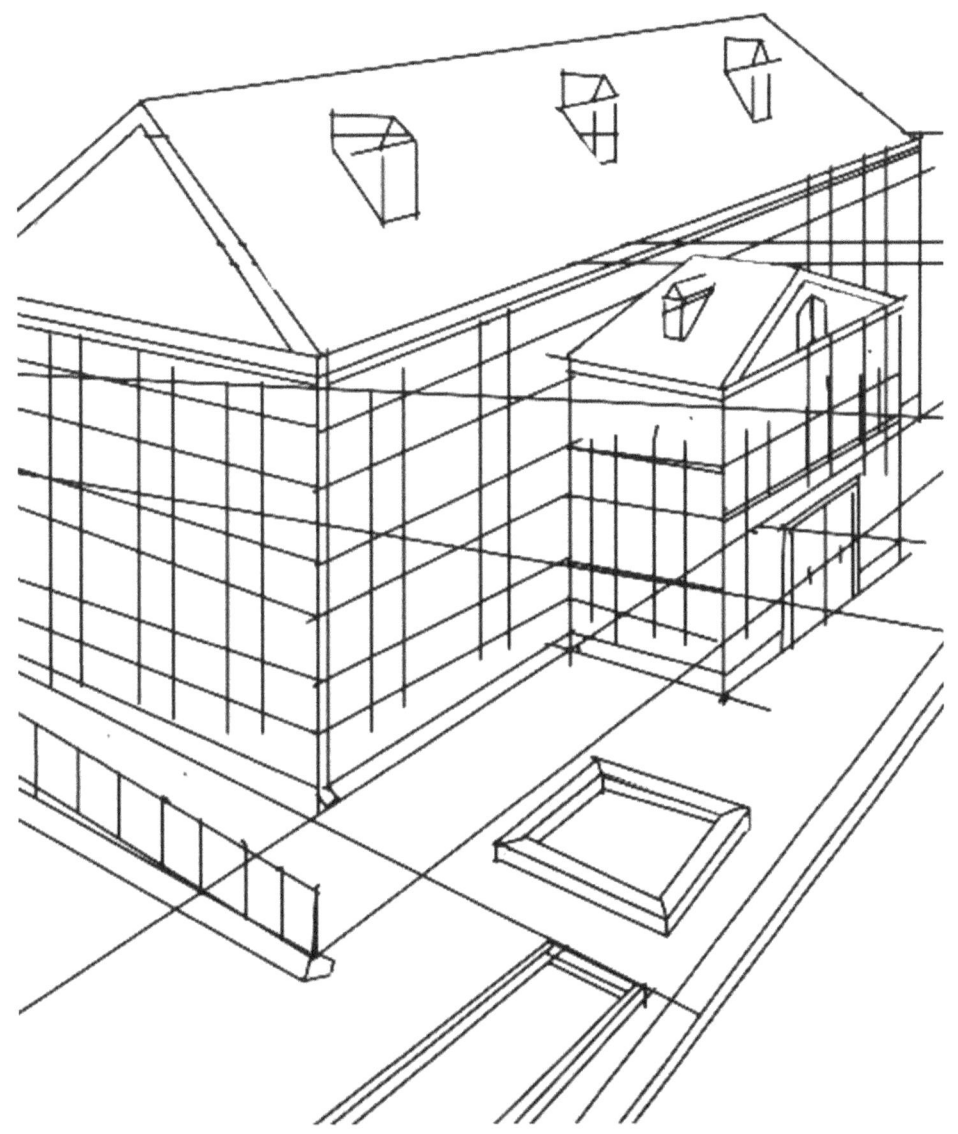

Okay, now we add more lines to the roof, and then remove some from the main front of the estate as well as the windows. As you see the estate is coming along rather nicely and the image is really starting to take shape!

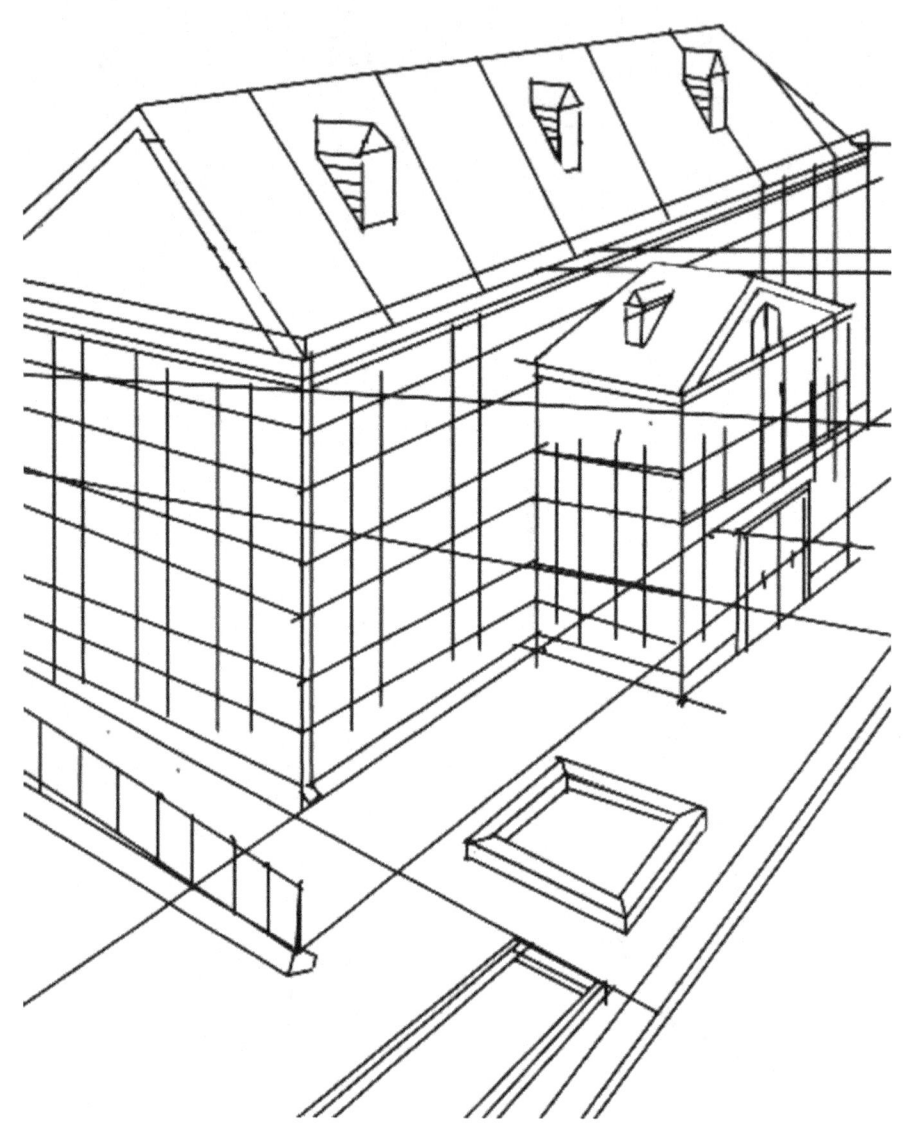

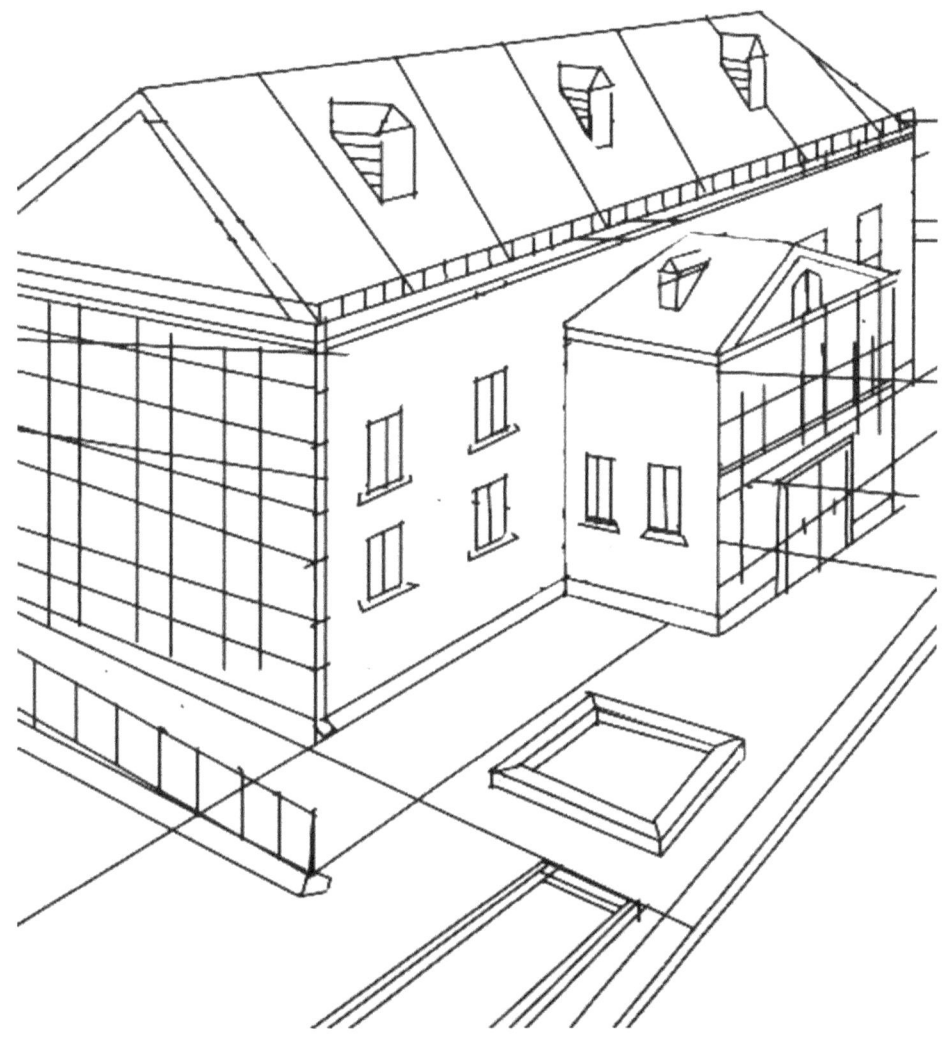

In these two images we see the final removal of the lines from the main estate, as well as the culmination of the windows created along all sides of the estate. The trim on the manors roof is a focal point as well, being something that could easily slip under the radar. Not only that but there are subtle additions to the main entrance to look out for

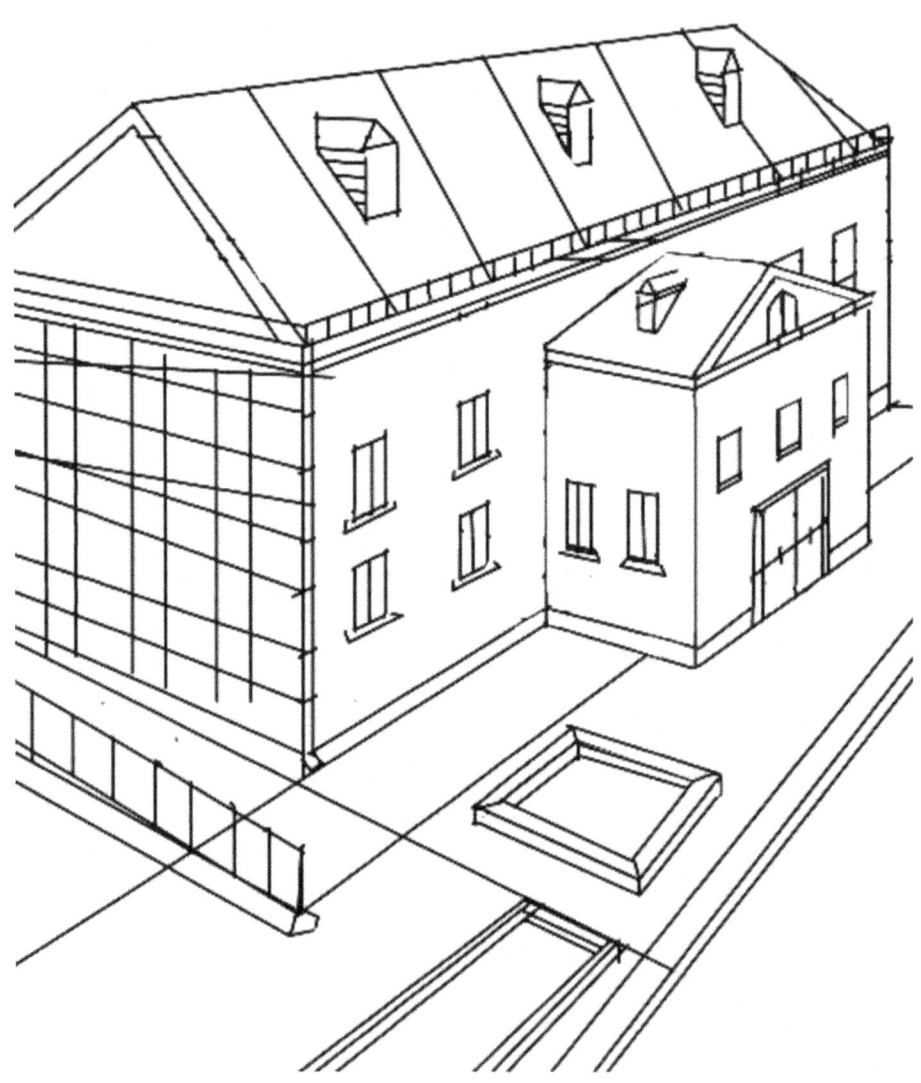

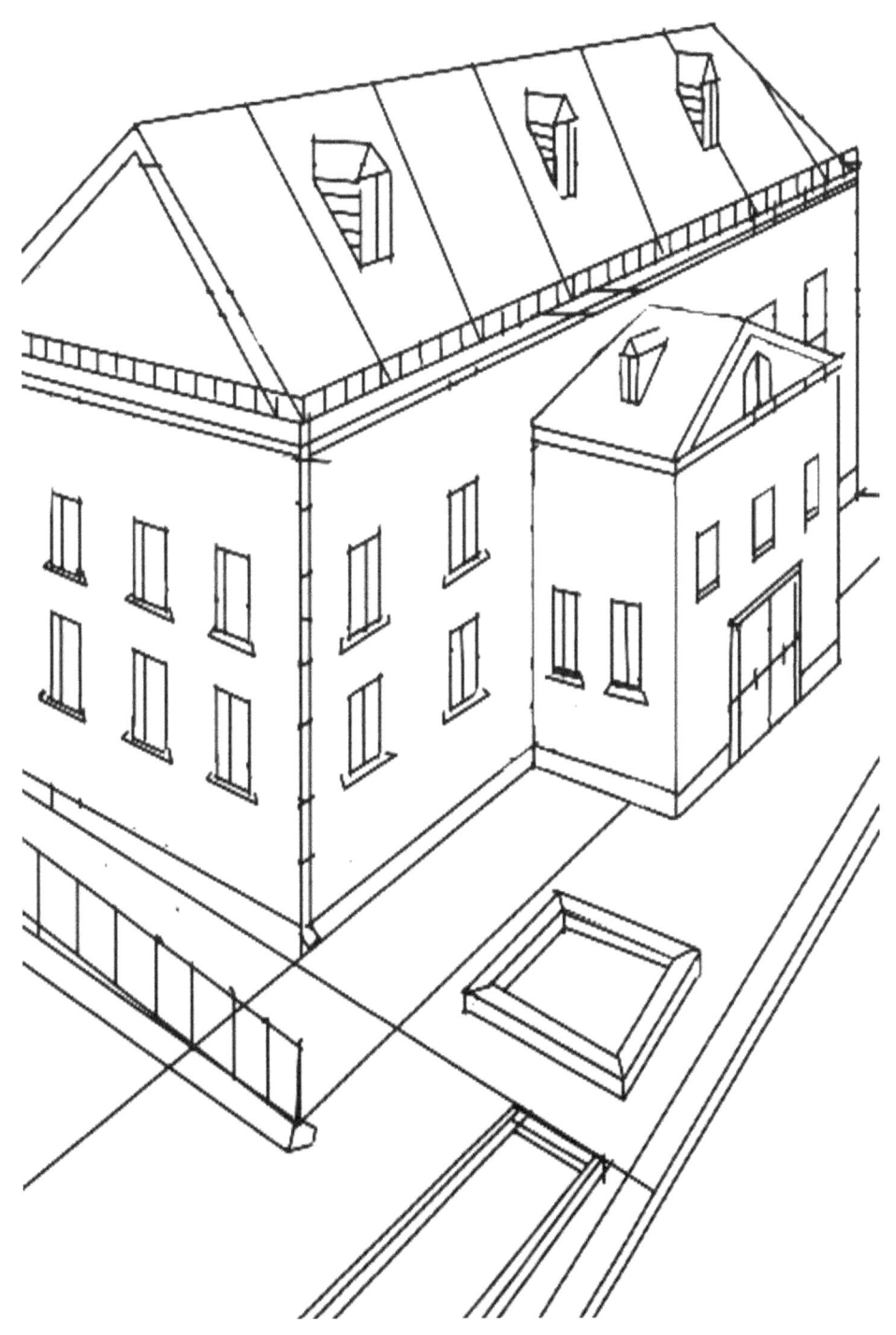

At long last we see that tree go in the planter at the bottom of the estate along the grounds, as well as some shrubs in the other one. There's also several subtle additions to the main entrance to look out for. Then when done those its time to start shading. You'll see a larger focus on darker shades the closer the building is to the perspective. Watch your blending.

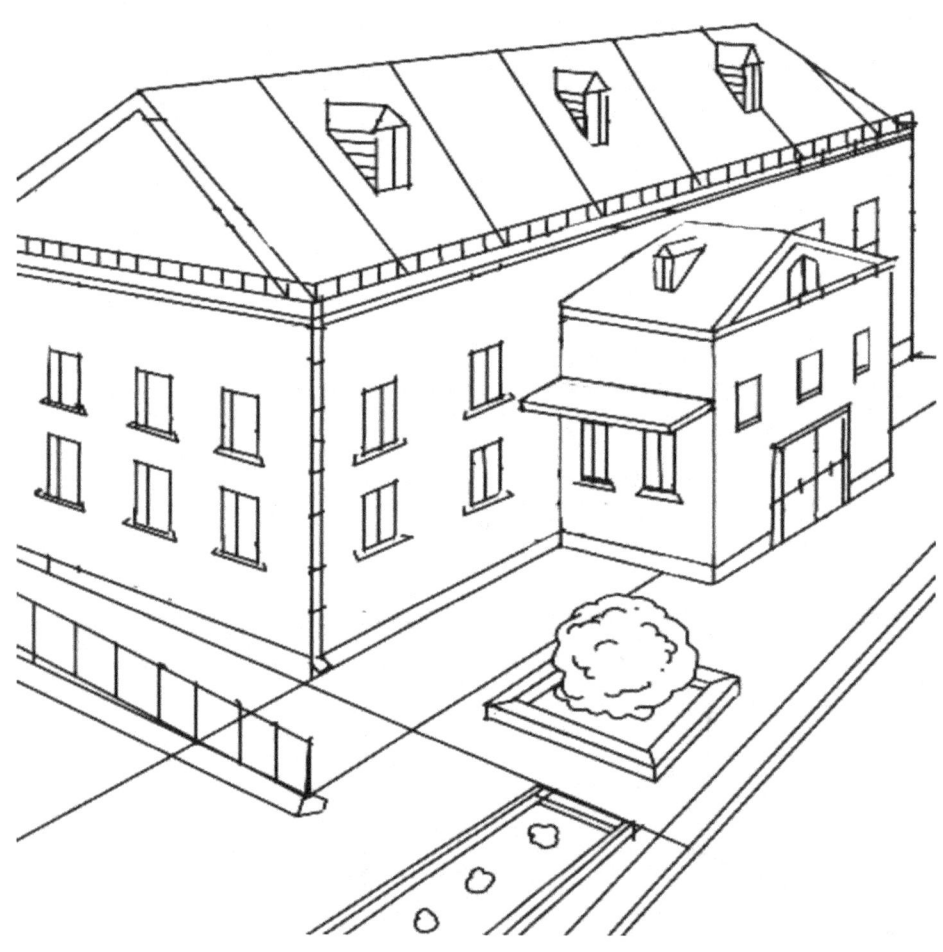

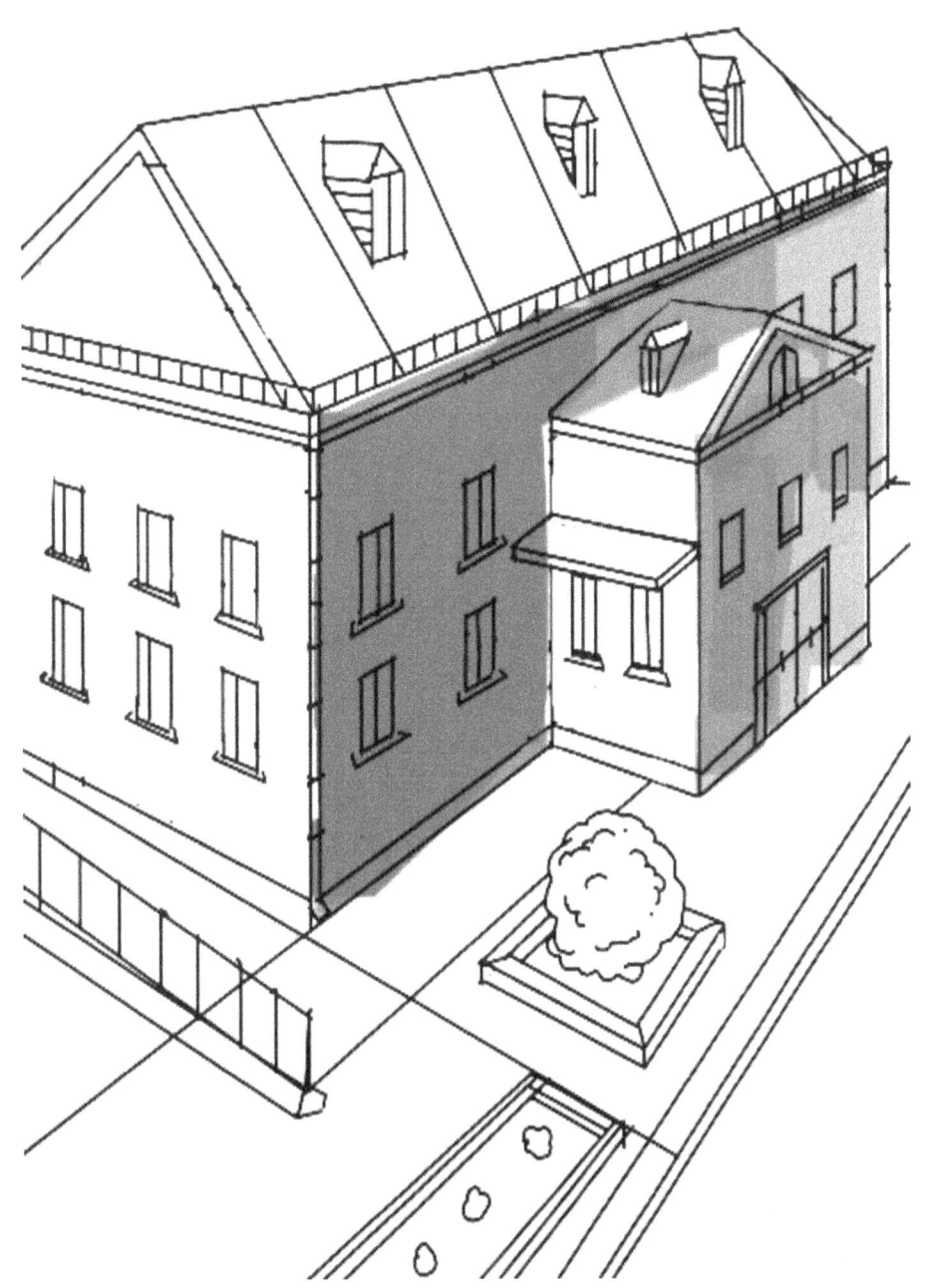

Here we reach the final two steps which again focus on shading and blending. As you'll see the main shadow falls across the very front of the estate and the fence. The lightest of tones is in the upper right corner and blends lighter outwards. This specific perspective drawing was a vast deal more intricate than others and is an impressive feat. Congratulations on completing this one!

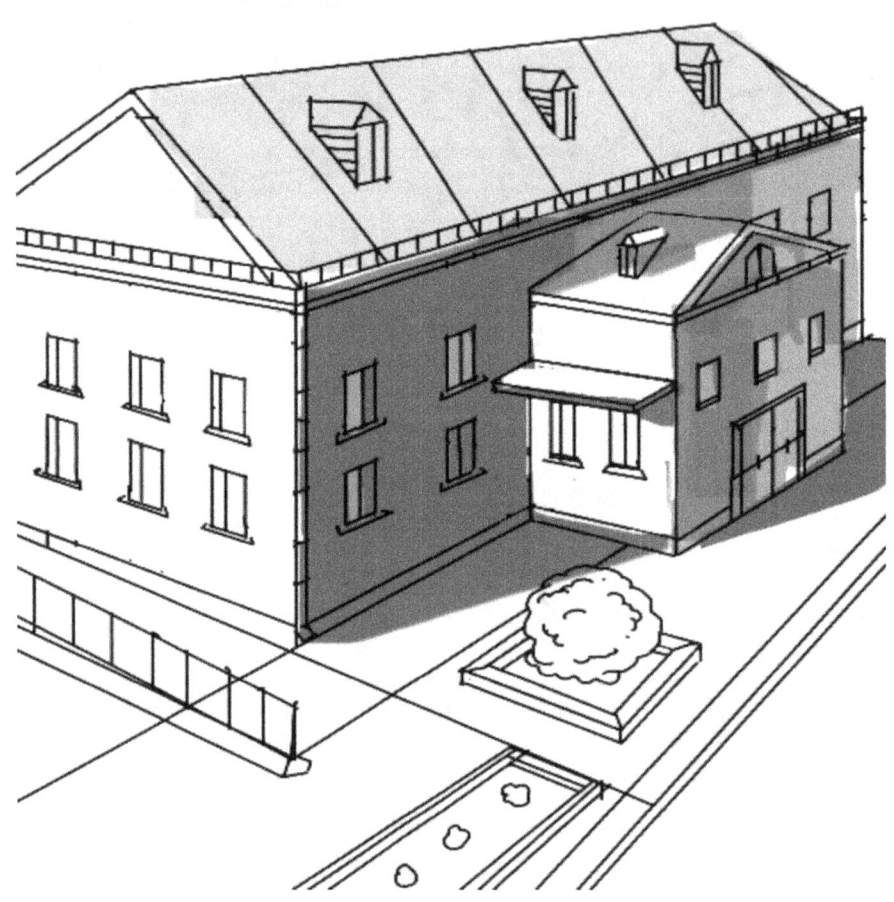

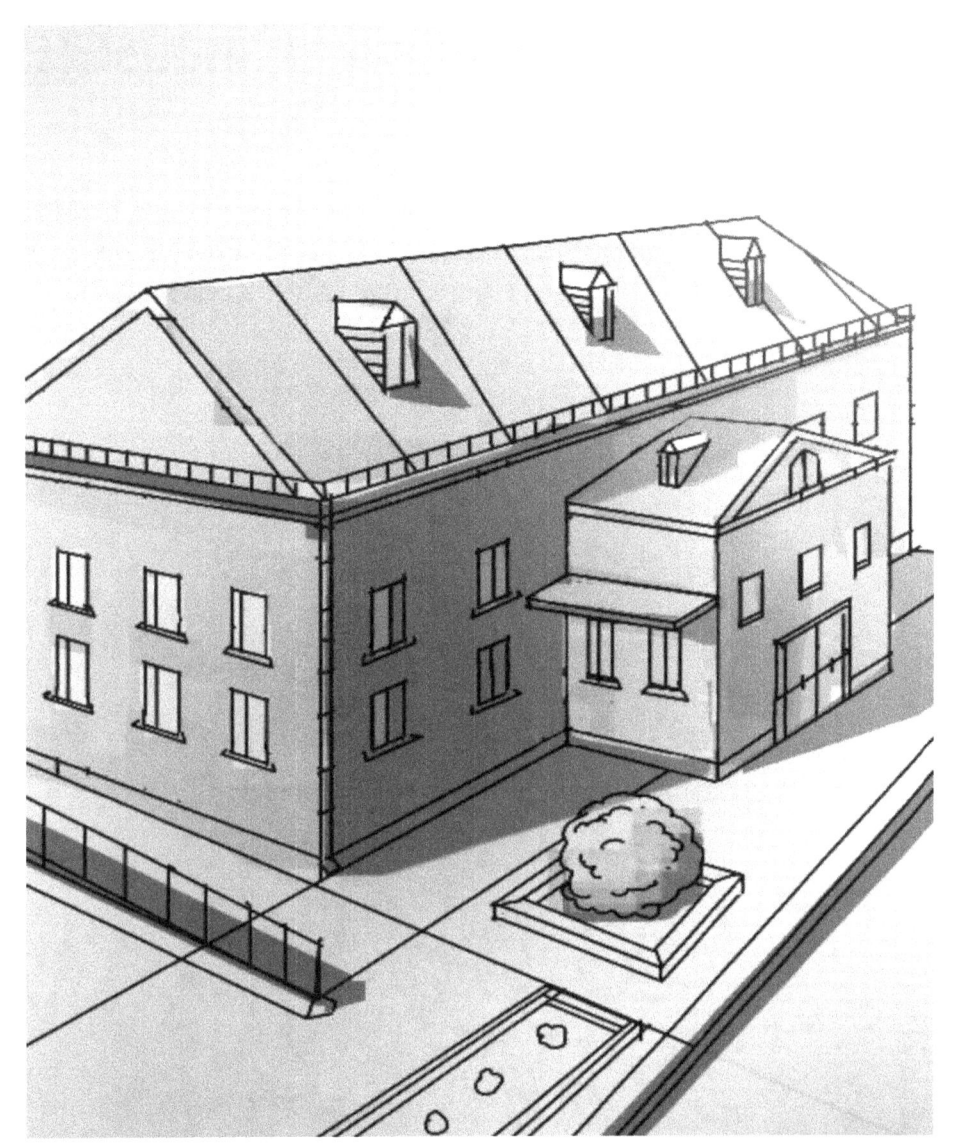

Seventh Perspective Drawing: Industrial Building

This next one is a lot like the last perspective image you crafted. Another exterior aerial shot with a lot of intricate line work. Start with the image on the right and follow its example closely.

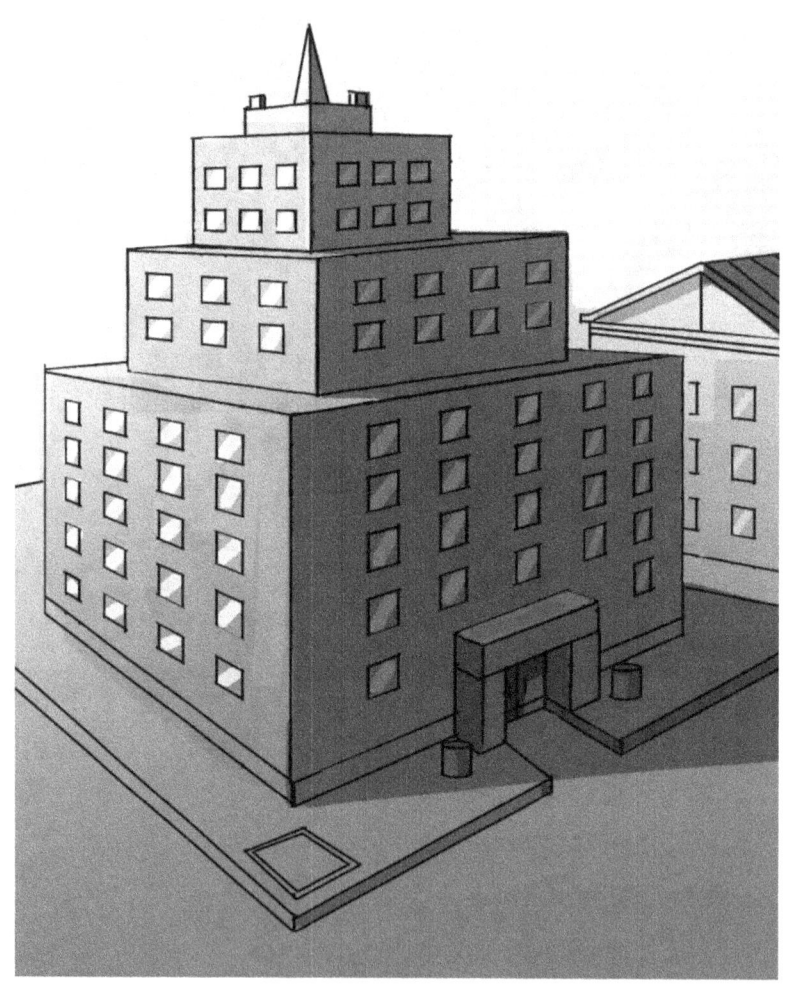

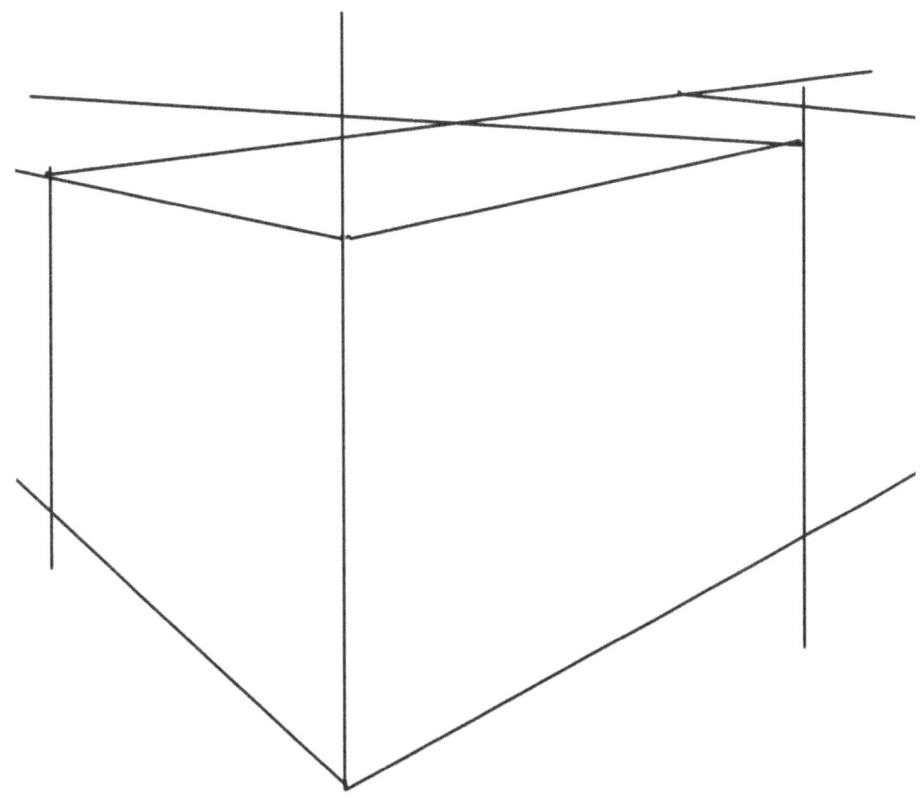

Once you have the original line work in place, follow these next two steps which shows more of the upper building structure being crafted by cross work and through lines. Keep in pace with those and then in the next step add even more. Try not to get overwhelmed with it.

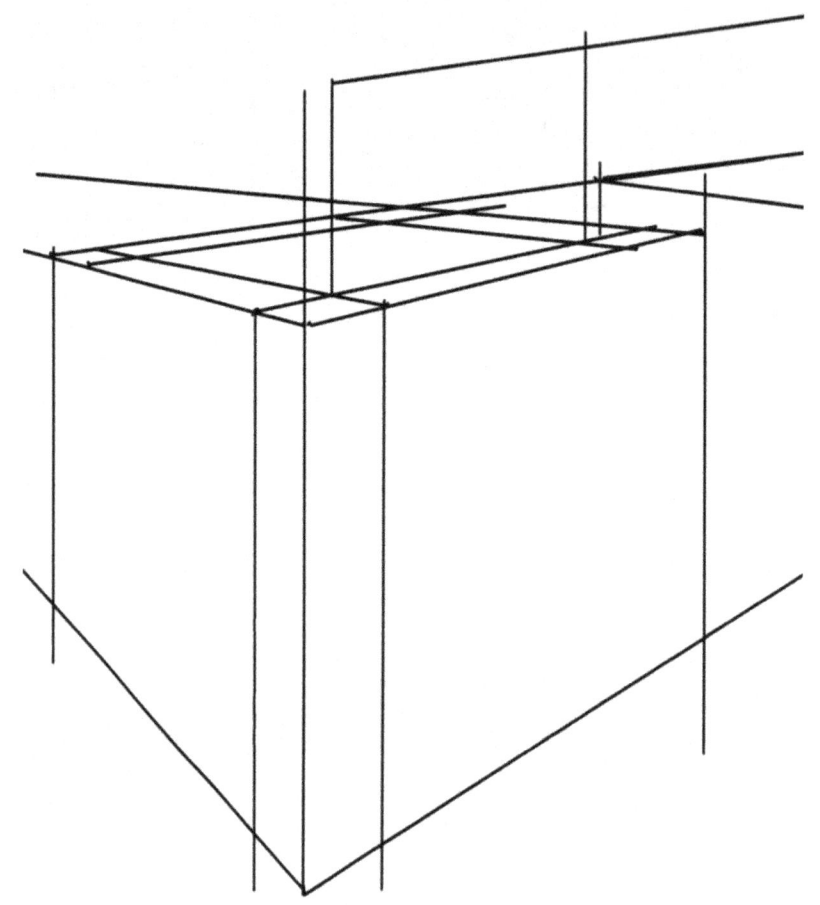

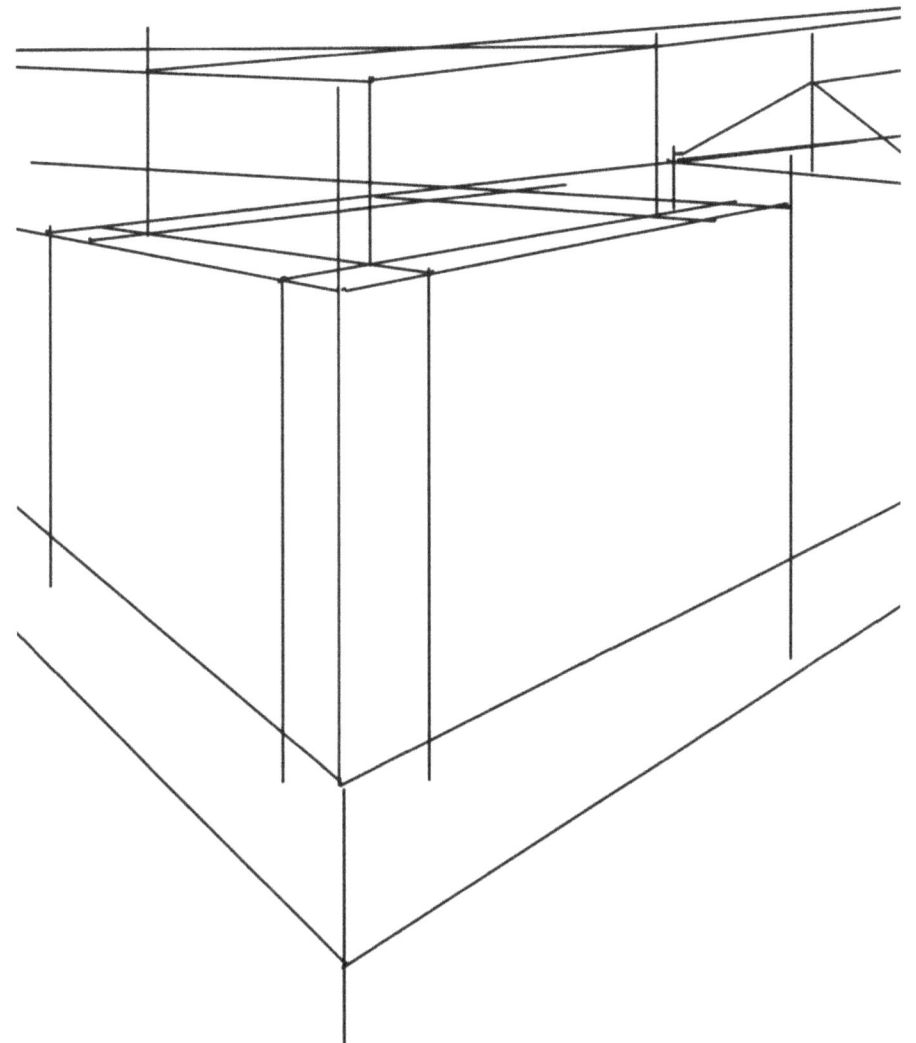

Here you see the foundation starting to really come together. In the image on the left it really begins to come together with more conjoining lines and then in the one on the right it looks more solid with the extra lines added in. There's an excess but they all play an important role in the creation of the building.

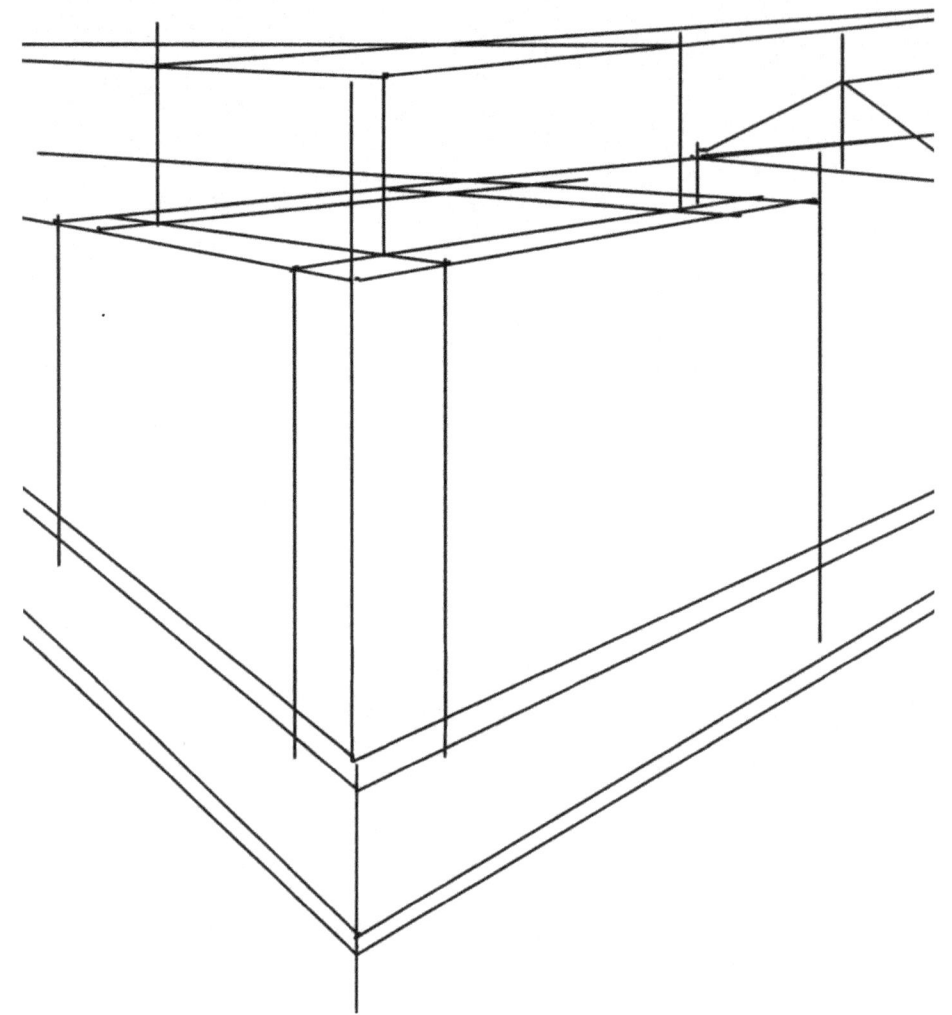

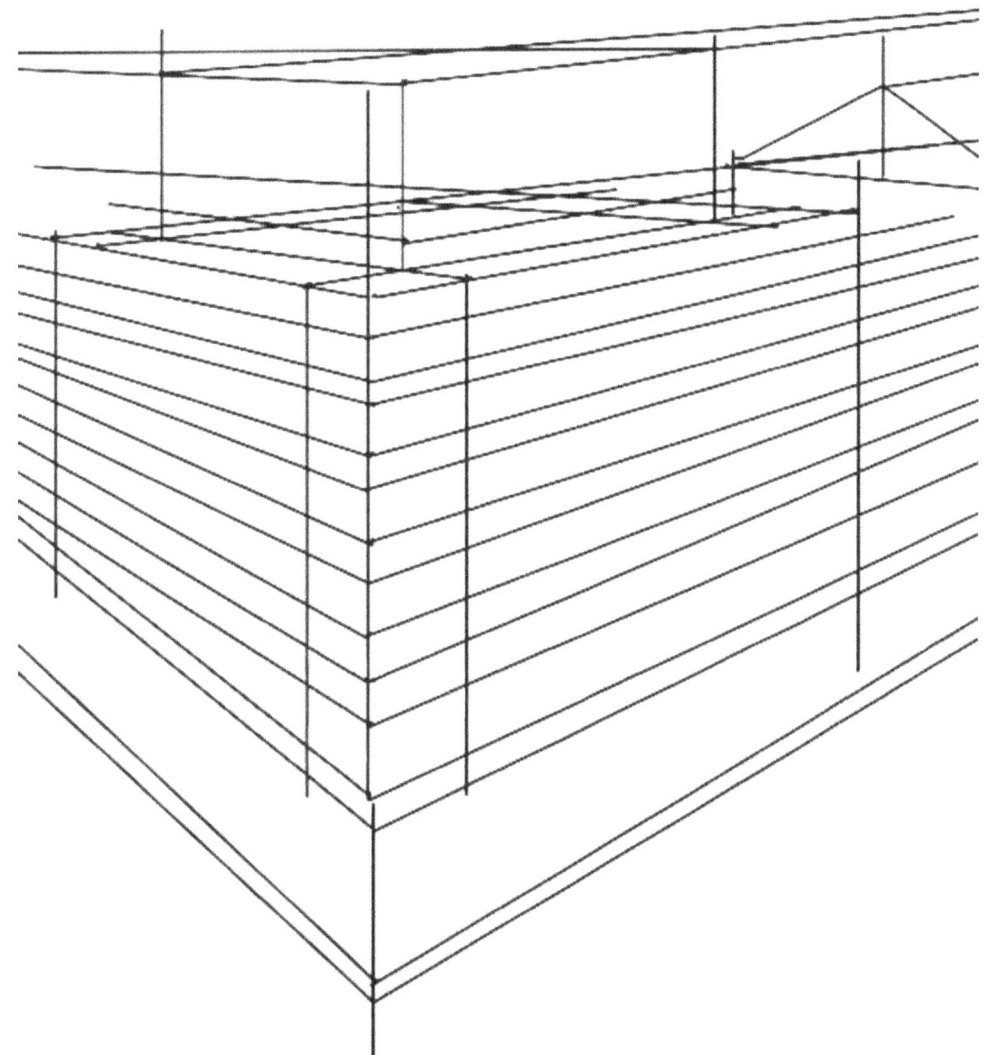

We start moving up the other levels in these next couple steps, as you'll see here in the next two steps we start on the middle and upper levels as well as the main entrance. Lines are added as well as removed as we proceed.

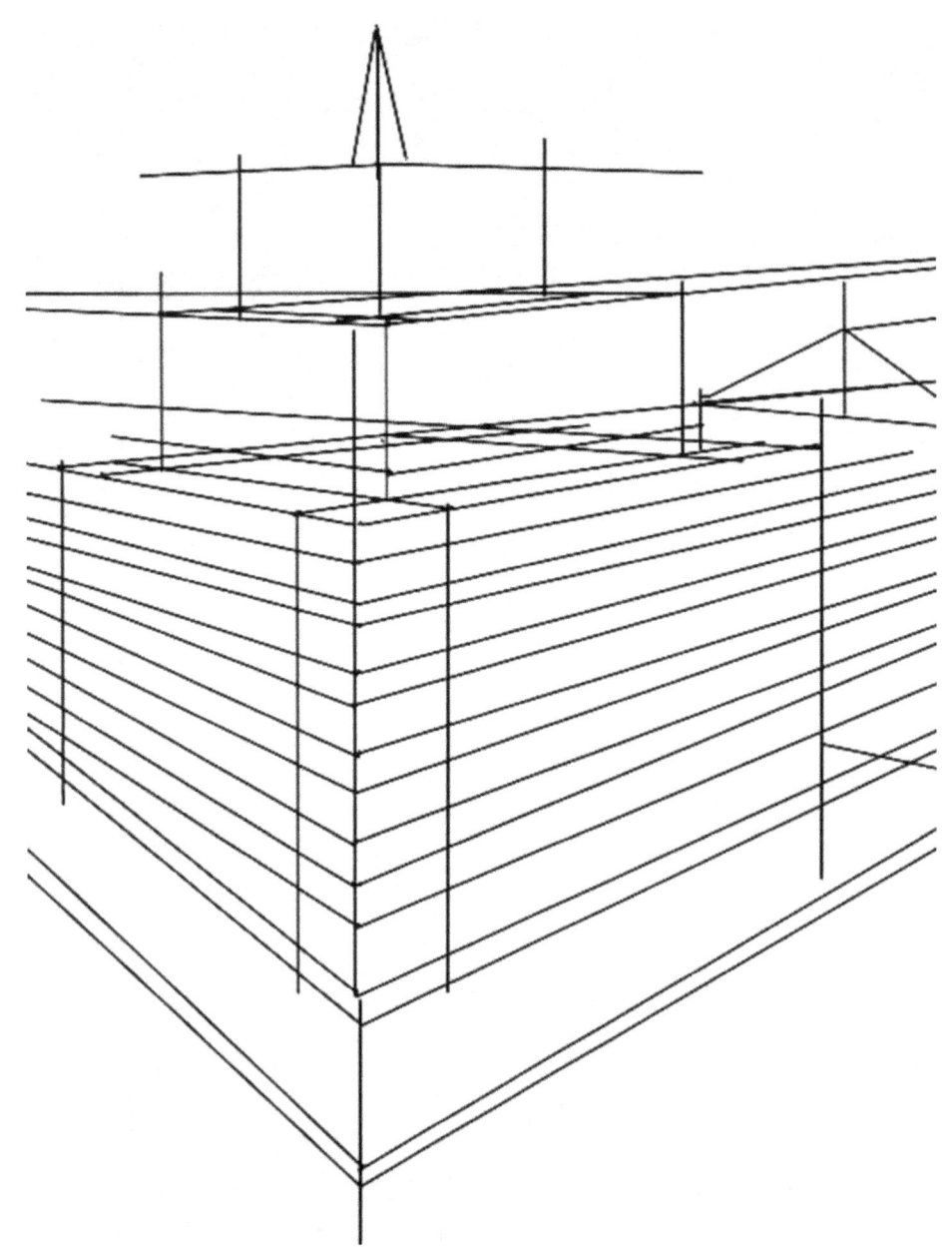

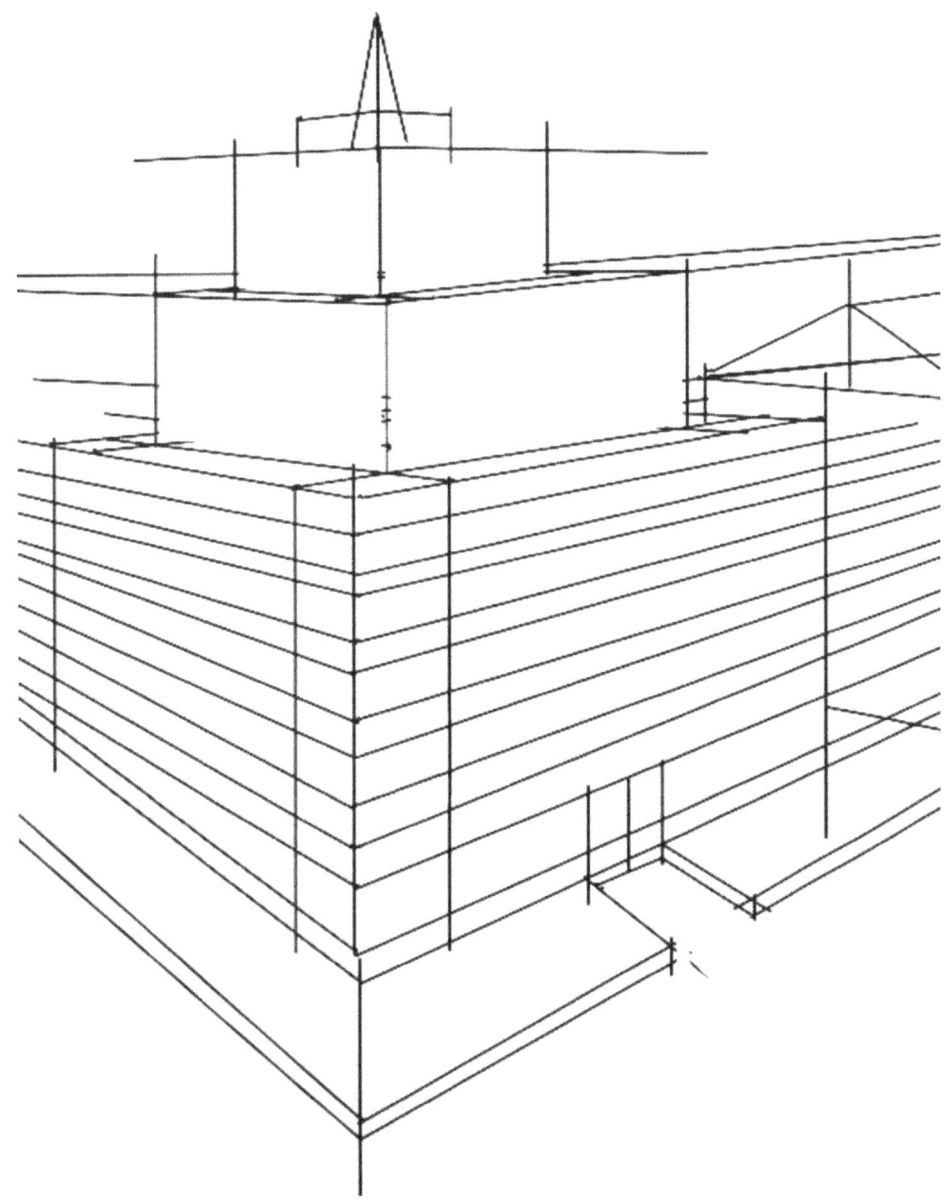

As we continue to add structural integrity to the building it looks more complicated. The lines become a lot more self involved and the final product can be hard to see. Yet in the image on the right you can see the image starting to develop. Watch those cross lines and the second building at the back as you continue.

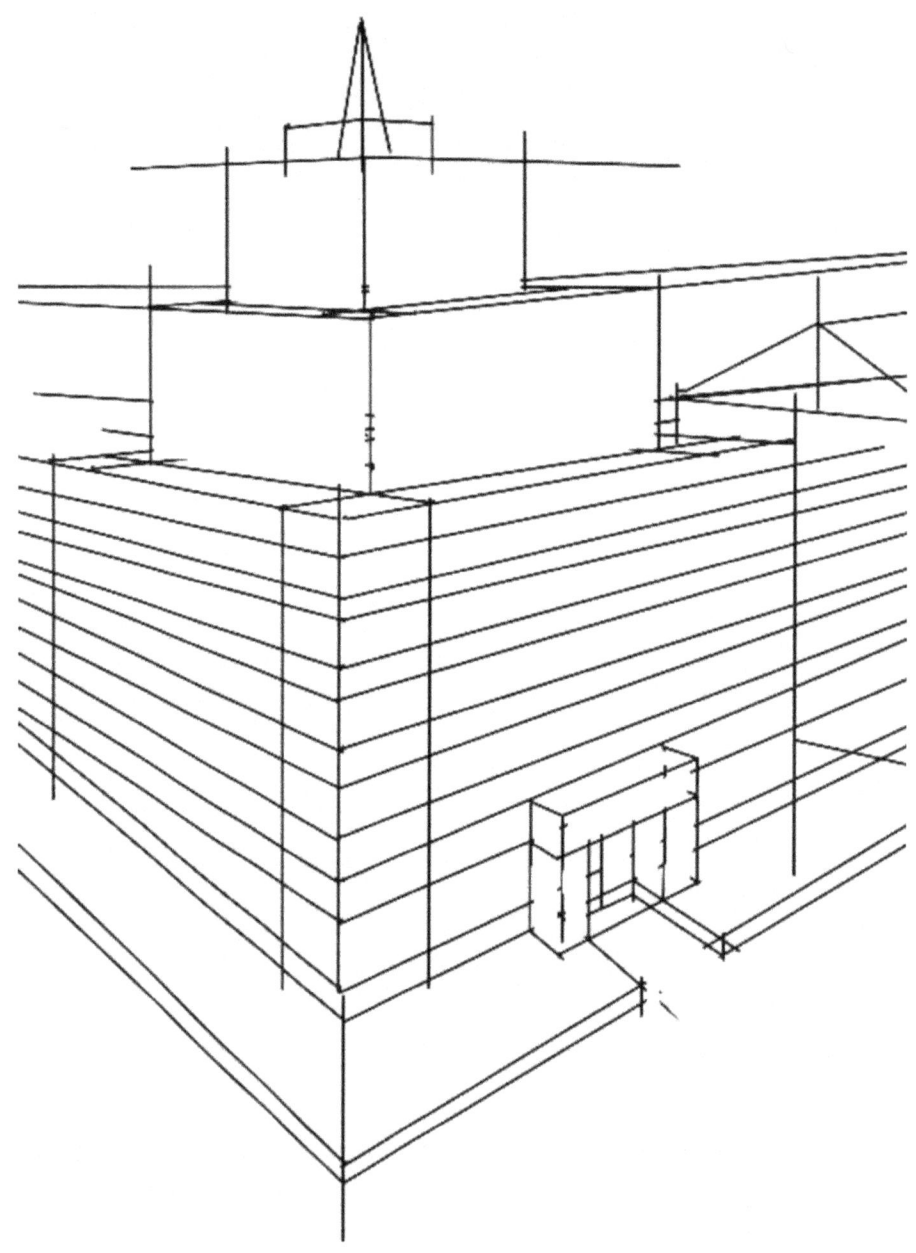

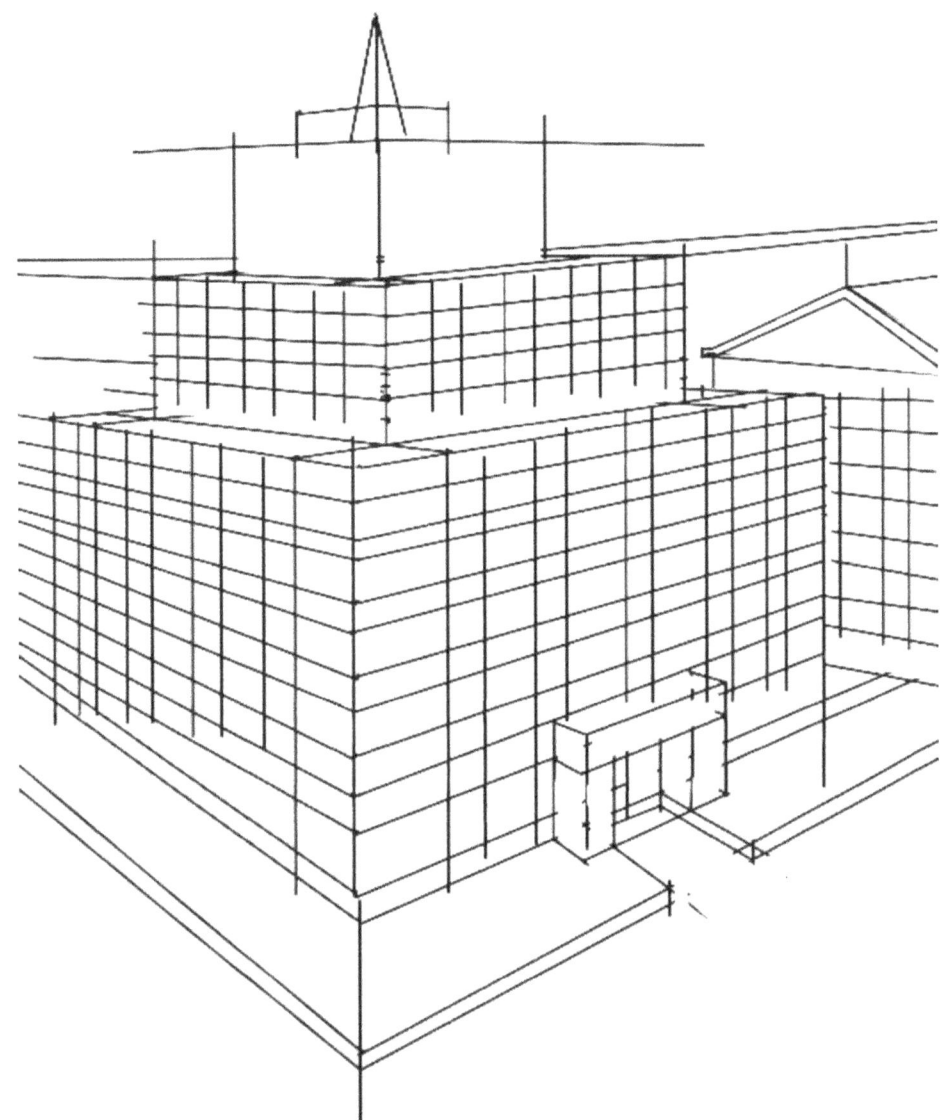

As you continue to add to the building keep an eye on your edges and your straight lines. try not to let the intricacies confuse you or take you by surprise. Then in the image on the right you finally have those windows developed. Watch out for those and make sure you get a clean look for it.

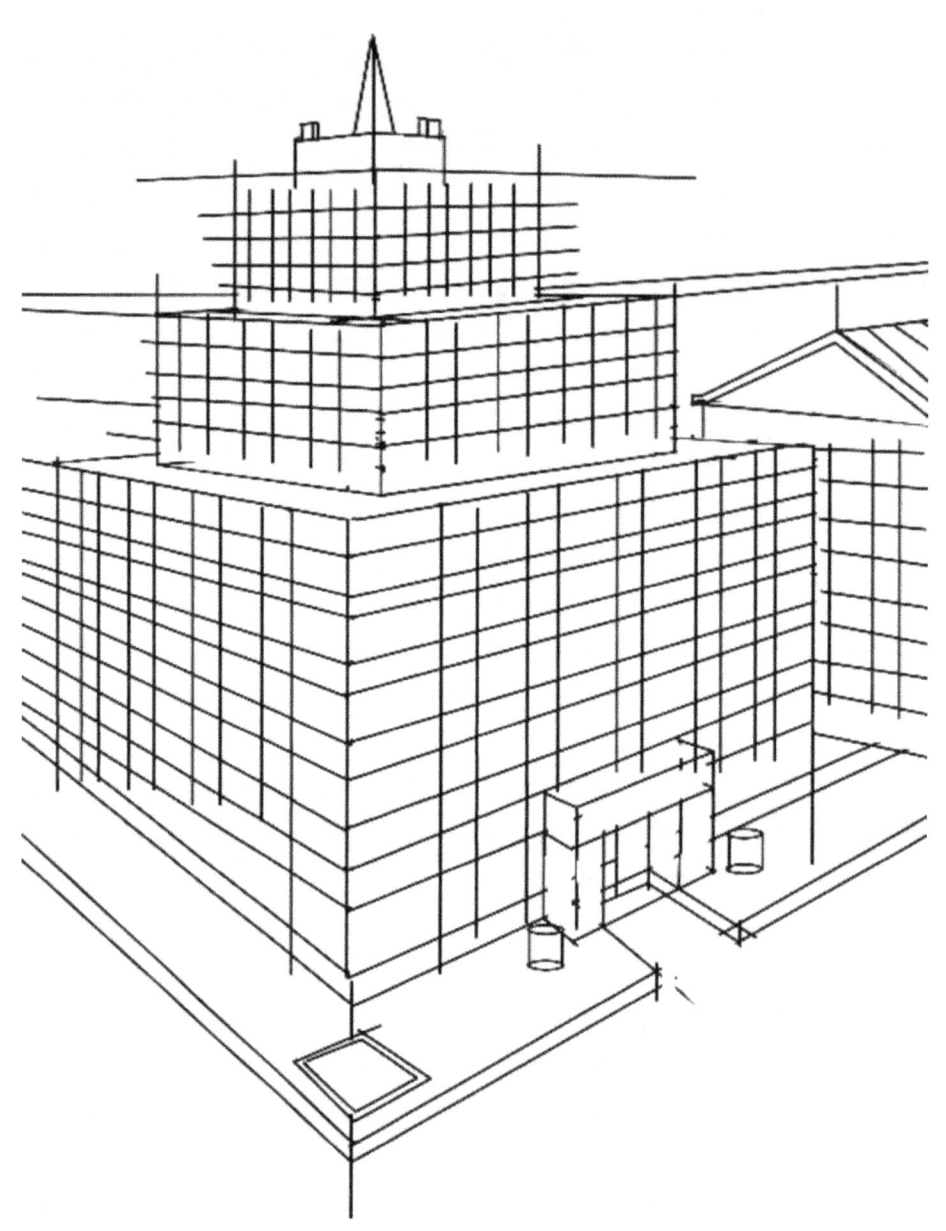

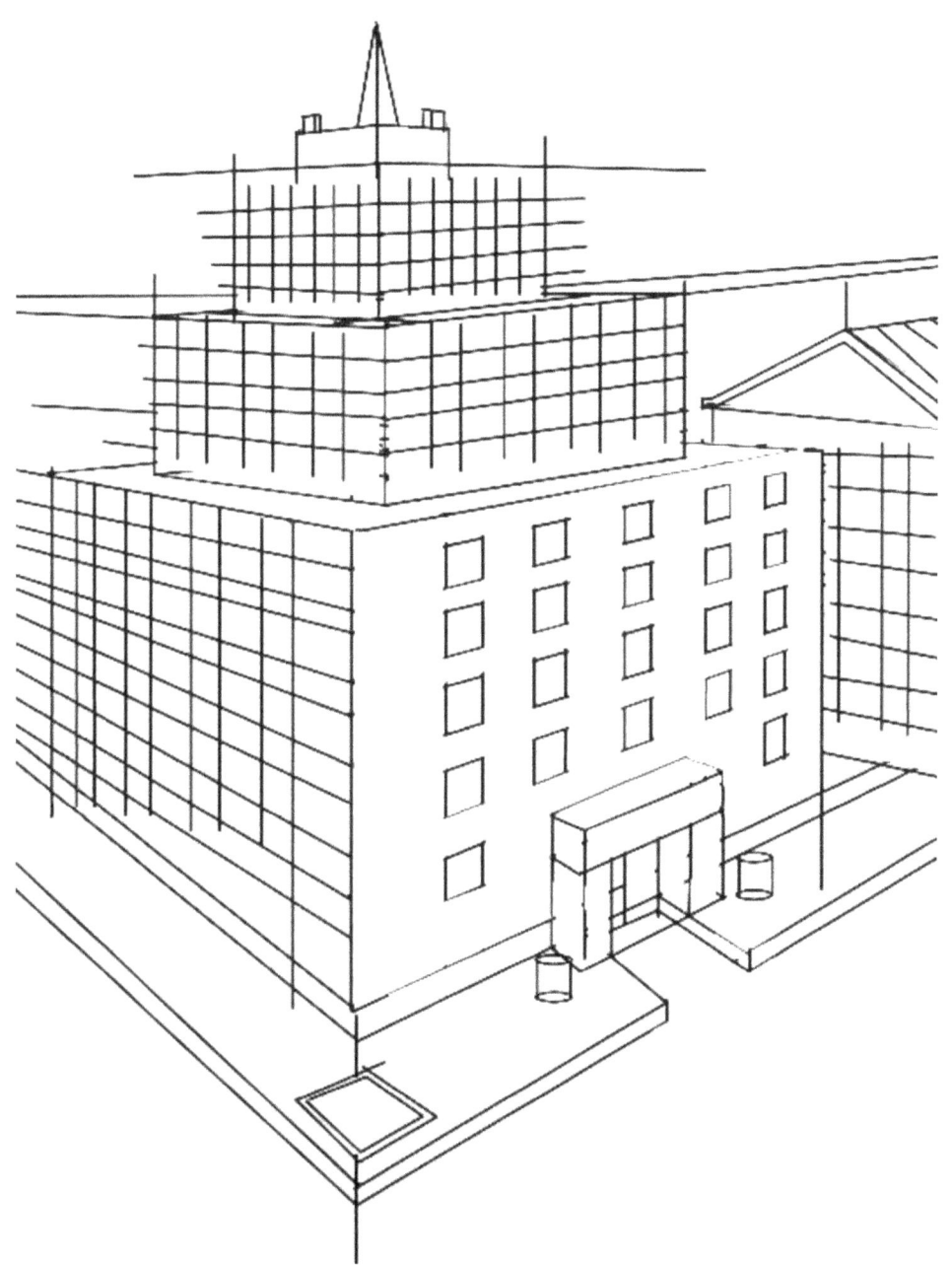

In these next two steps we focus on the windows for both the main building as well as the one in the background. Not just for the main level but the second as well. You'll also the that the cross lines are more focused in the second to just the upper building. In preparation for adding the windows.

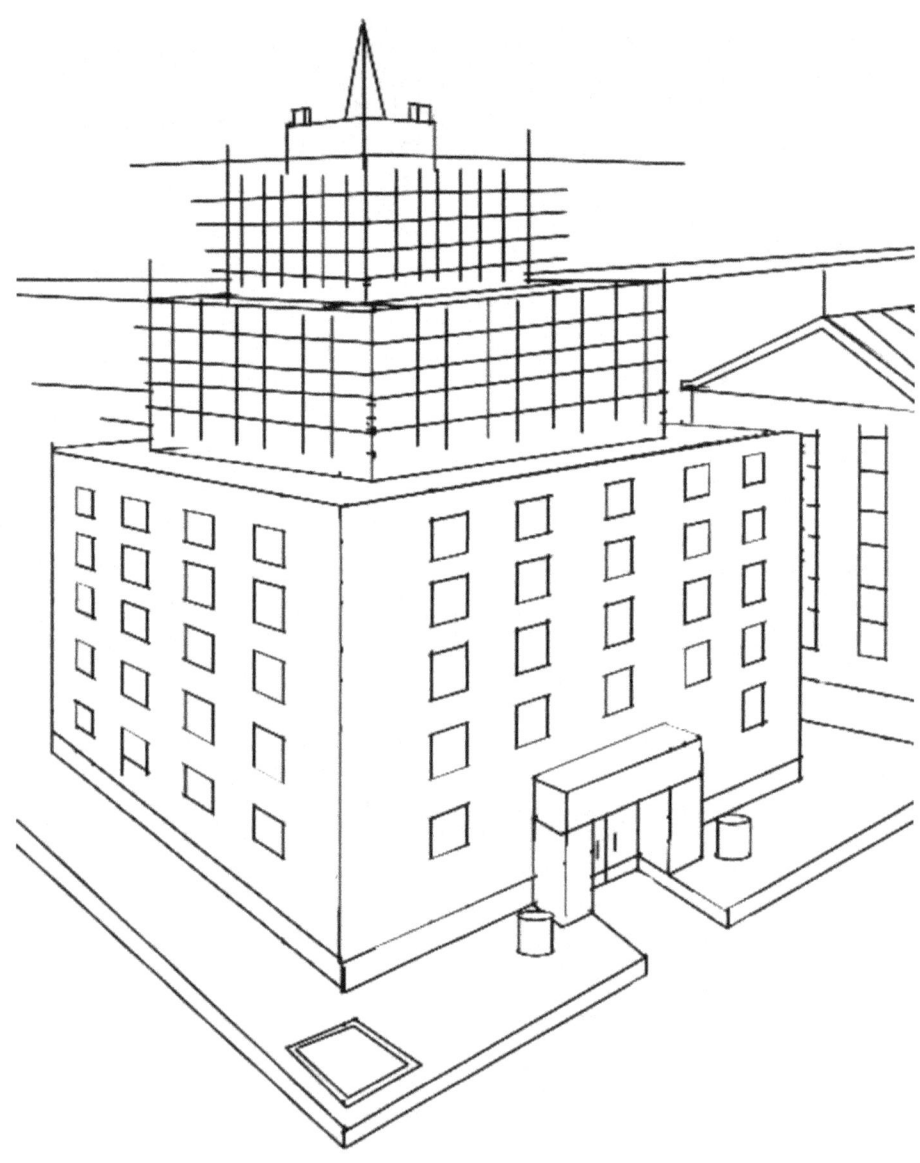

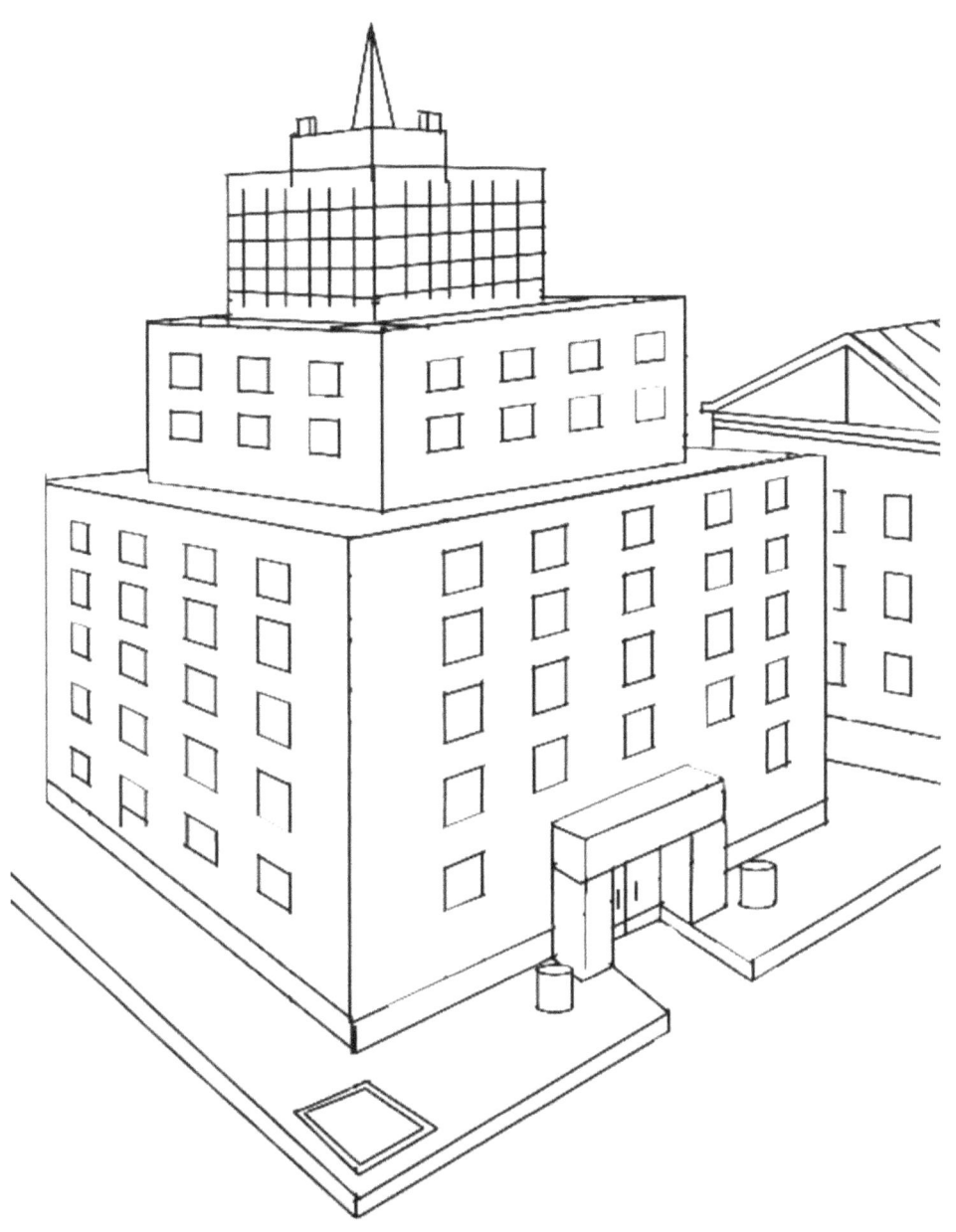

Now the final level of the building has its windows and we embark on the journey of shading. Again this is another important thing to remember but the location of light is a huge part of these perspective drawings. If you know where the sun is coming from its beneficial for outside shots. Indoors its important to take note of sources of light. Either way, start getting the shading on the building done then proceed to the next set of steps.

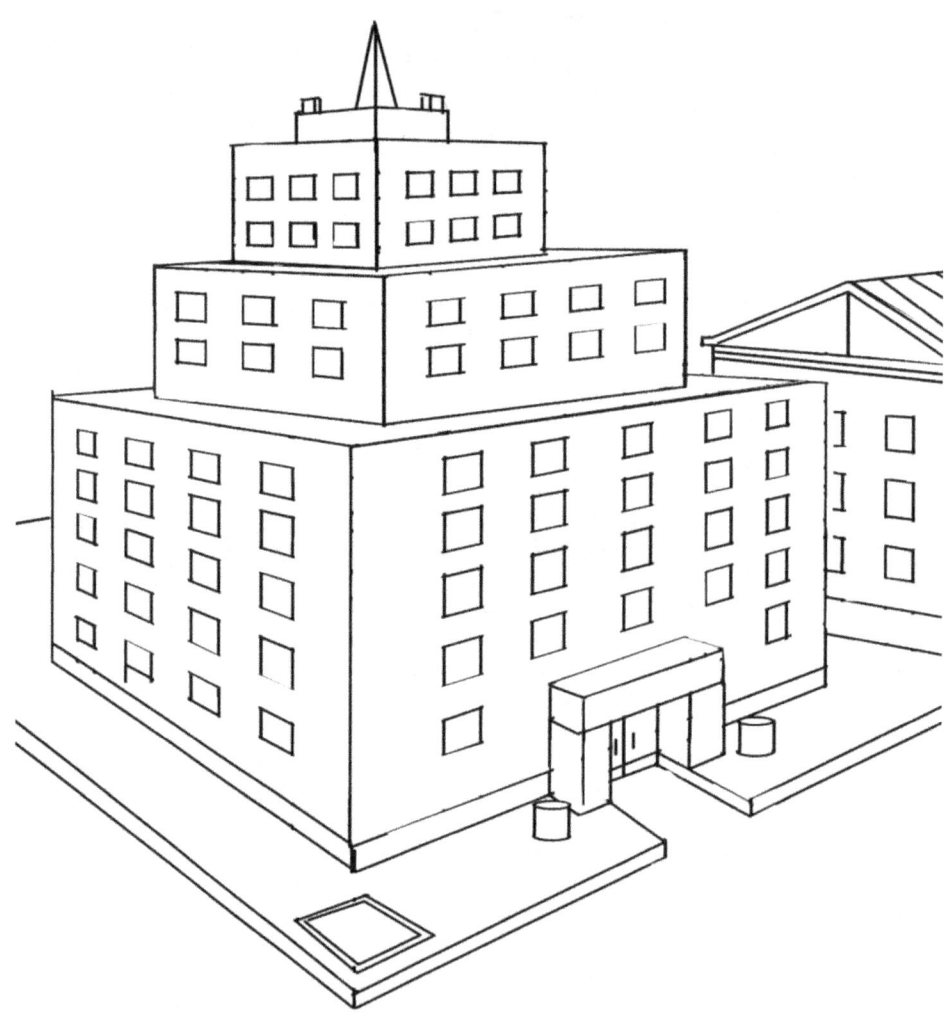

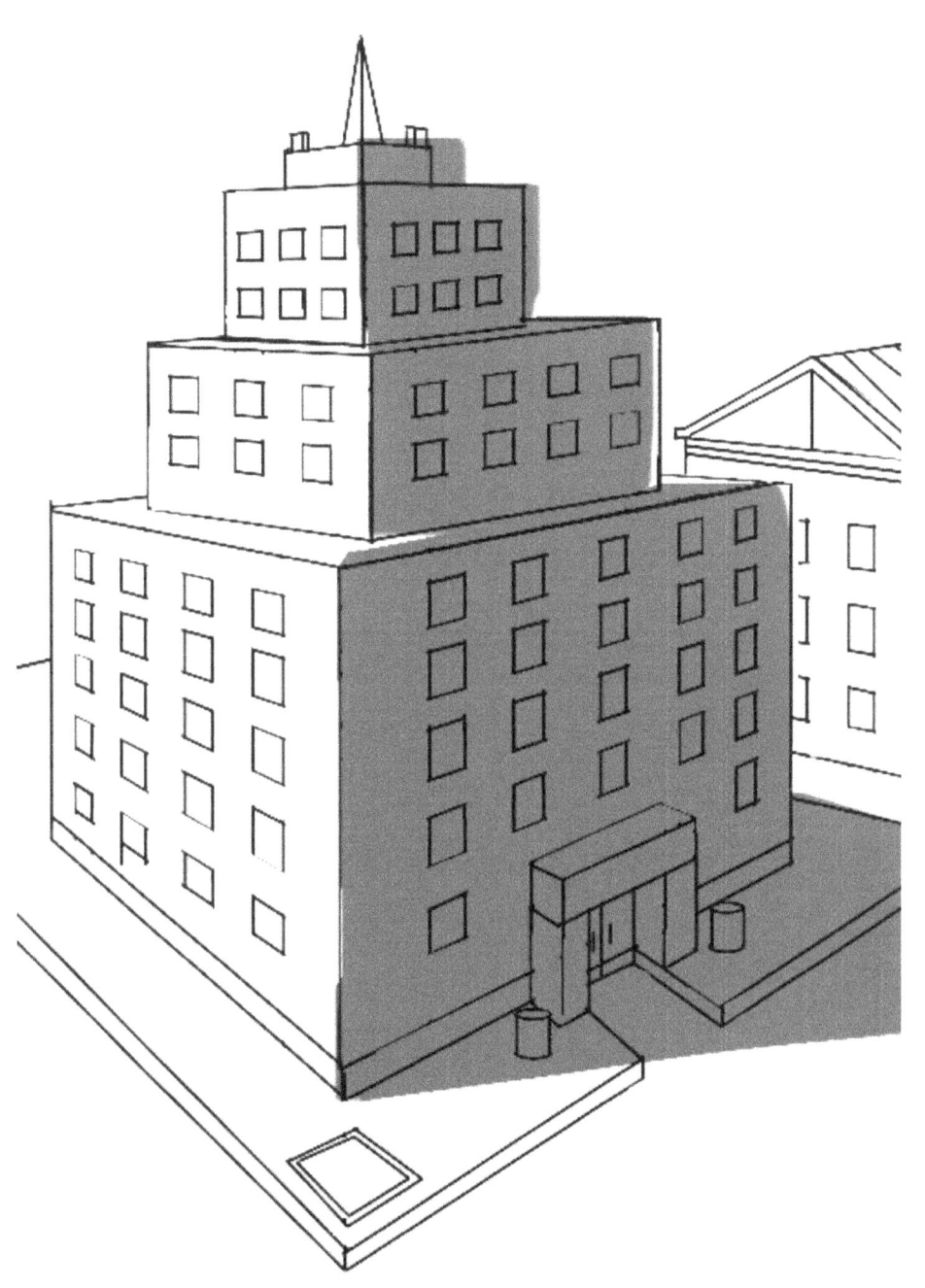

Again as always you'll notice the blending taking shape here. The darker shades on the right hand most side of both buildings and the angles at which the light hits each building. You'll notice in the second image on the right that the point at the top of the building is also affected by light positioning.

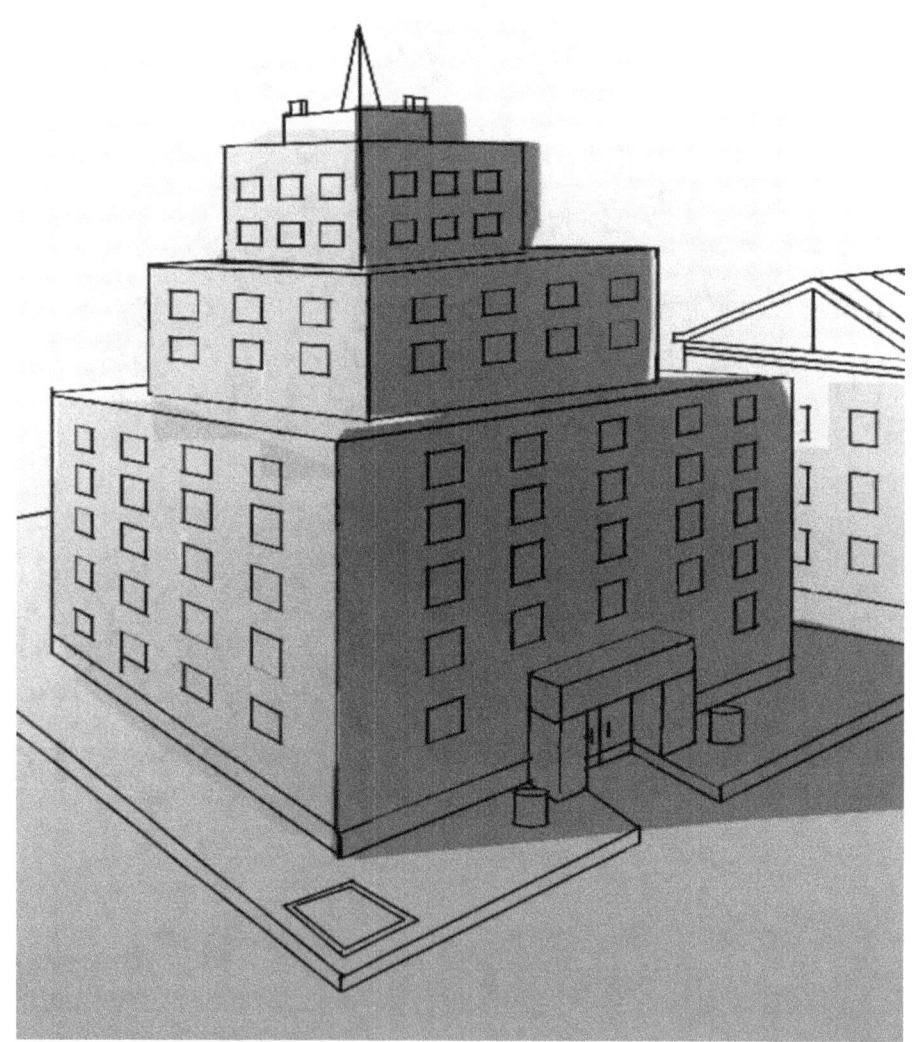

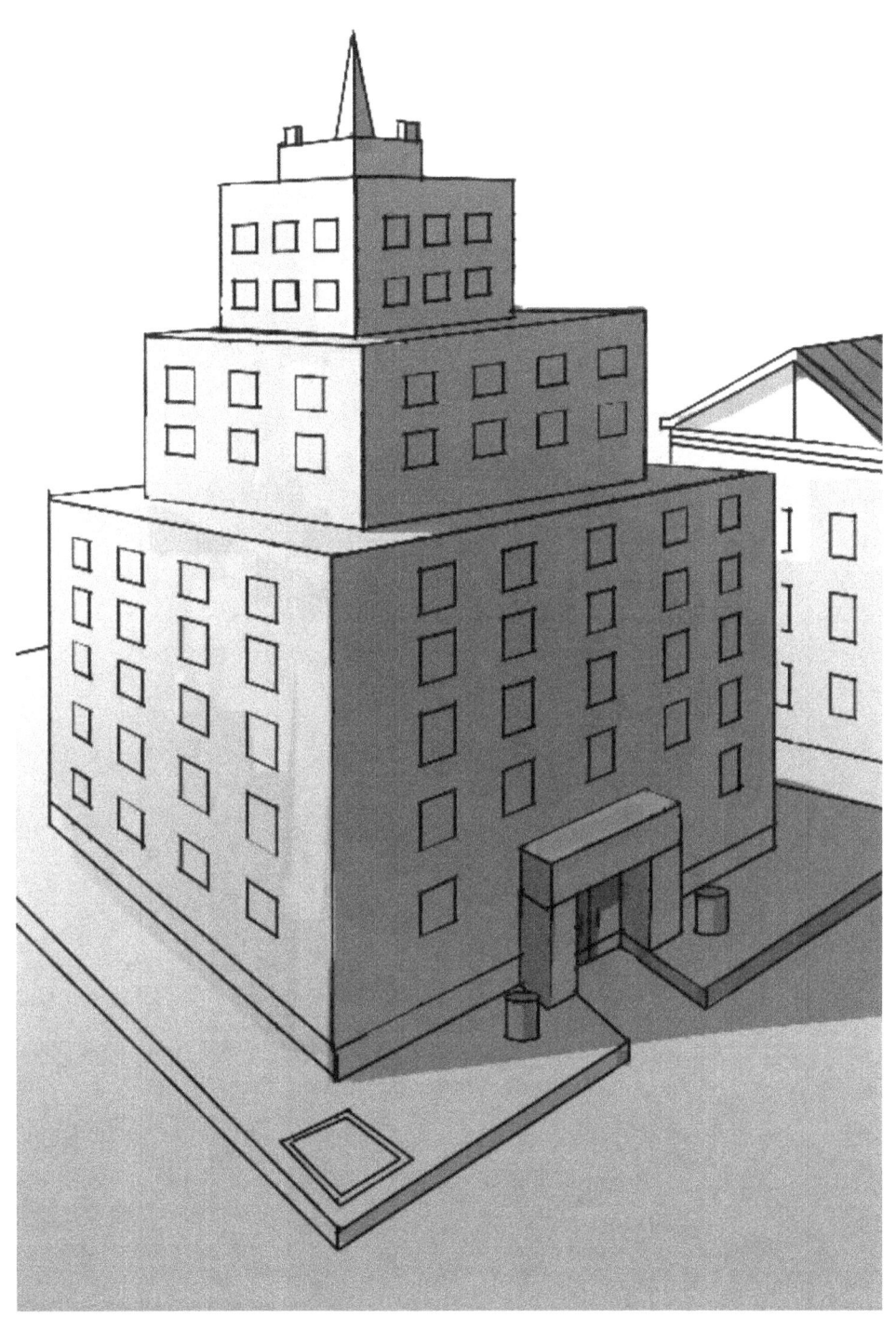

Here we see the shine of the windows is an integral addition as well as the final aspect of blending, then the image is complete! This one was monstrous. Proceed to the next one and remember techniques learned from this one.

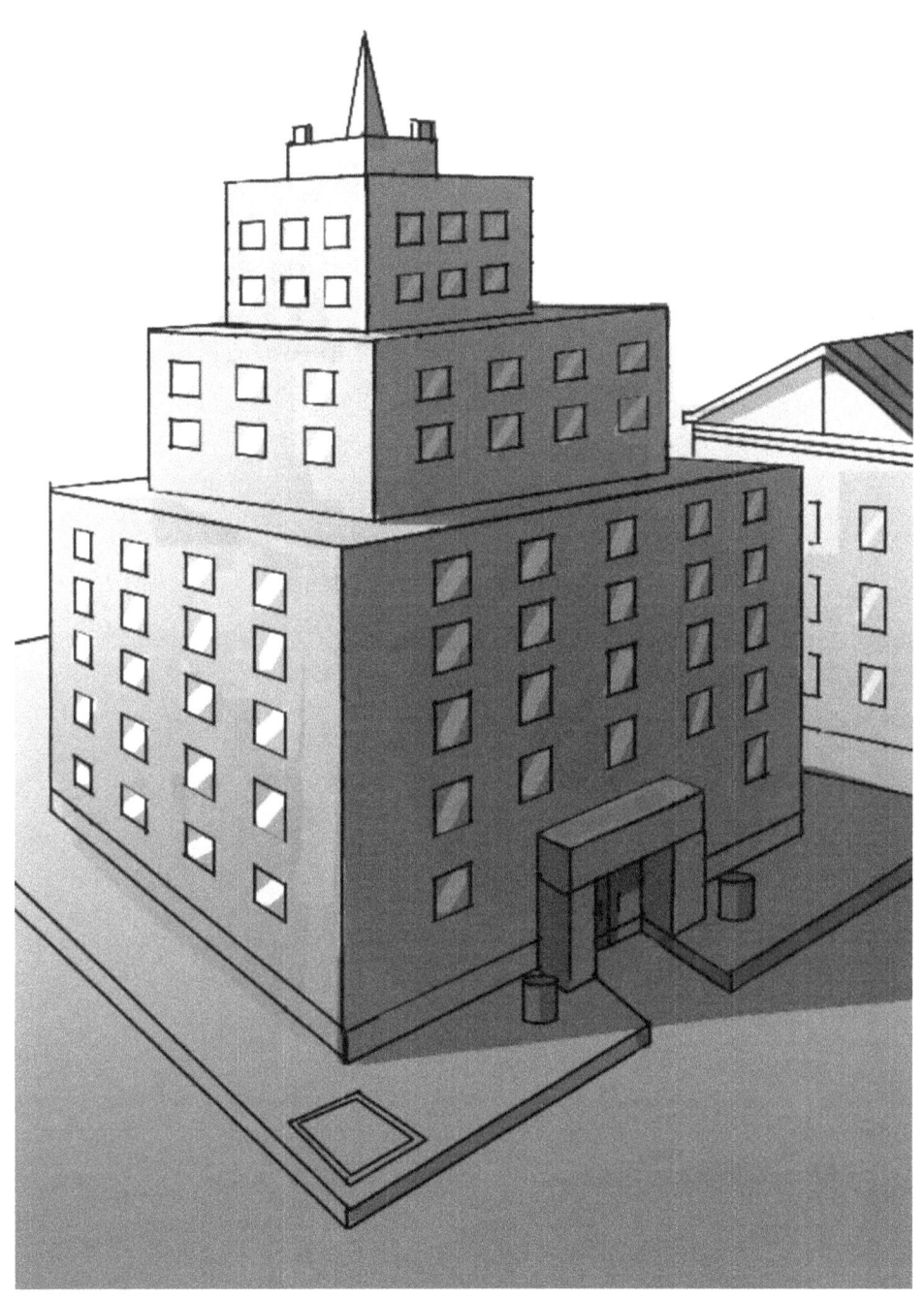

Eighth Perspective Drawing: Storefront

This next one is a ground level view of a storefront. It's got the perspective shading as well as intricacies. It's also one of my favorite images from this set of ten. So moving forward take a good look at the image on the left and then at the image on the right. Evaluate where those lines are going to take you and how they relate to the final product. Then jump right in and get started.

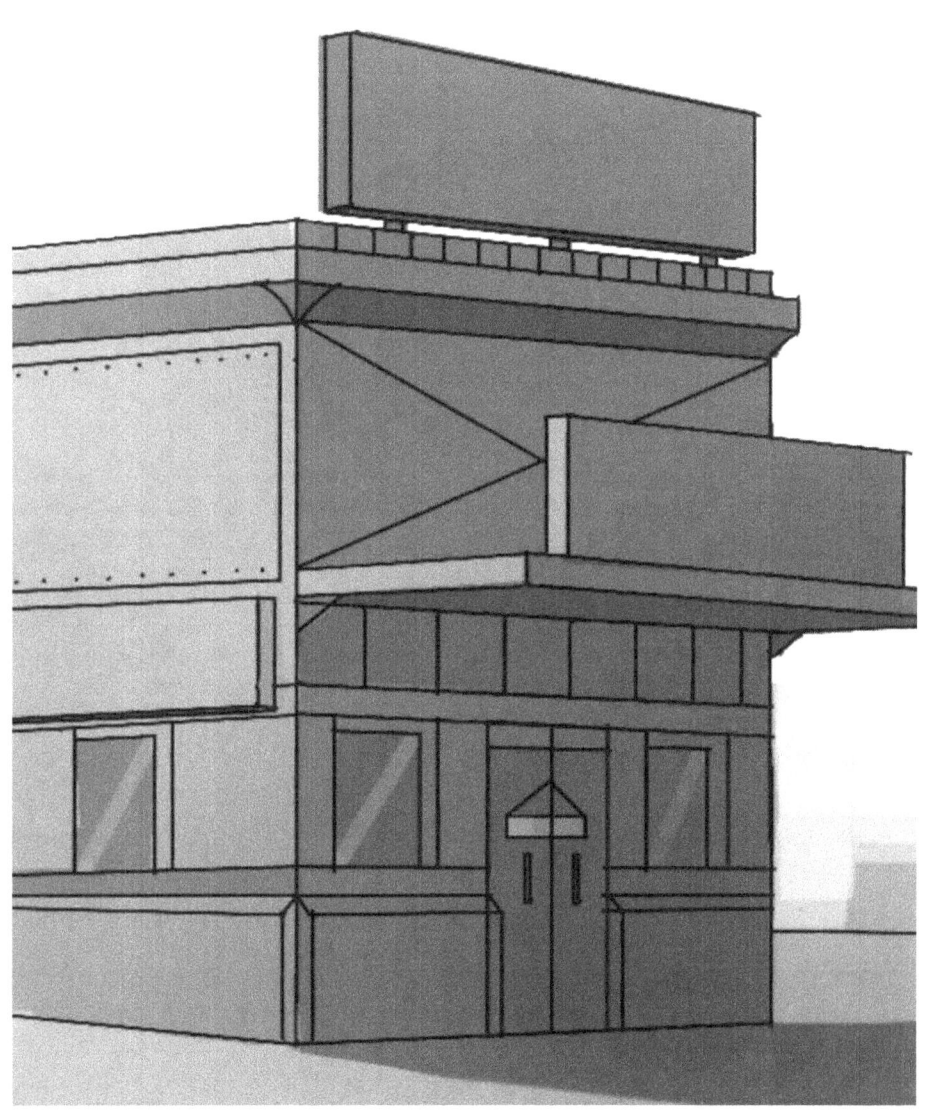

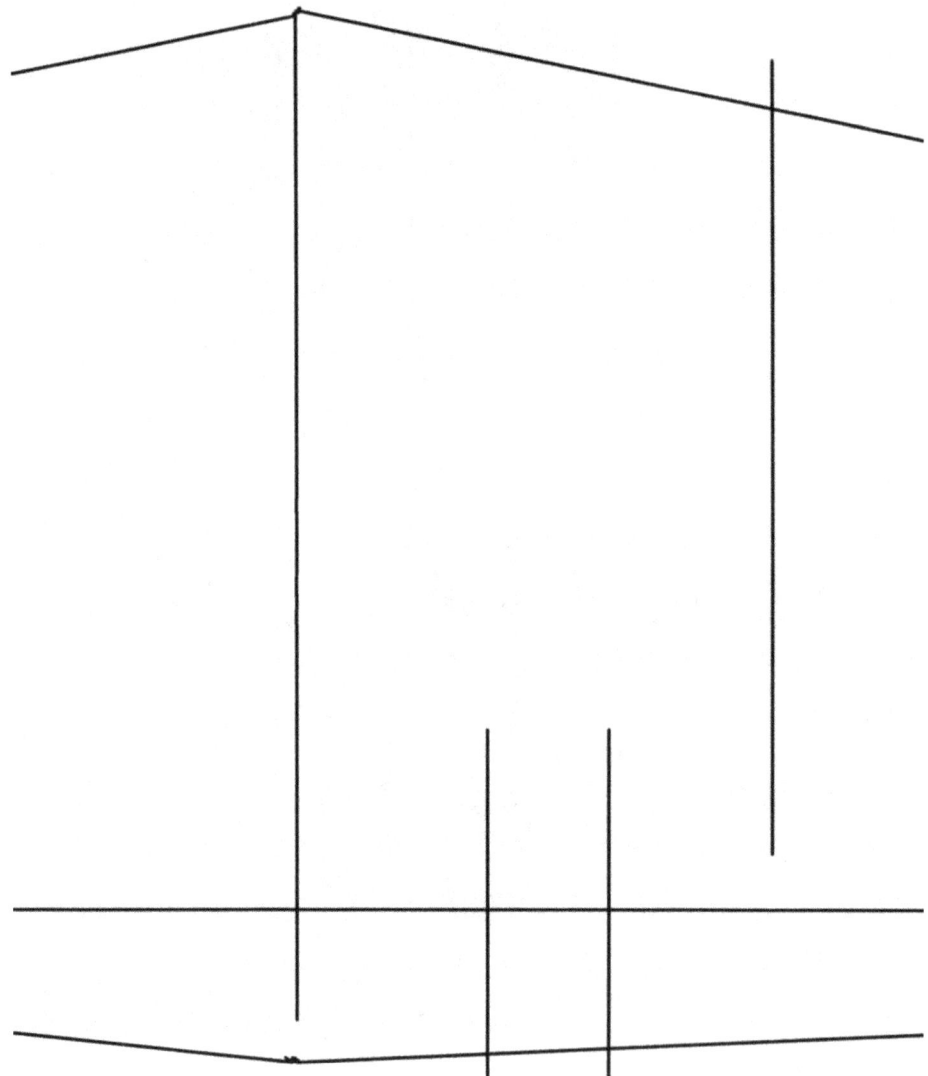

As you advance through these steps you'll see the line work reflect that of a larger building then the final product.

Understand the extra lines are to create the actual imagery required for this project.

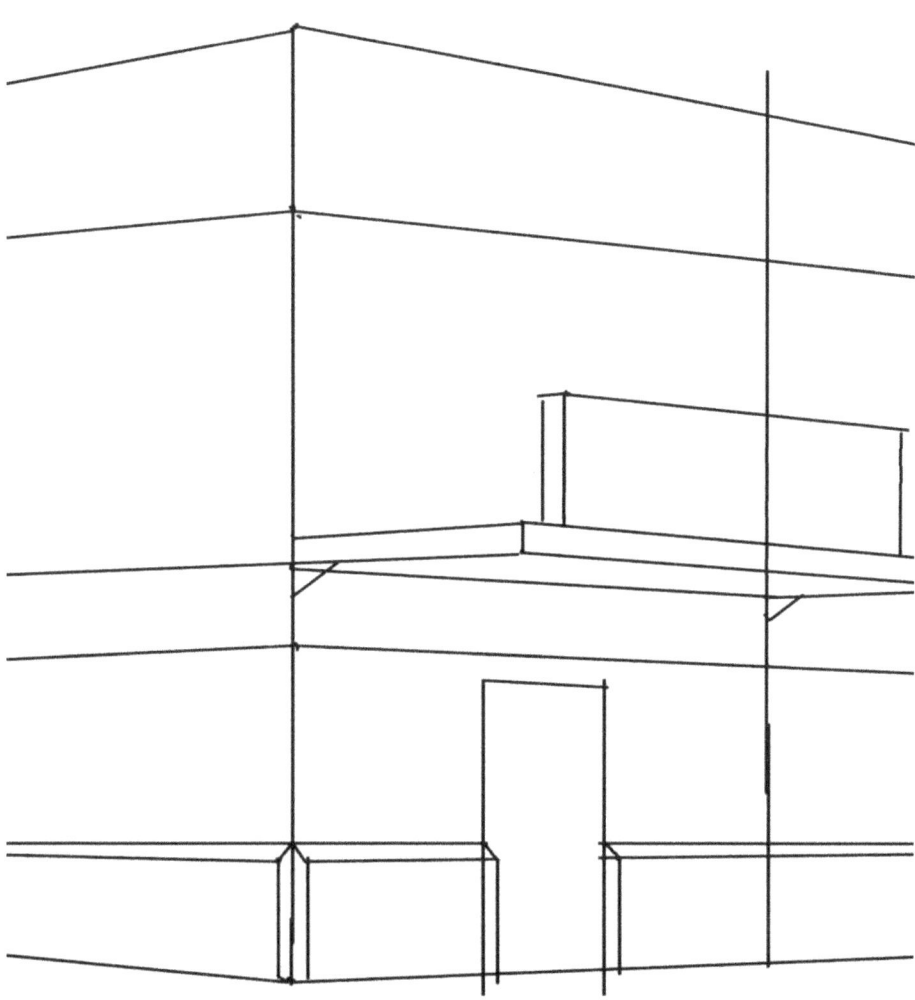

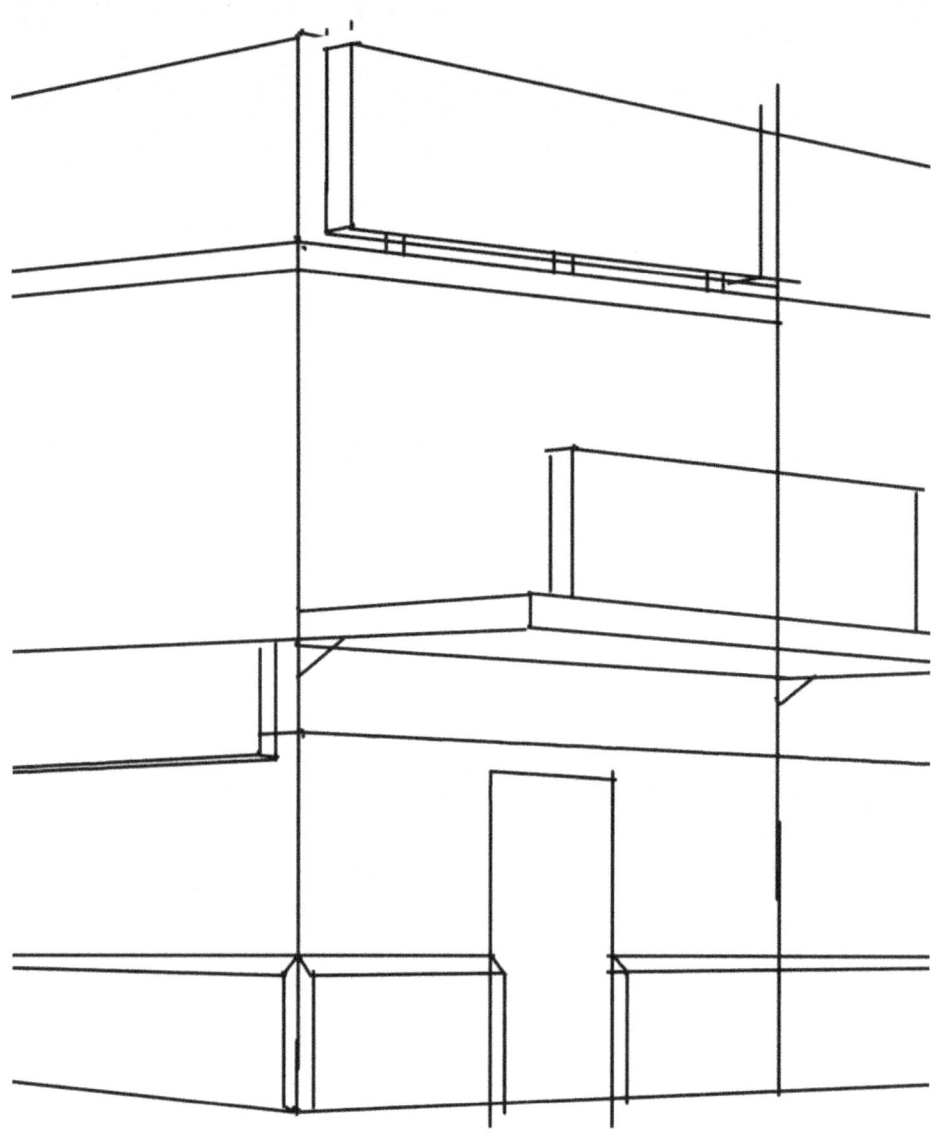

Next you'll see the first level of the store taking shape. As well as the awning and all other features. You'll have to keep on that line work. And watch for the subtle details in the outer walls of the storefront.

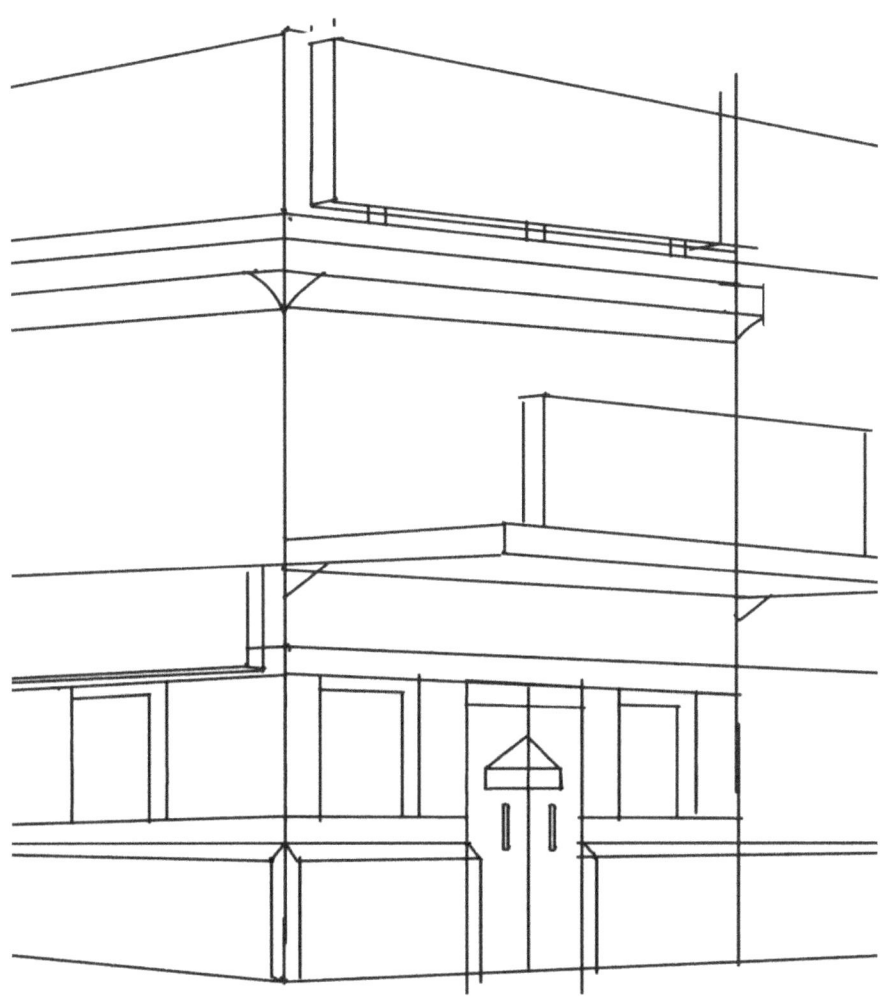

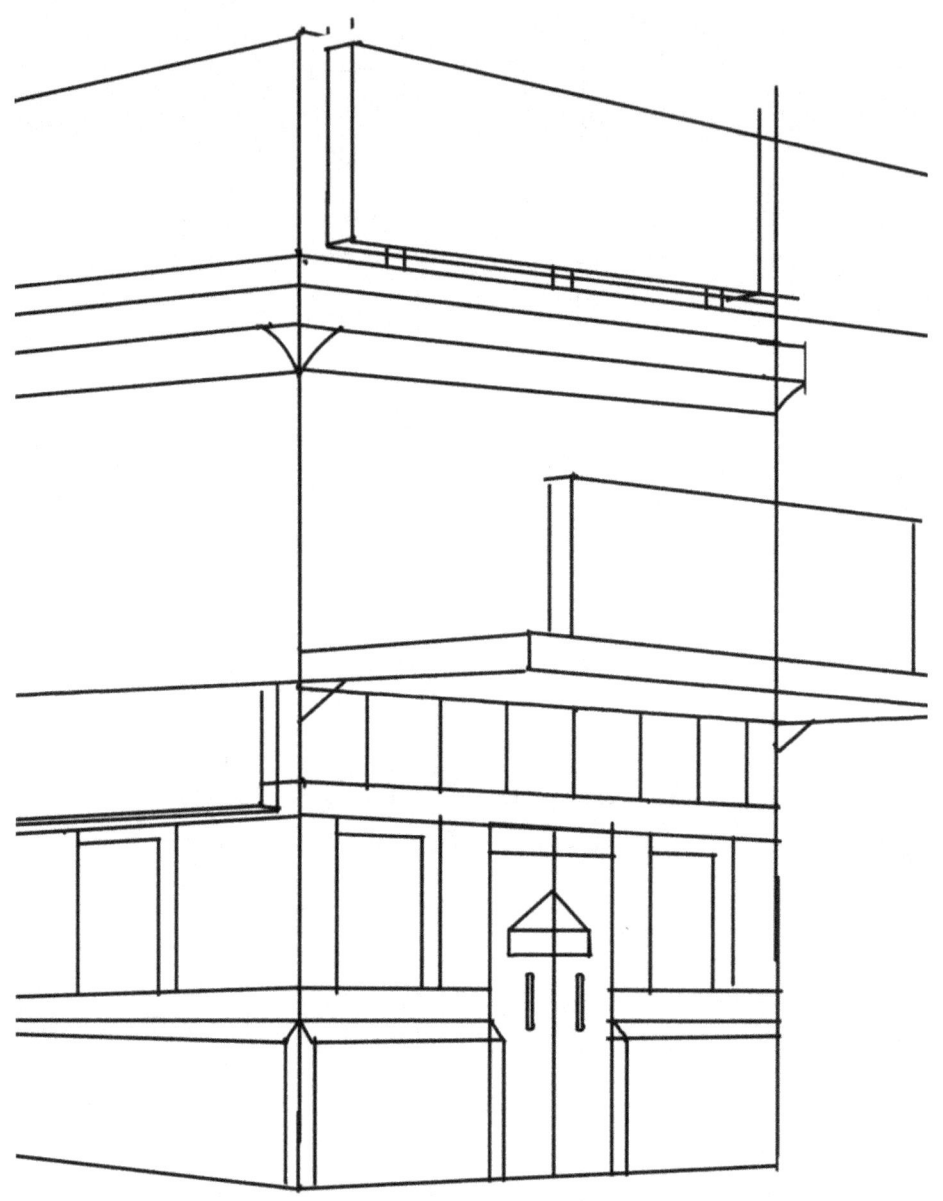

Now we see the upper levels of the storefront finishing up
and coming to fruition. The signage and the displays all looking well

edged and straight. Then the shading is next up, starting dark on the front and light on the side.

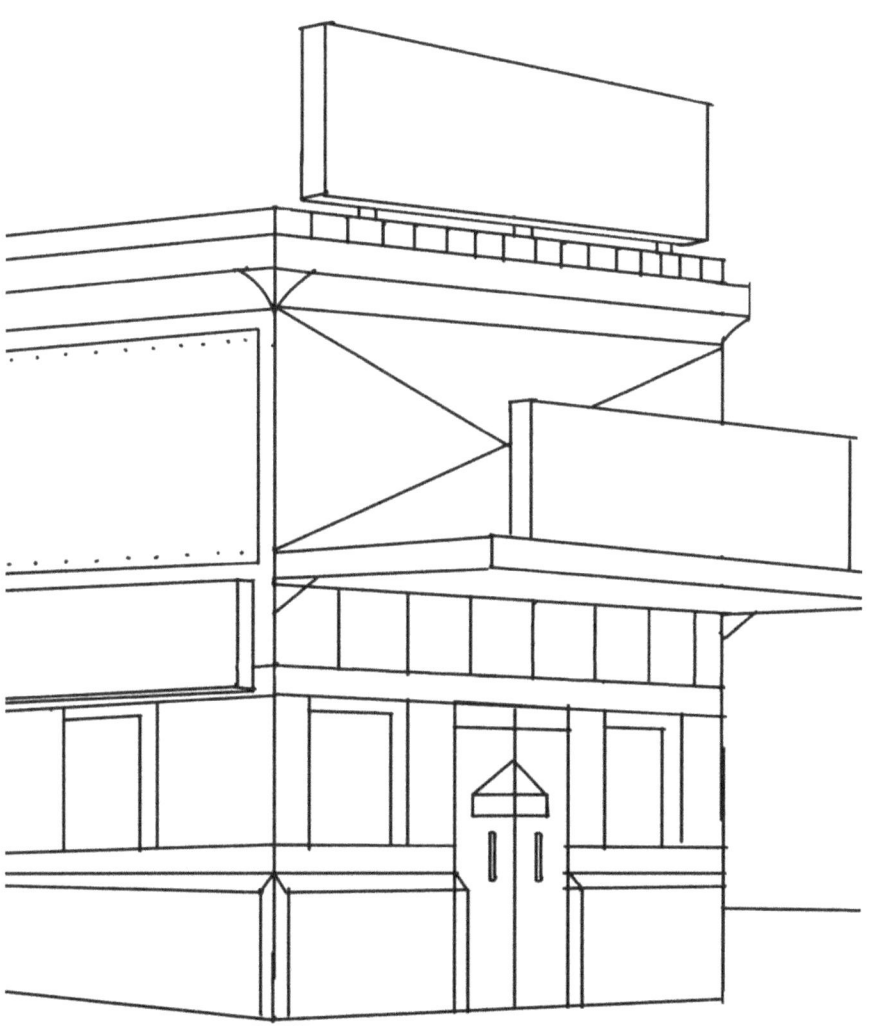

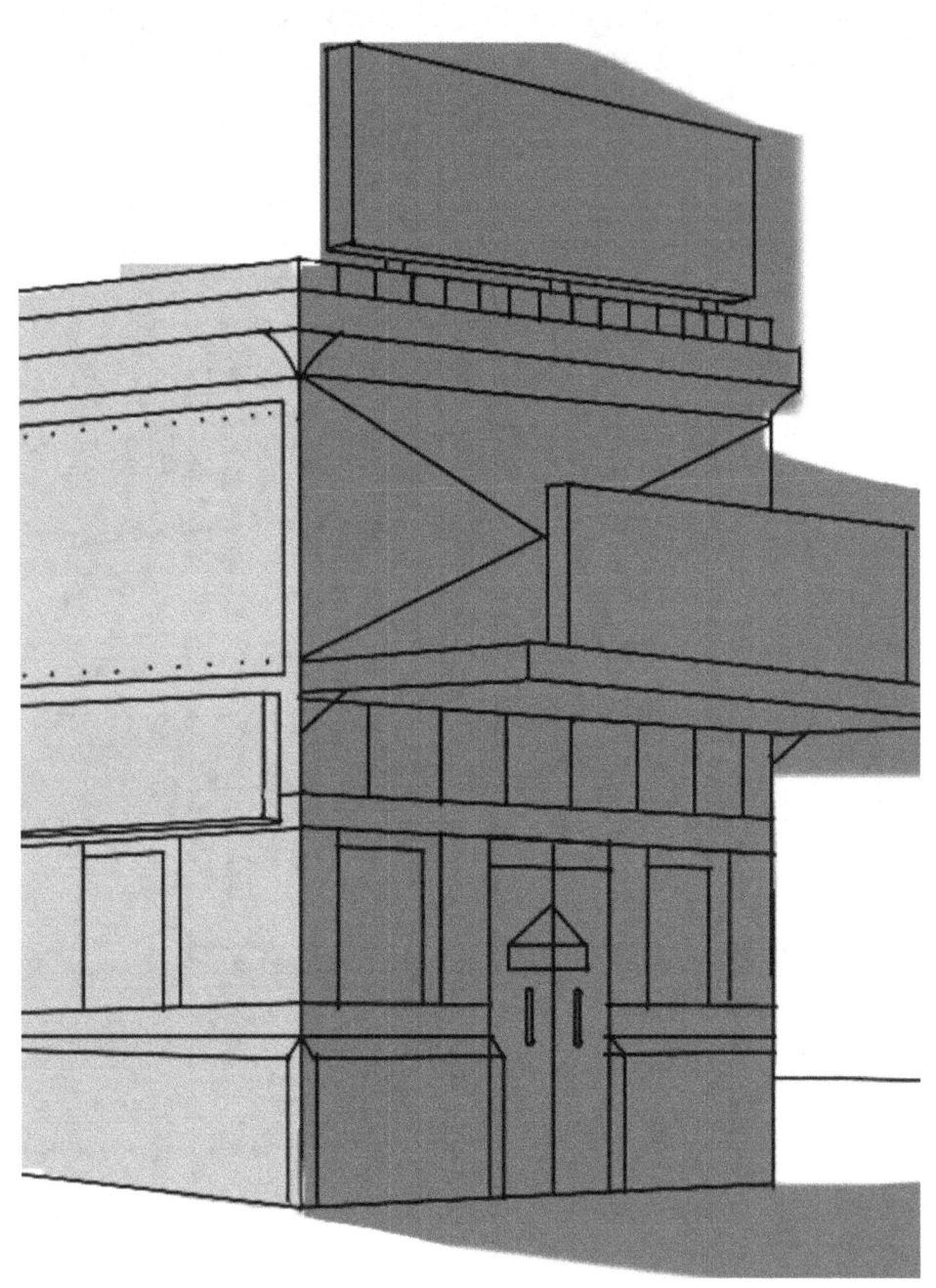

In the first image we see some light blending happening, and then we really see the effect that shading has take hold in the second image. It really adds a dimension to the perspective that wasn't already there a moment before.

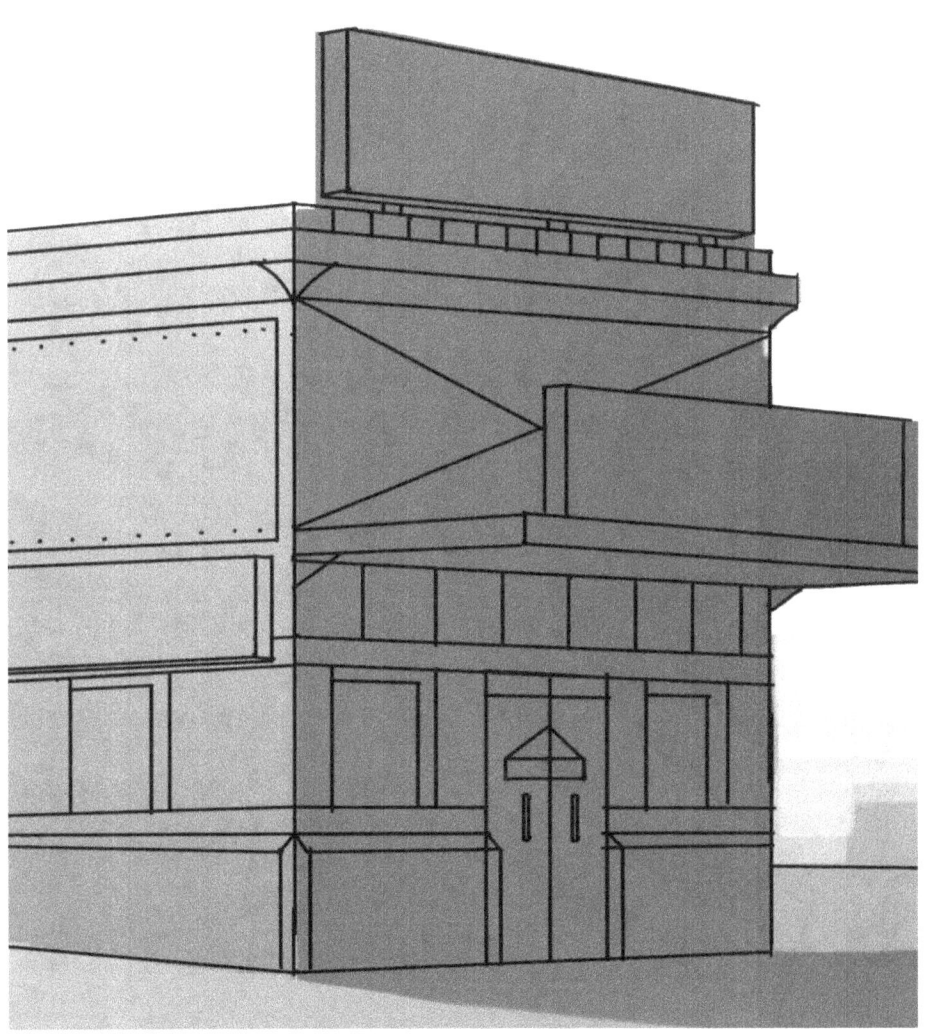

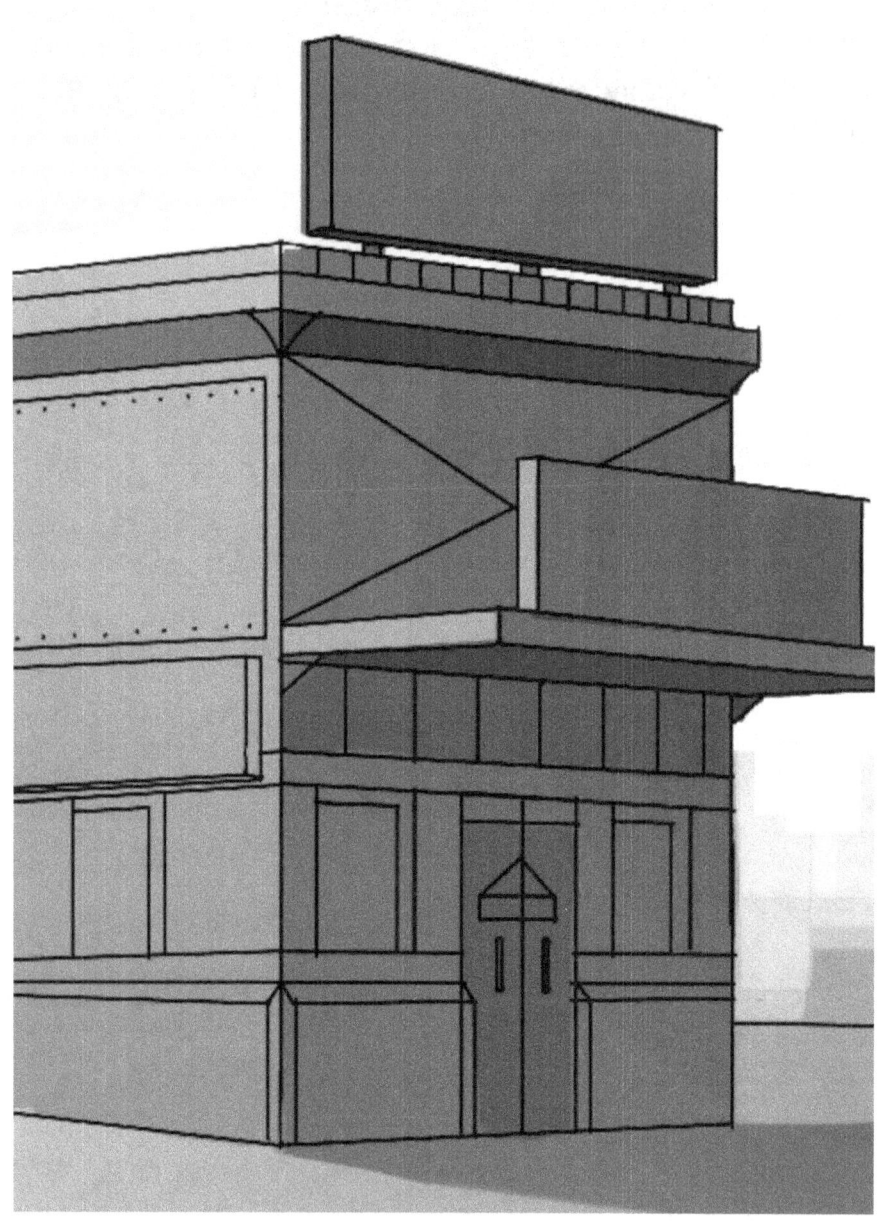

In these final two steps you'll see the expert shading skill put to use. So its a good chance for you to sharpen the skills you've learned on the last few drawings here. Shine up those windows in the last step and then you're about ready to call this one cased!

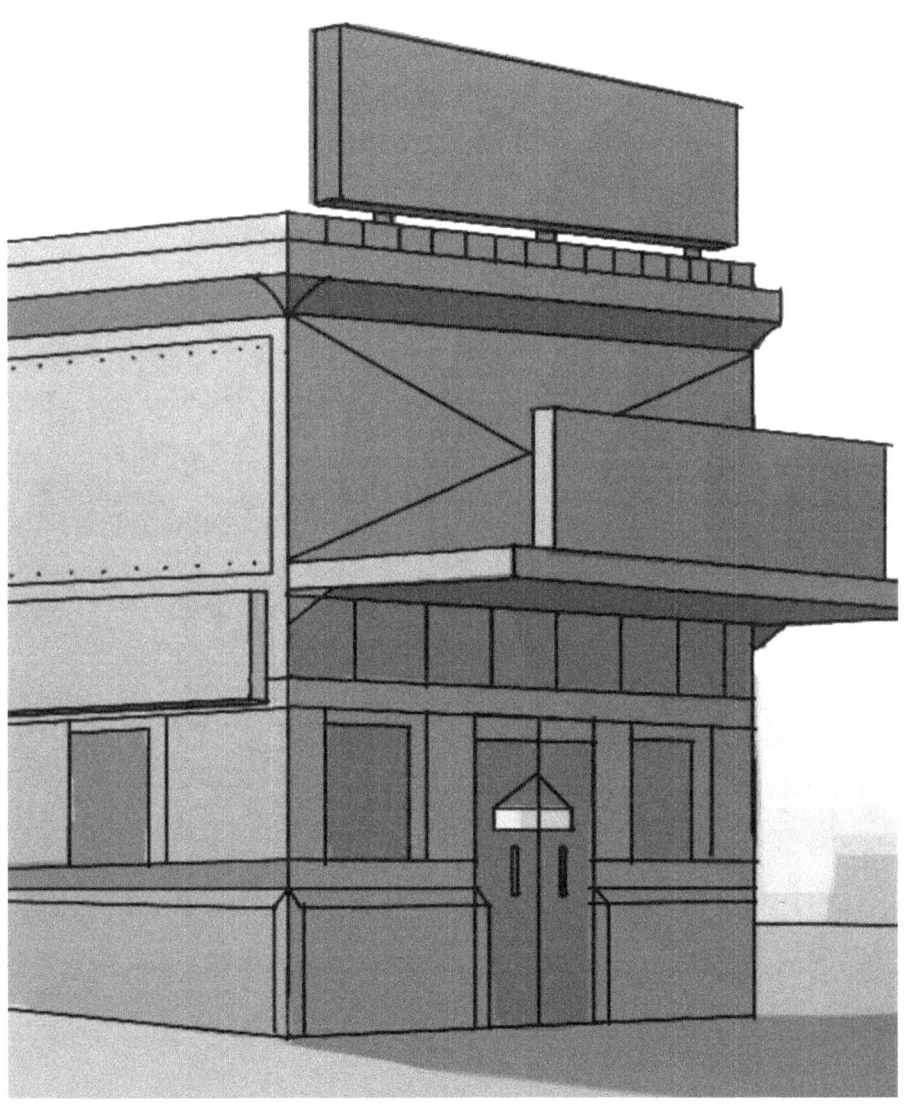

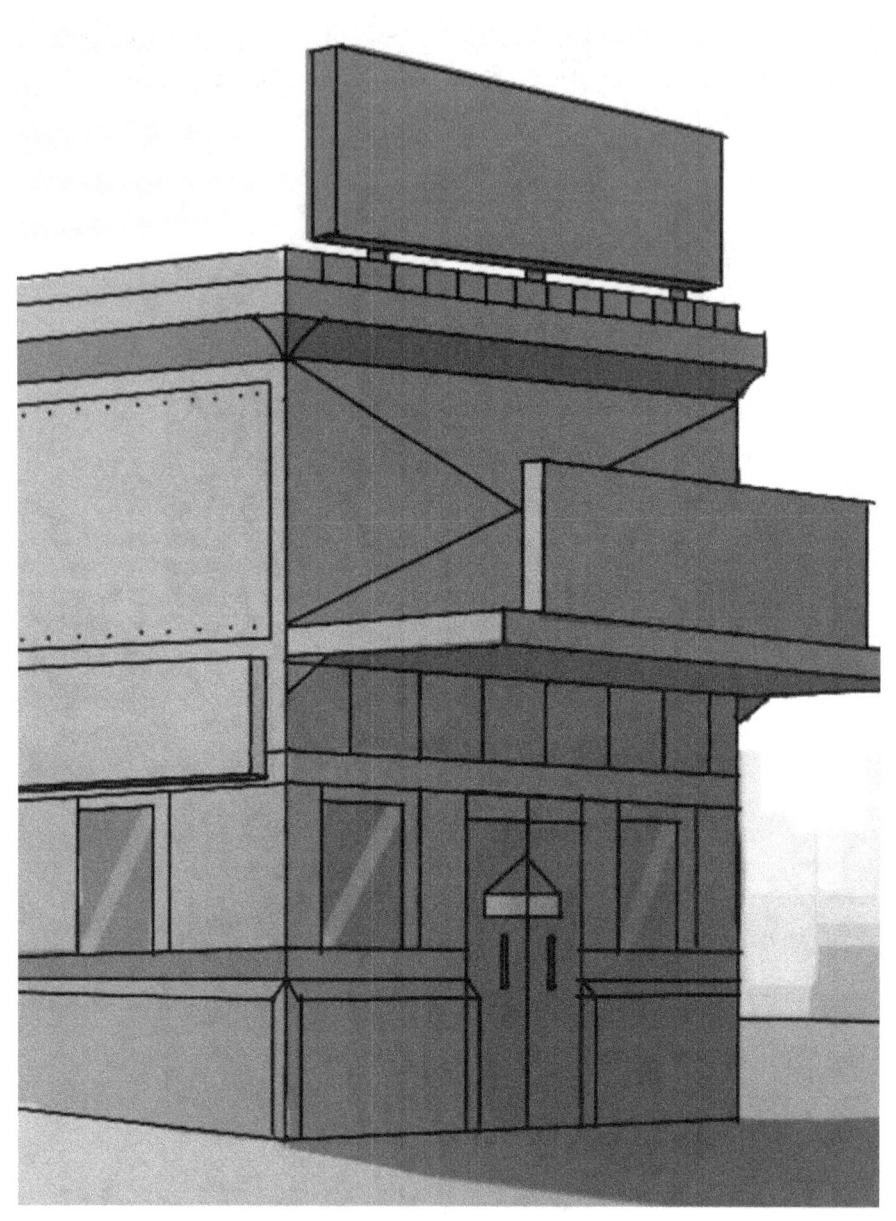

Ninth Perspective Drawing: Industrial Exterior

For this next one you're going to design the exterior of an industrial building. You'll notice the completed image on the left like with the other ones. Ignore that for now and start on the image on the right. Get those angled lines up as well as the cross work lining.

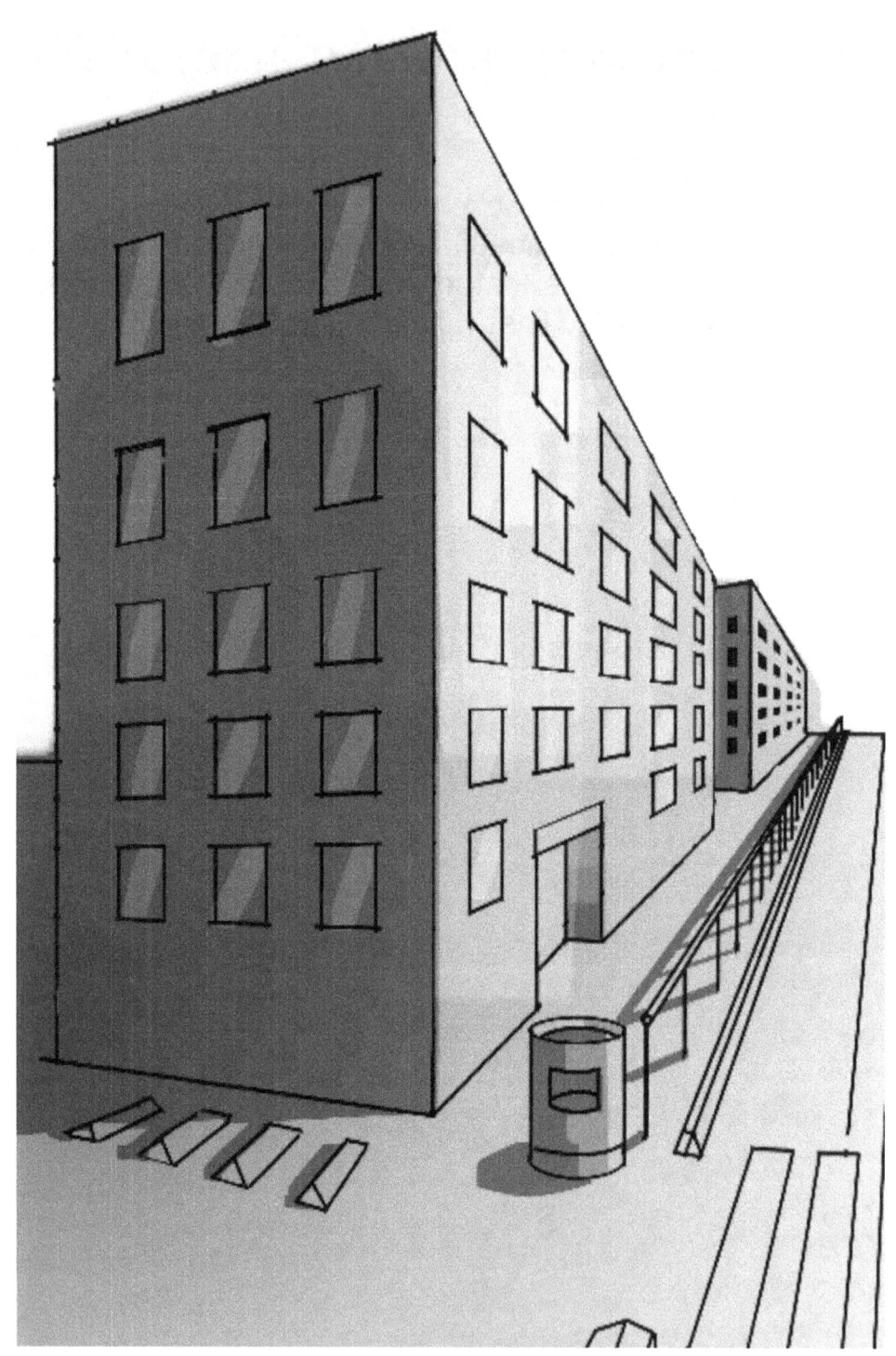

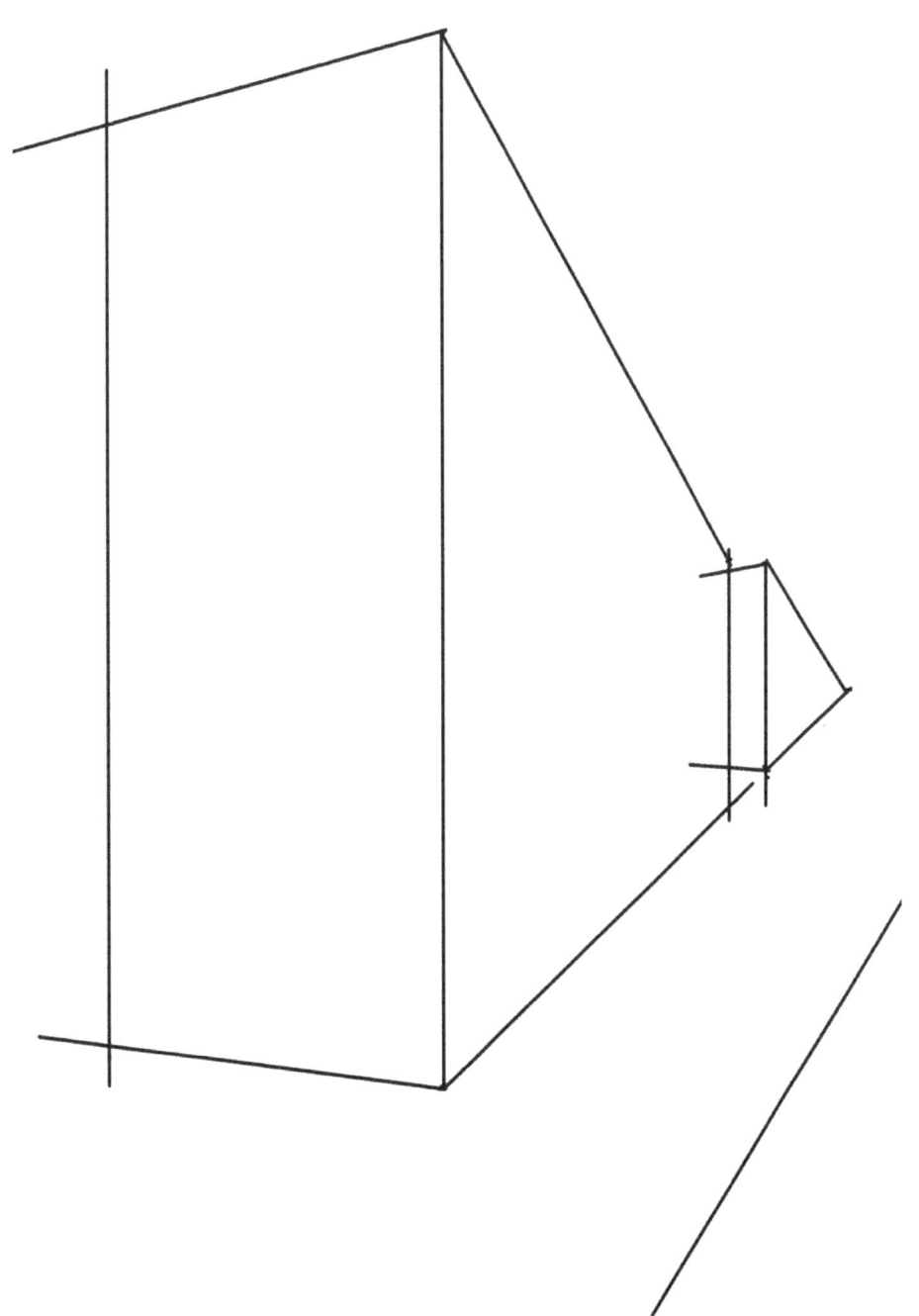

Next up you'll need to start with the basic foundation for the fence, and then build up on it in the next step. Also you'll see that the building wall has a few minor adjustments.

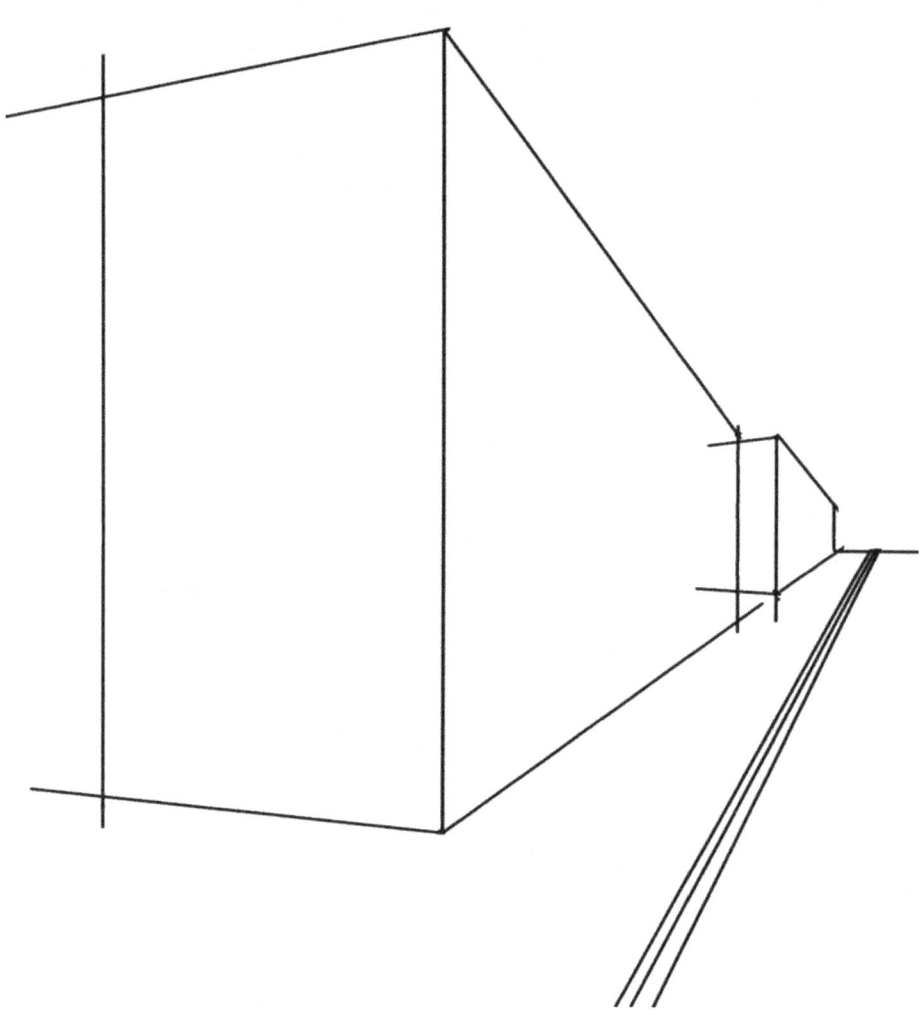

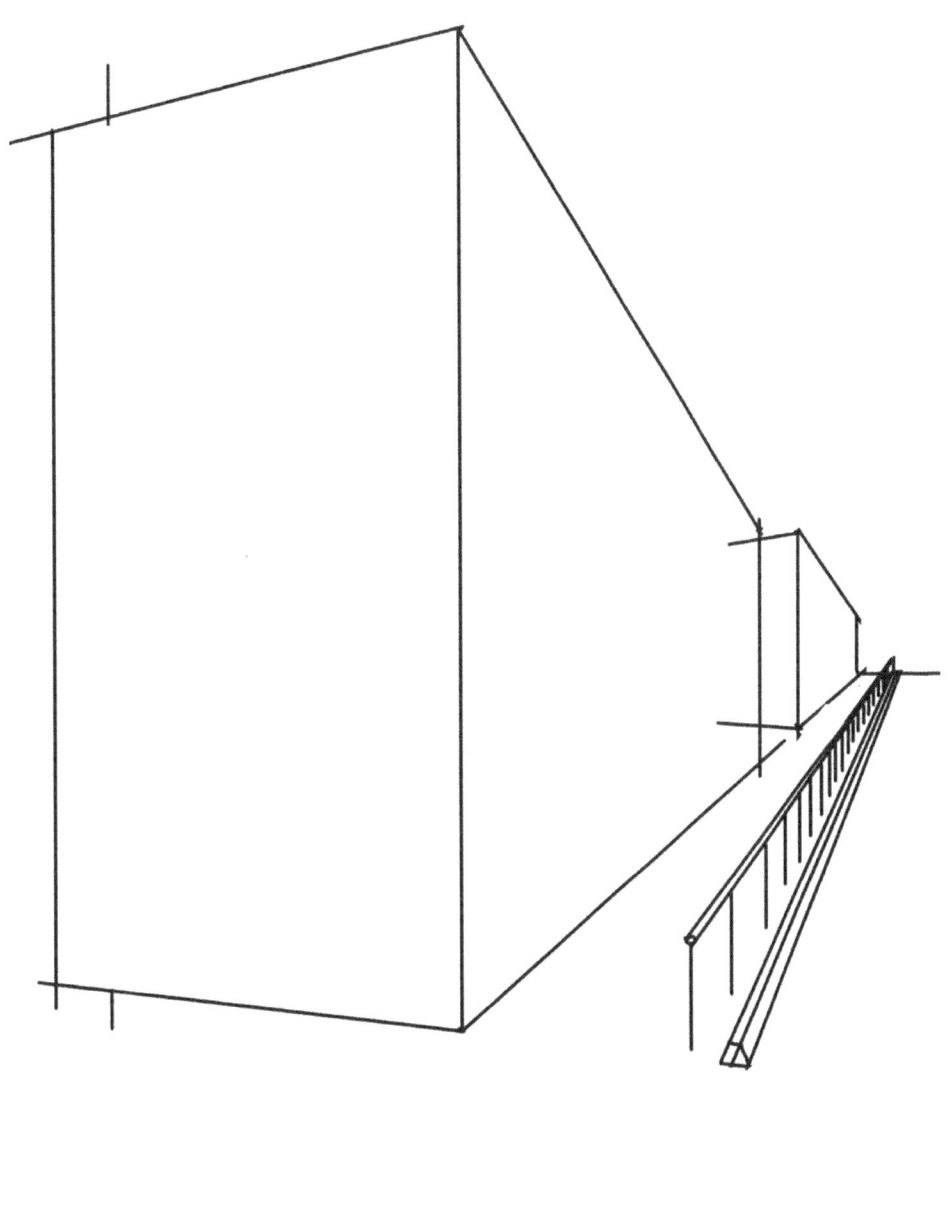

This is where it gets interesting. The horizontal lines will help set up the actual structure of the building. Theres also the line work on the ground, then the main entrance to consider.

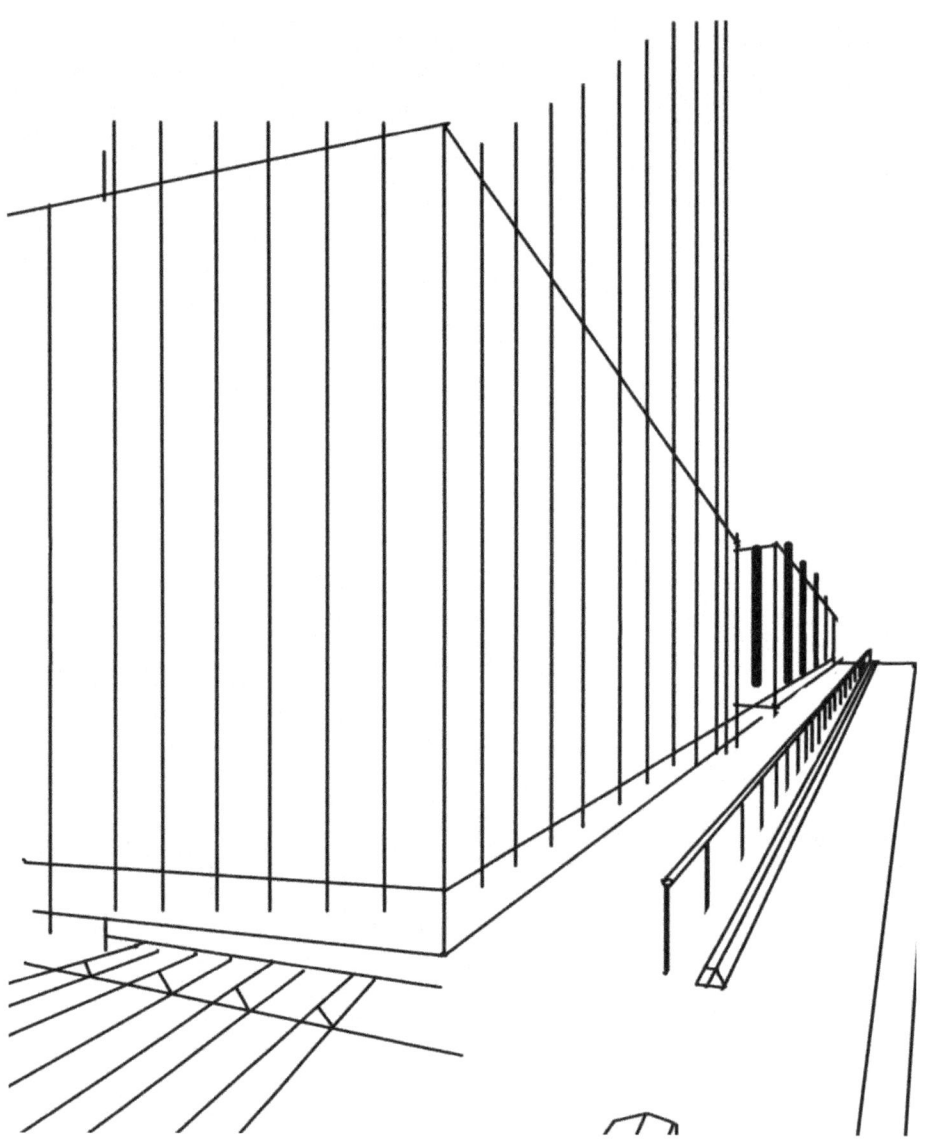

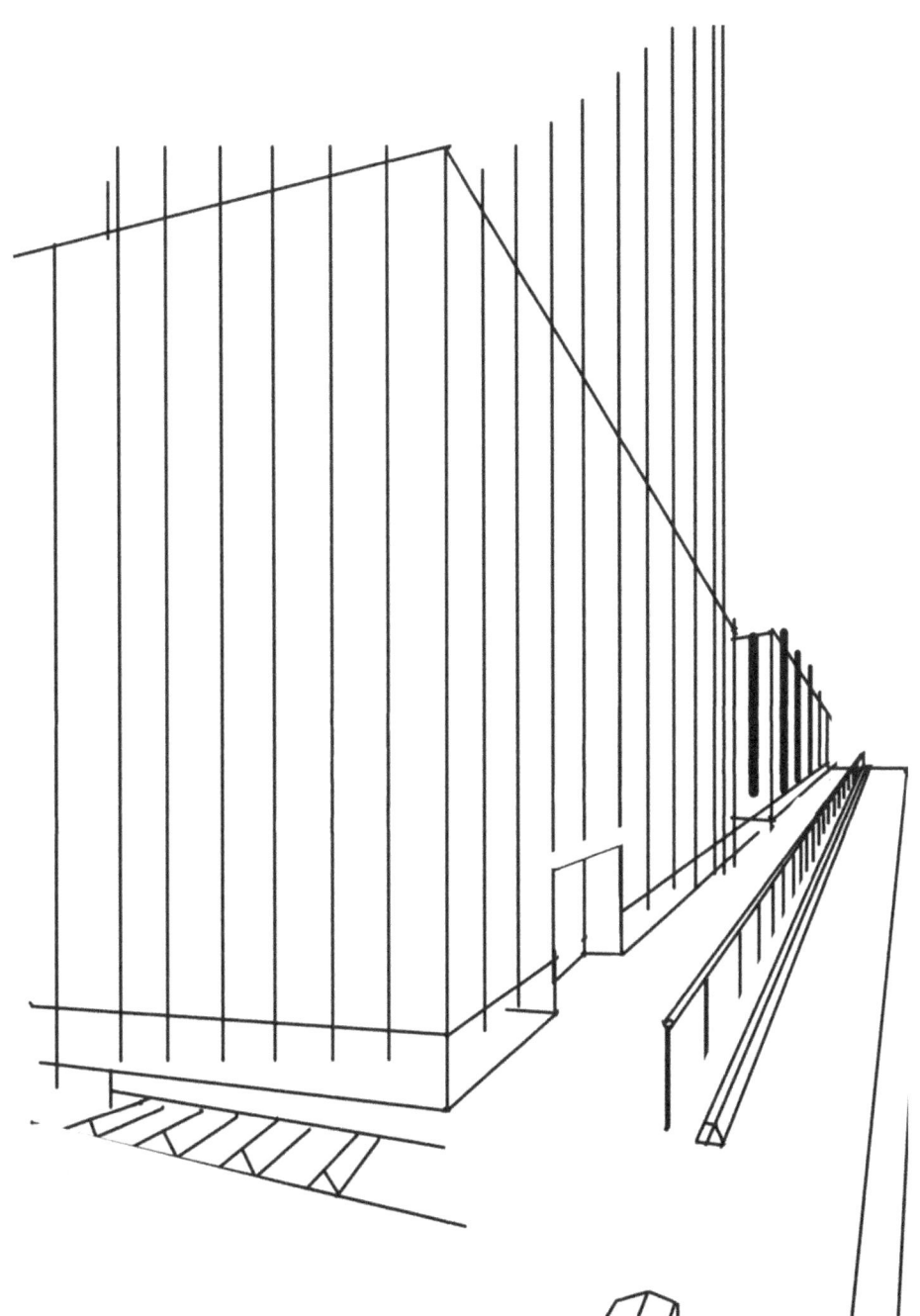

Then we add in the vertical lines to give the building that third dimension look and feel. In the second image we trim down the lines in order to add the true shape to the image. You can really see the perspective shot coming to life.

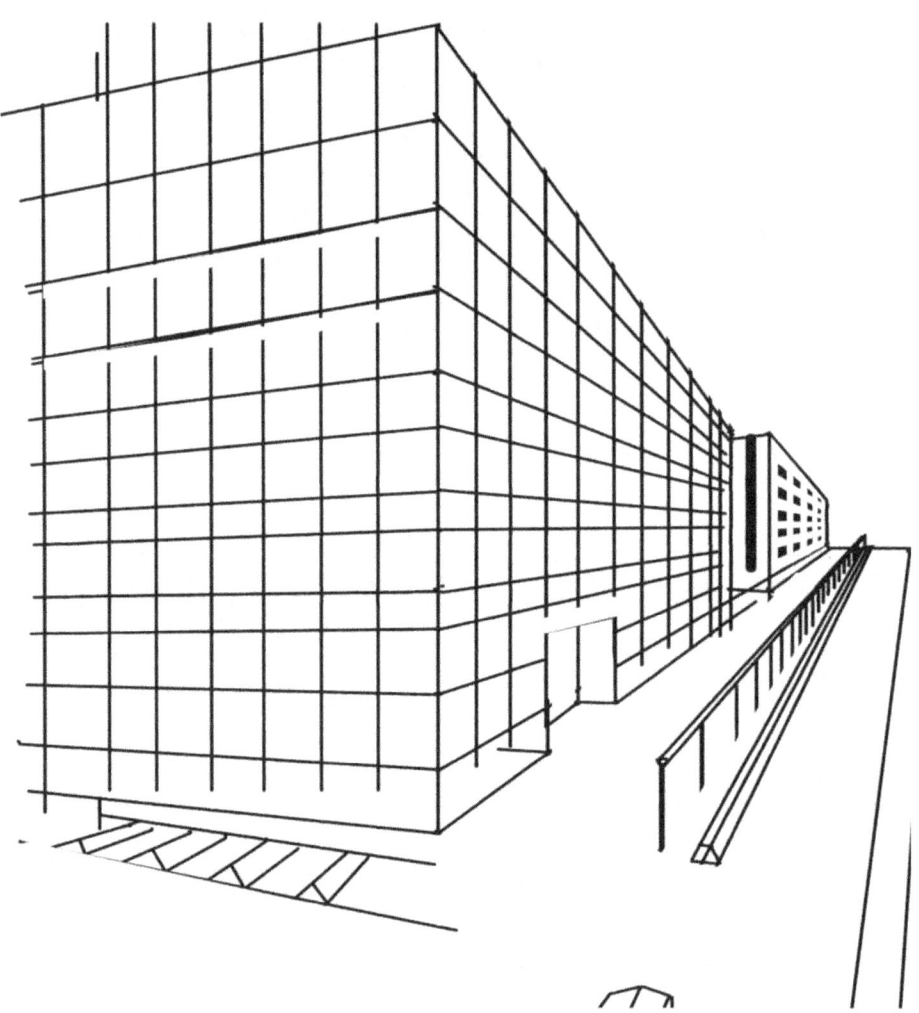

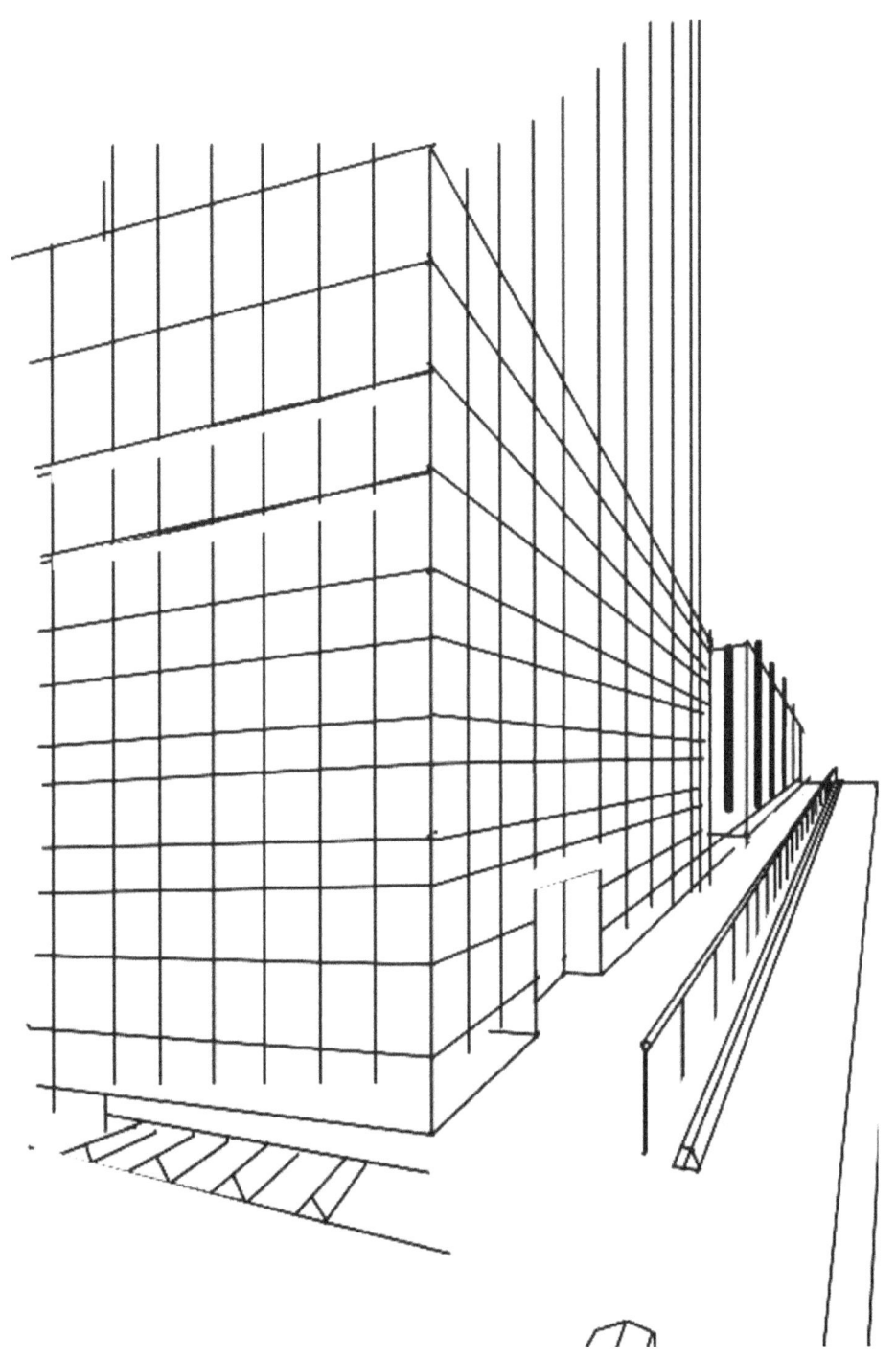

This time around we focus on the ground work and the items that litter the ground. There's also minute differences in the buildings line work.

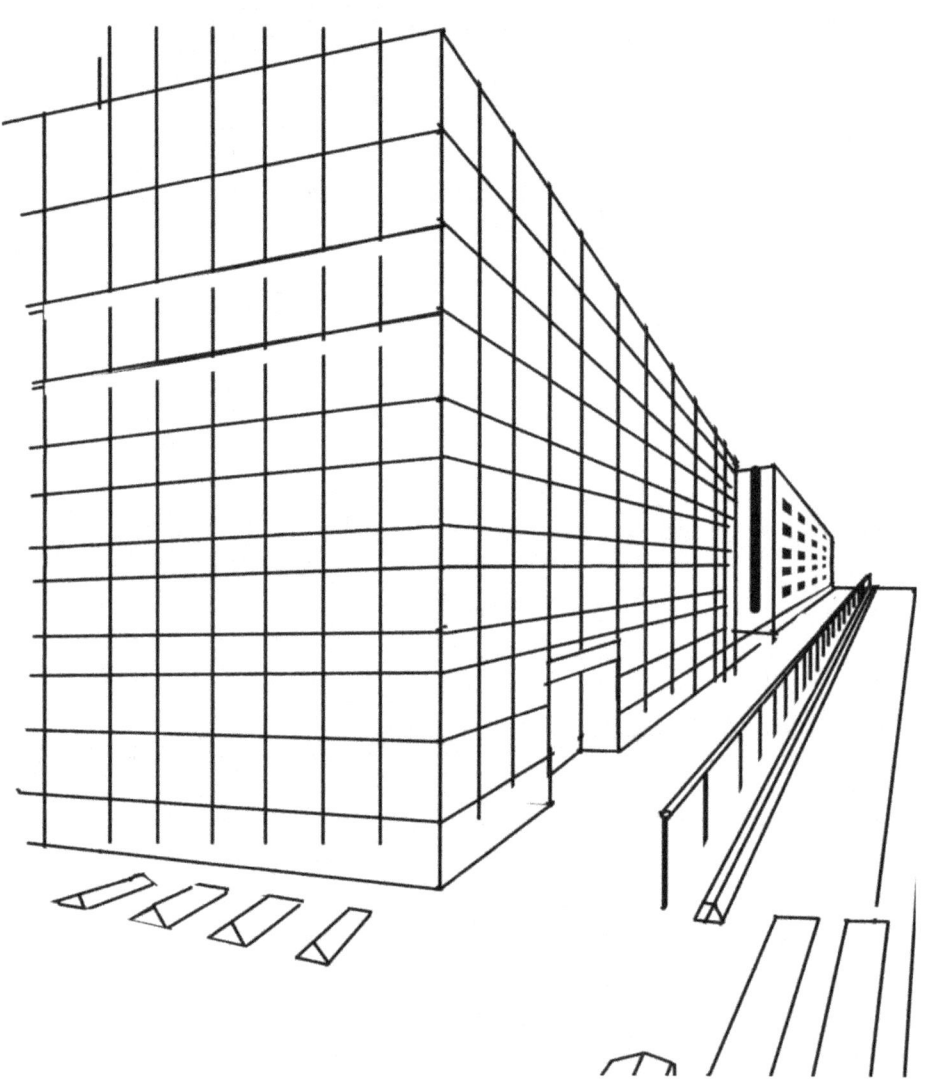

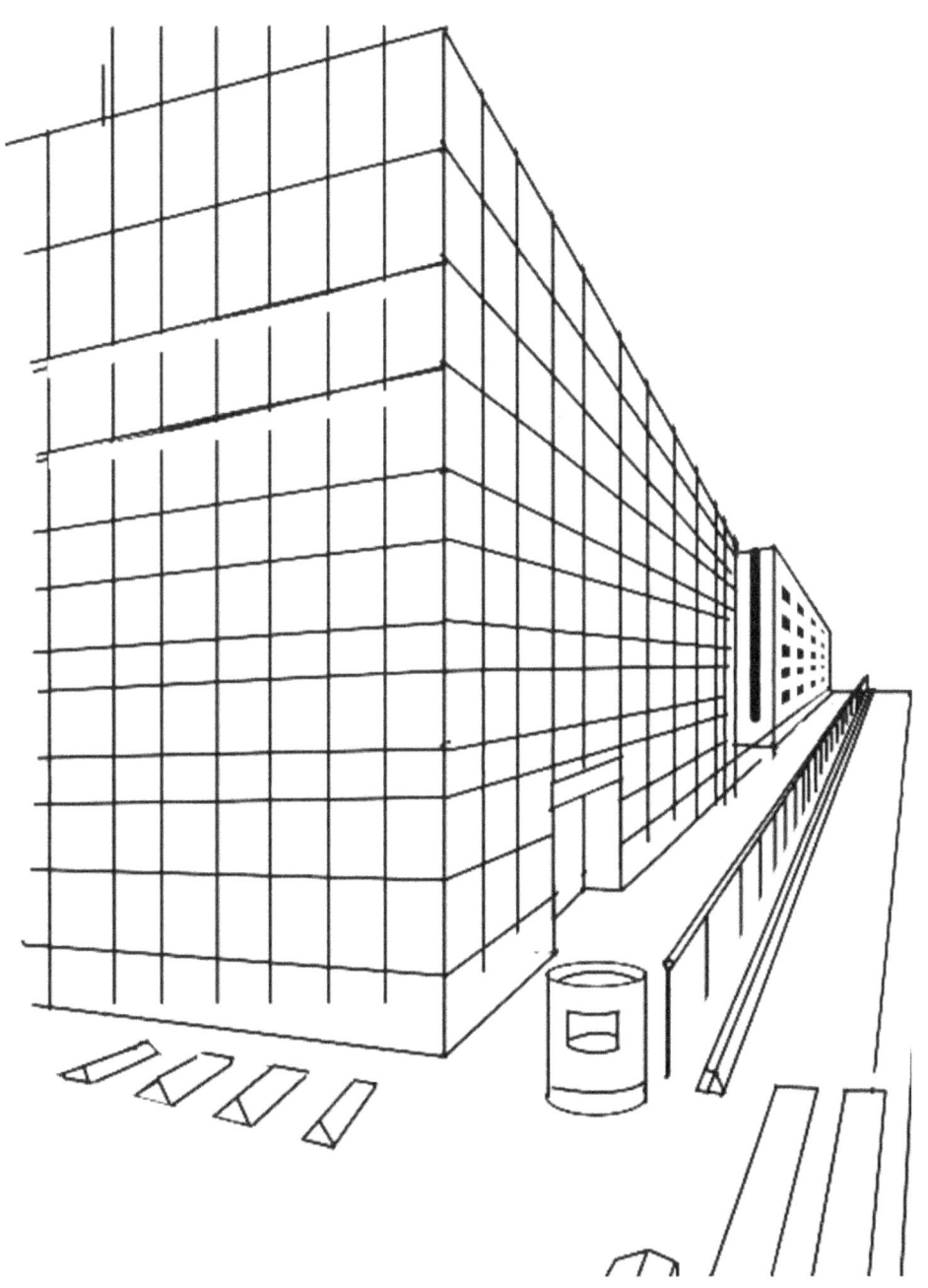

Time to move on to the windows, on the front of the first building. Then the side wall in the second image. Make sure to be careful with erasing the lines and double check your work.

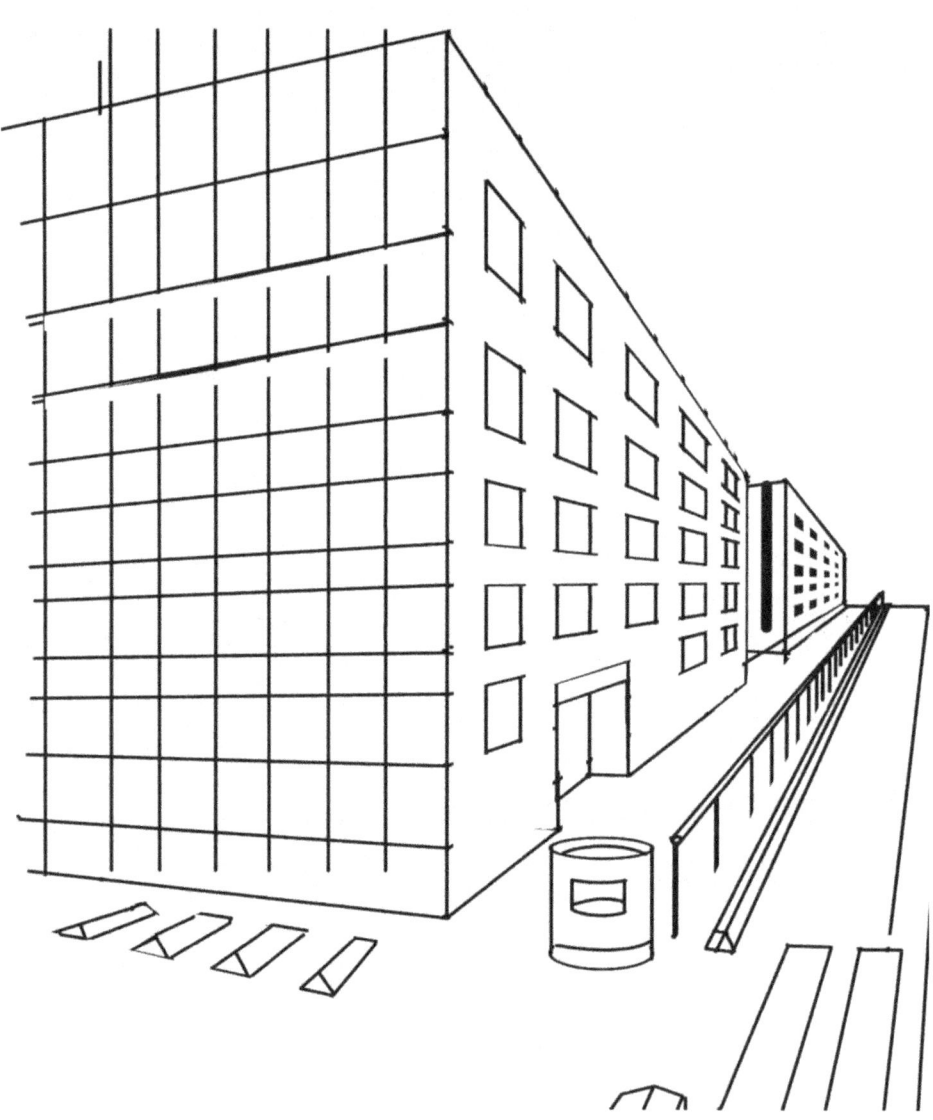

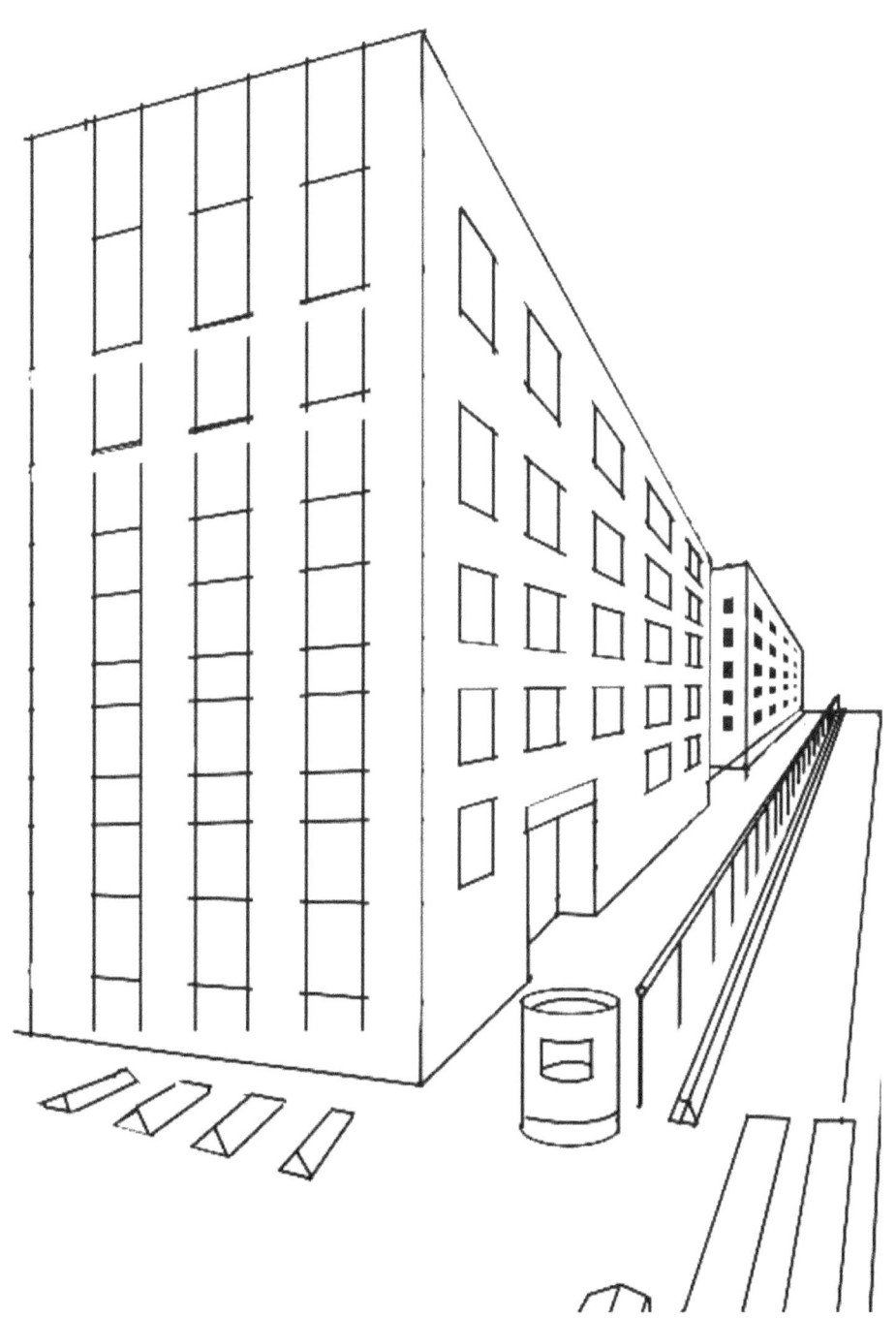

Finally the building gets a little bit of polish. You erase the final lines on the buildings leaving the windows finished and looking crisp.

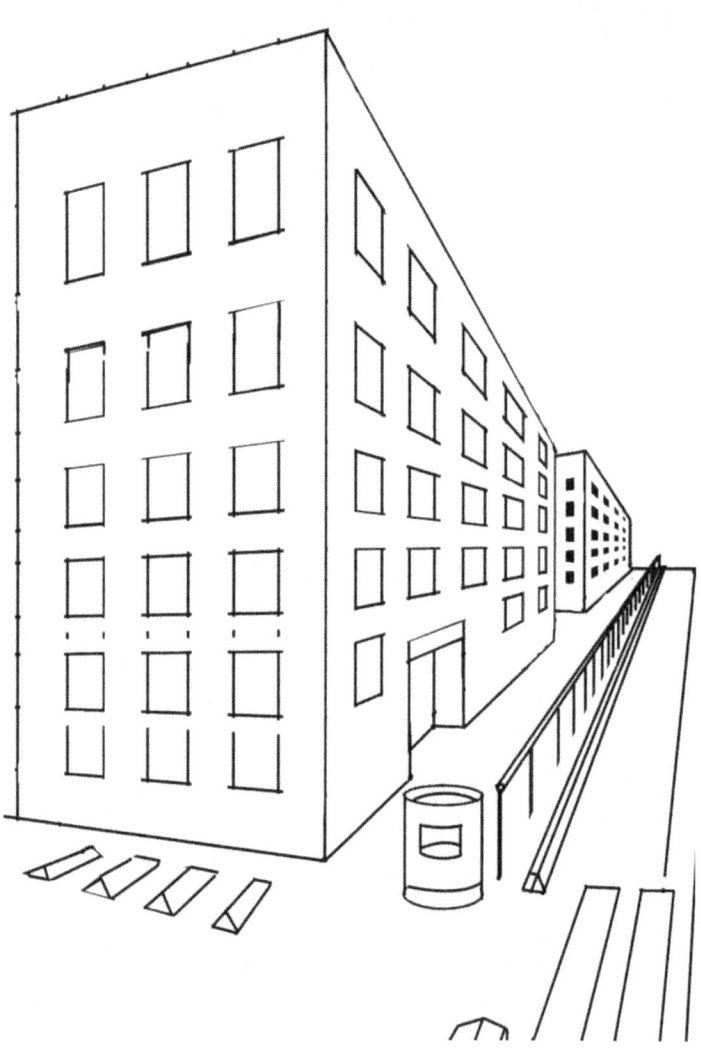

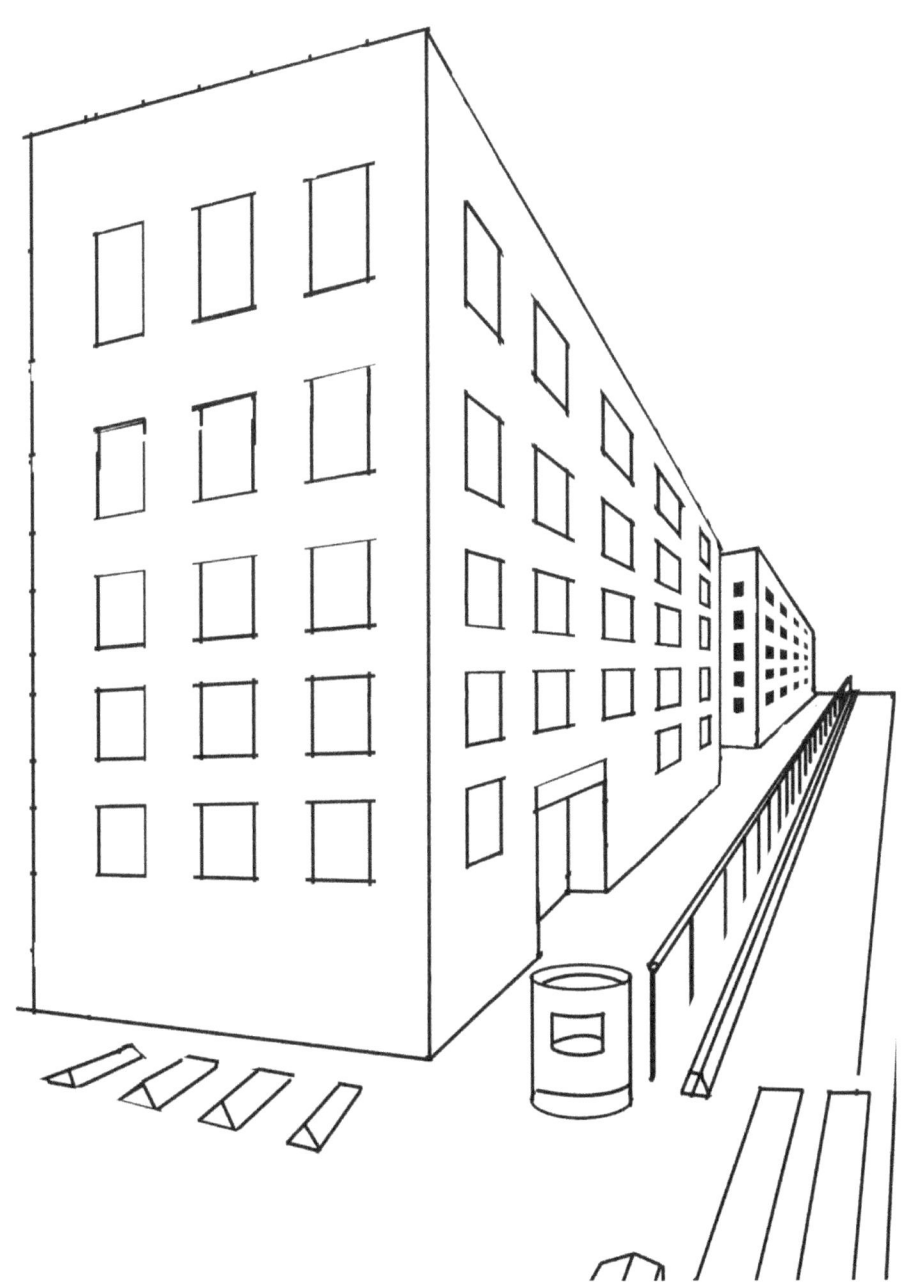

At first there's a couple minor details needed to be made in the first image. Then you can start the shading process in the right hand image. Start out with the darker wall.

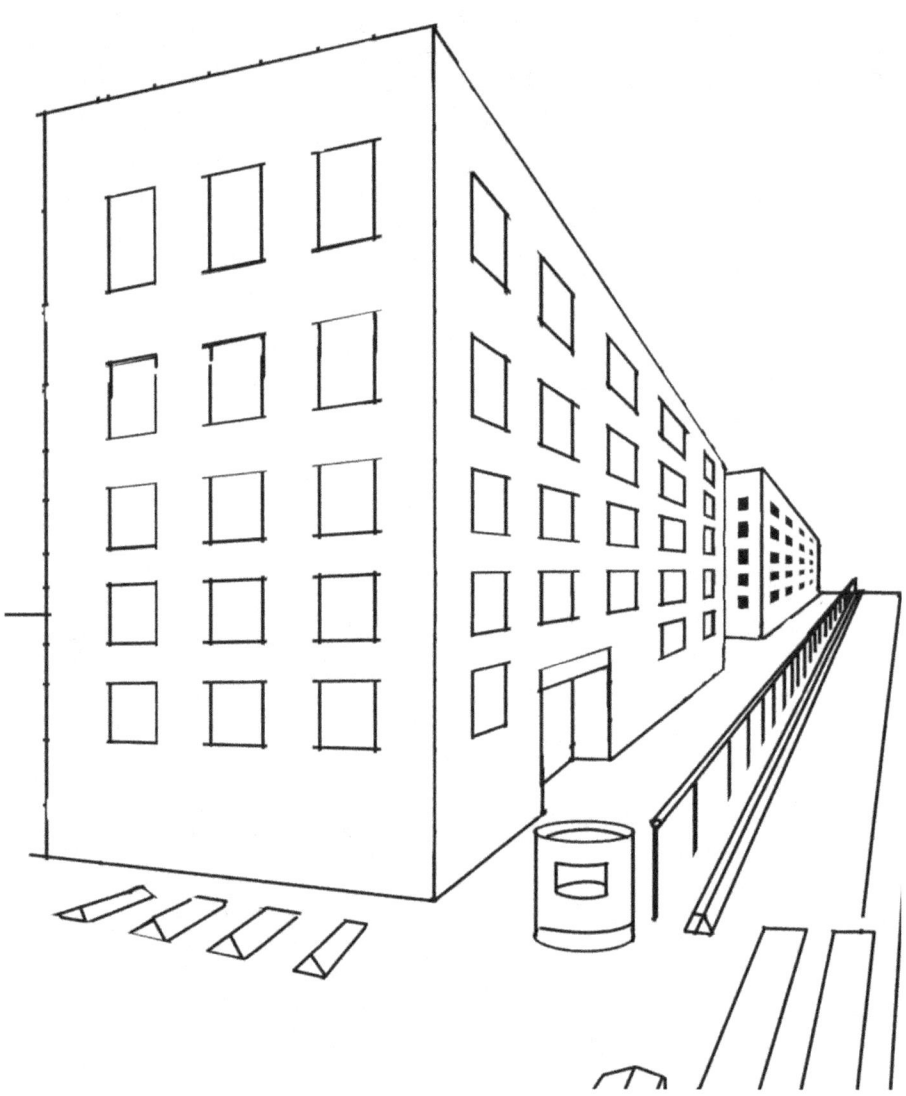

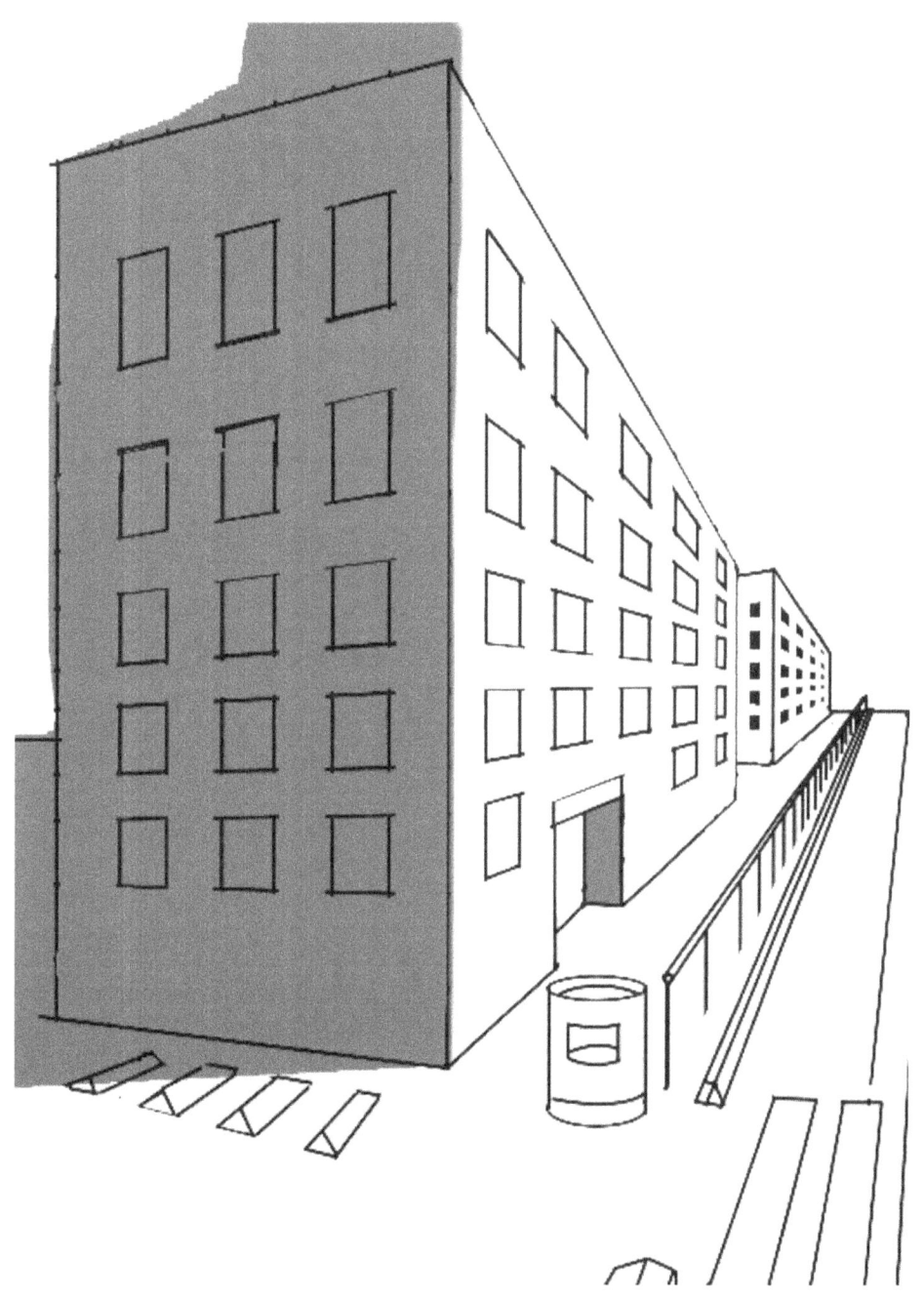

The next step in the shading is to get the perspective of the sun correct then adding in the lighter tones and blending what you see.

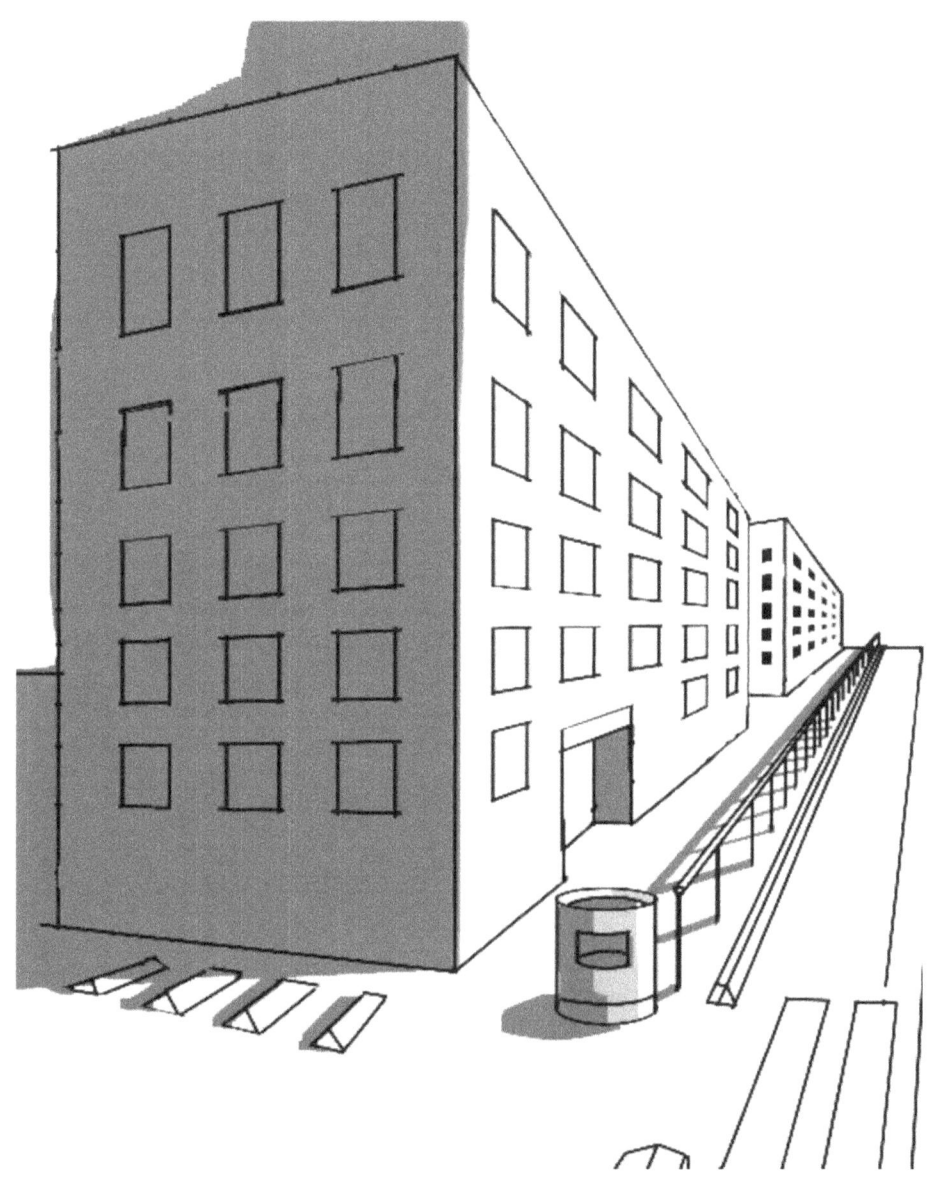

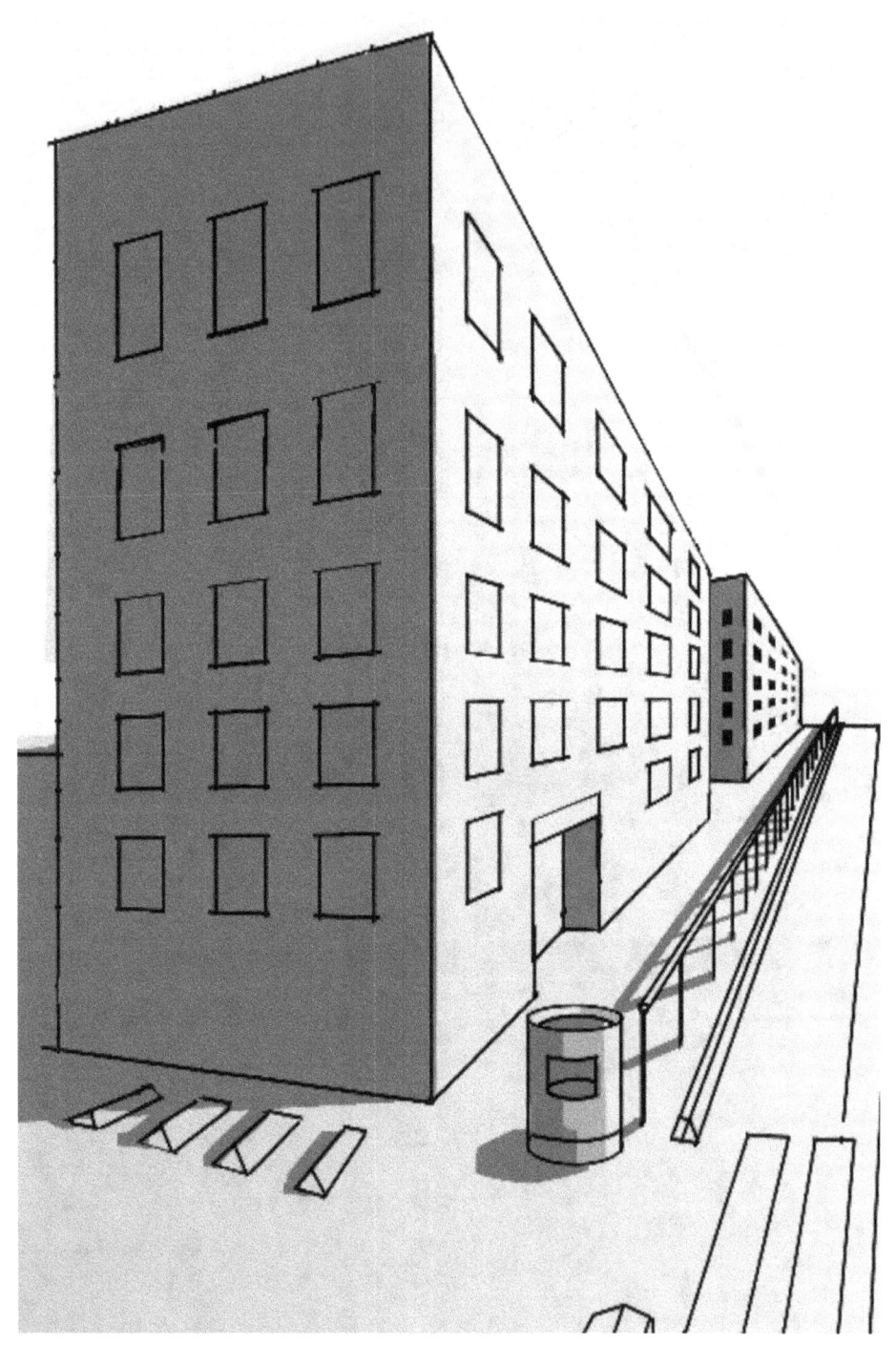

The final step is to make sure those windows are gleaming and you get all the proper blending in where it's supposed to be. By now you should be a professional at these perspective drawings, and following your instincts every step of the way.

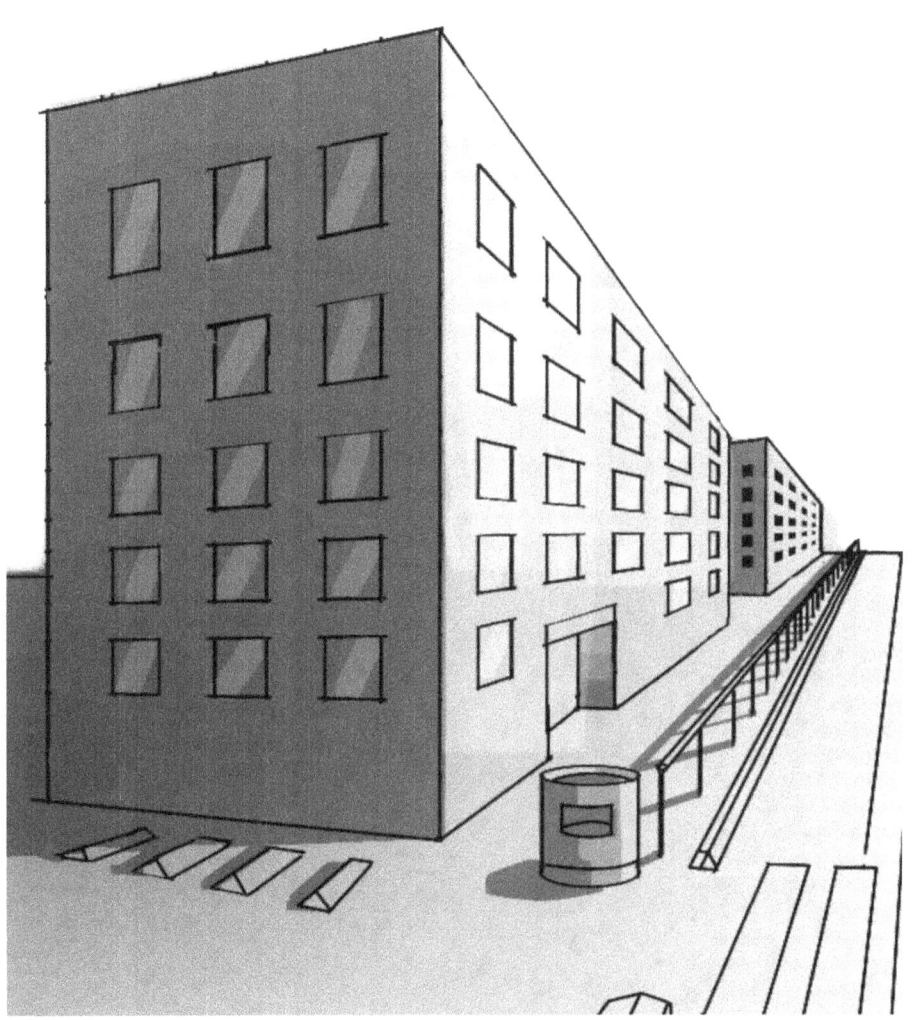

Tenth Perspective Drawing: Corporate Building

This is the tenth and last drawing to be completed in this book and you are finally finished. For this one, we will be doing the exterior of a corporate building. You can see the completed image on the left, and the base to start with on the right. Daunting at first perhaps, but follow the steps and it should be a breeze.

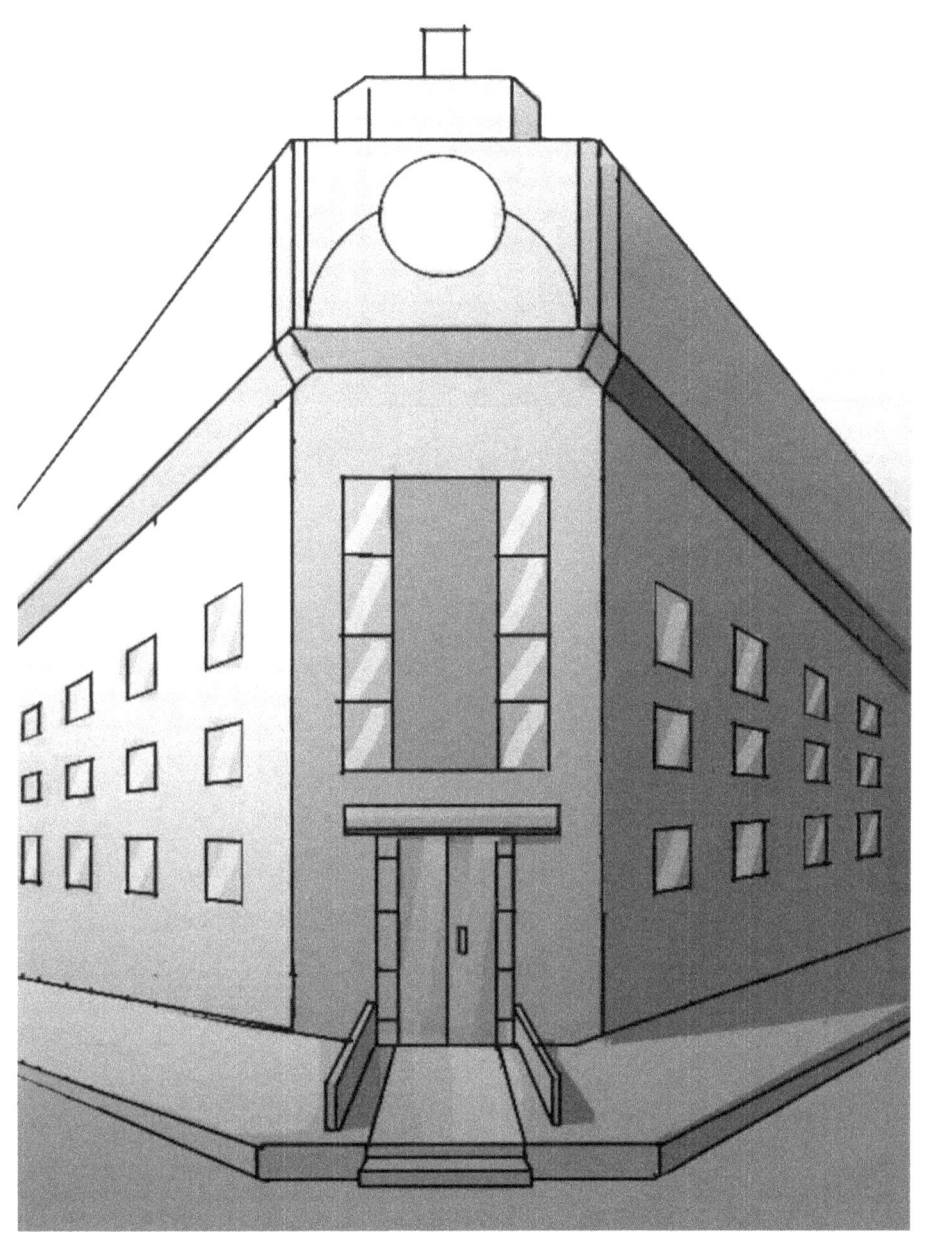

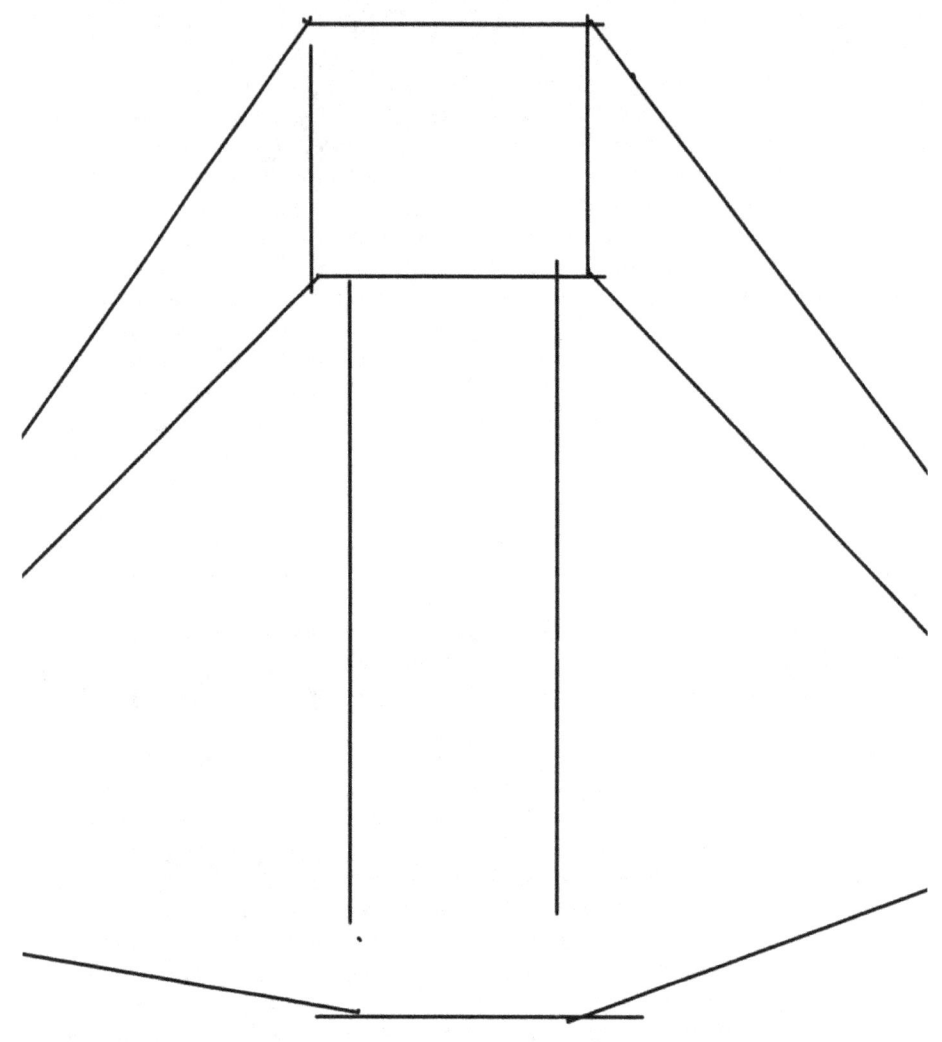

Here the line work begins its usual task of getting complex and intricate. You can see the outline of the building taking form. The vertical lines and horizontal ones intersect here and there creating points of intrigue to look out for.

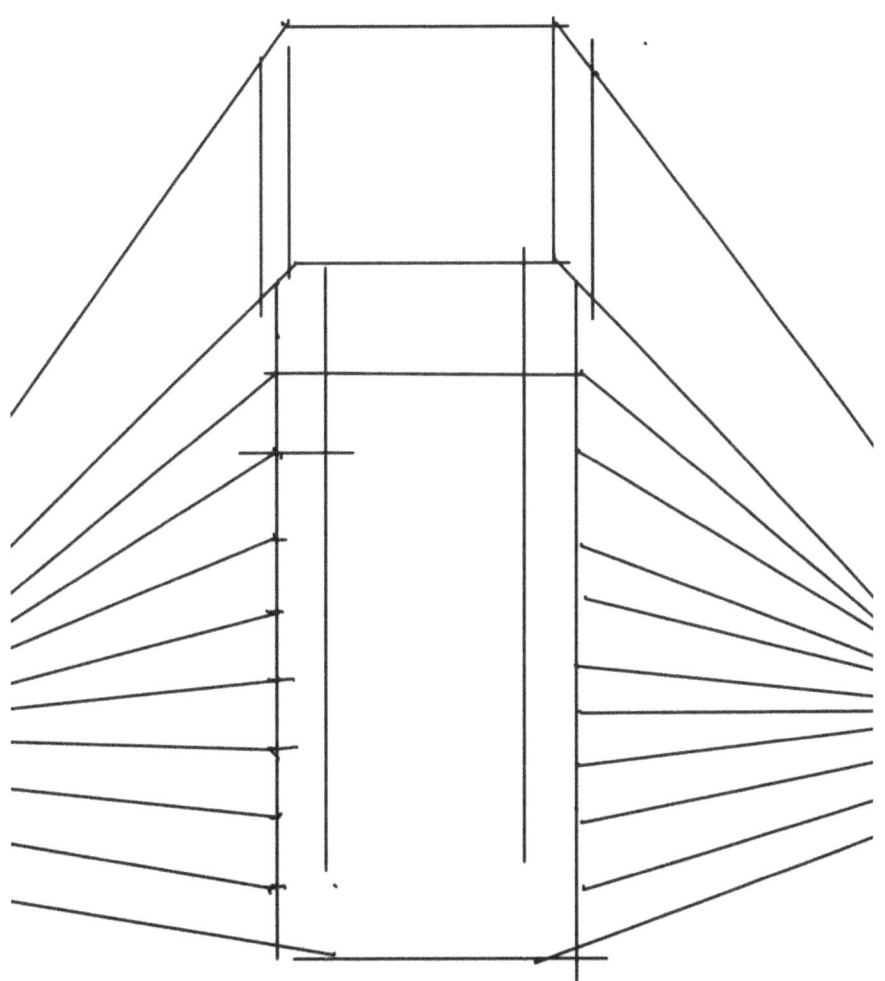

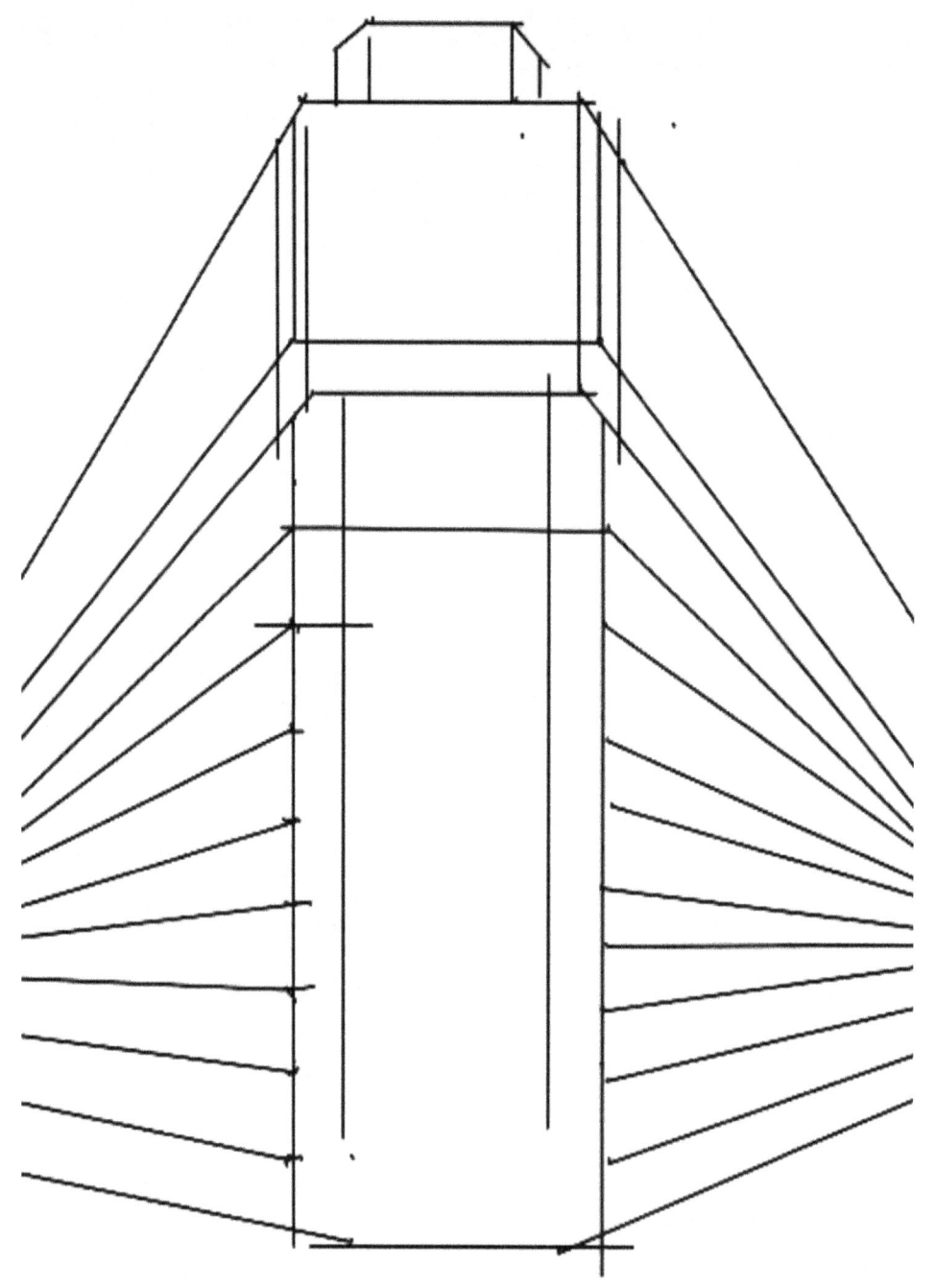

Then you start further cementing the front of the store in the first image, while in the second you start fleshing out the street corner and the main entrance of the building.

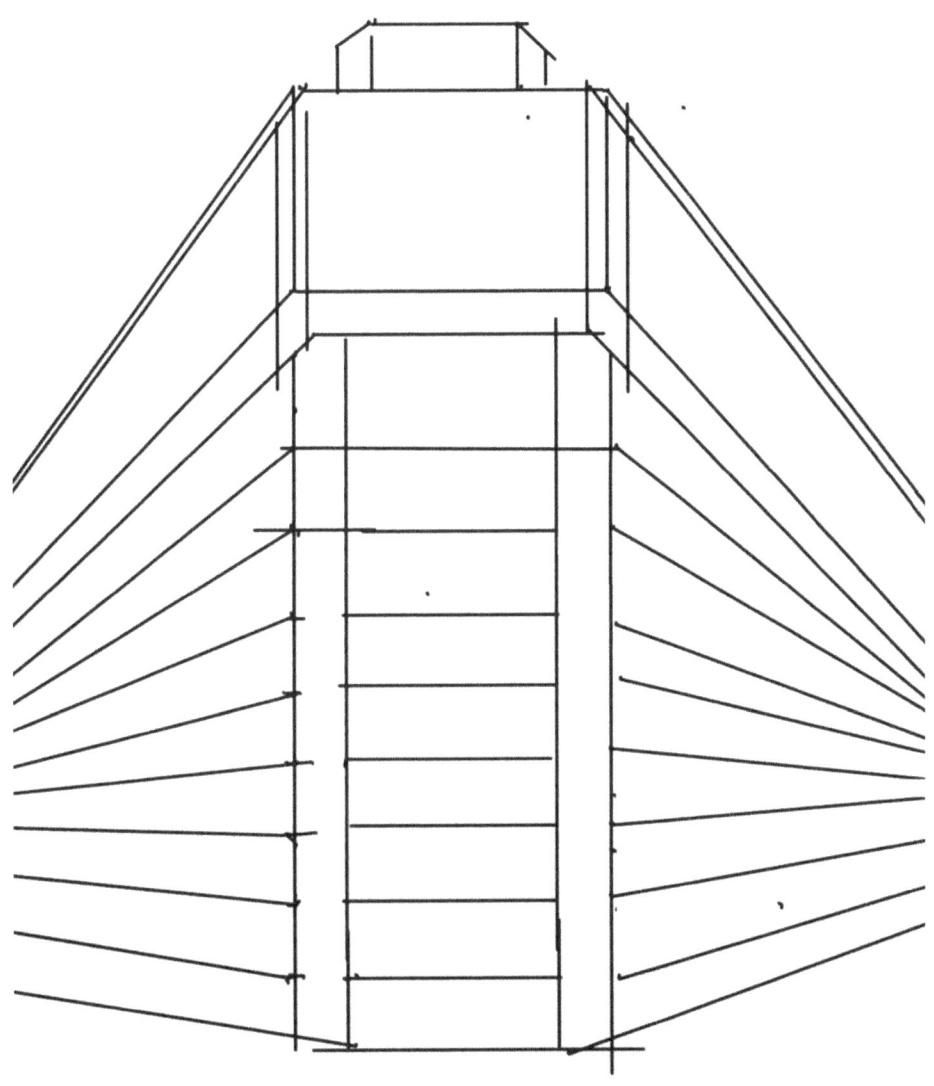

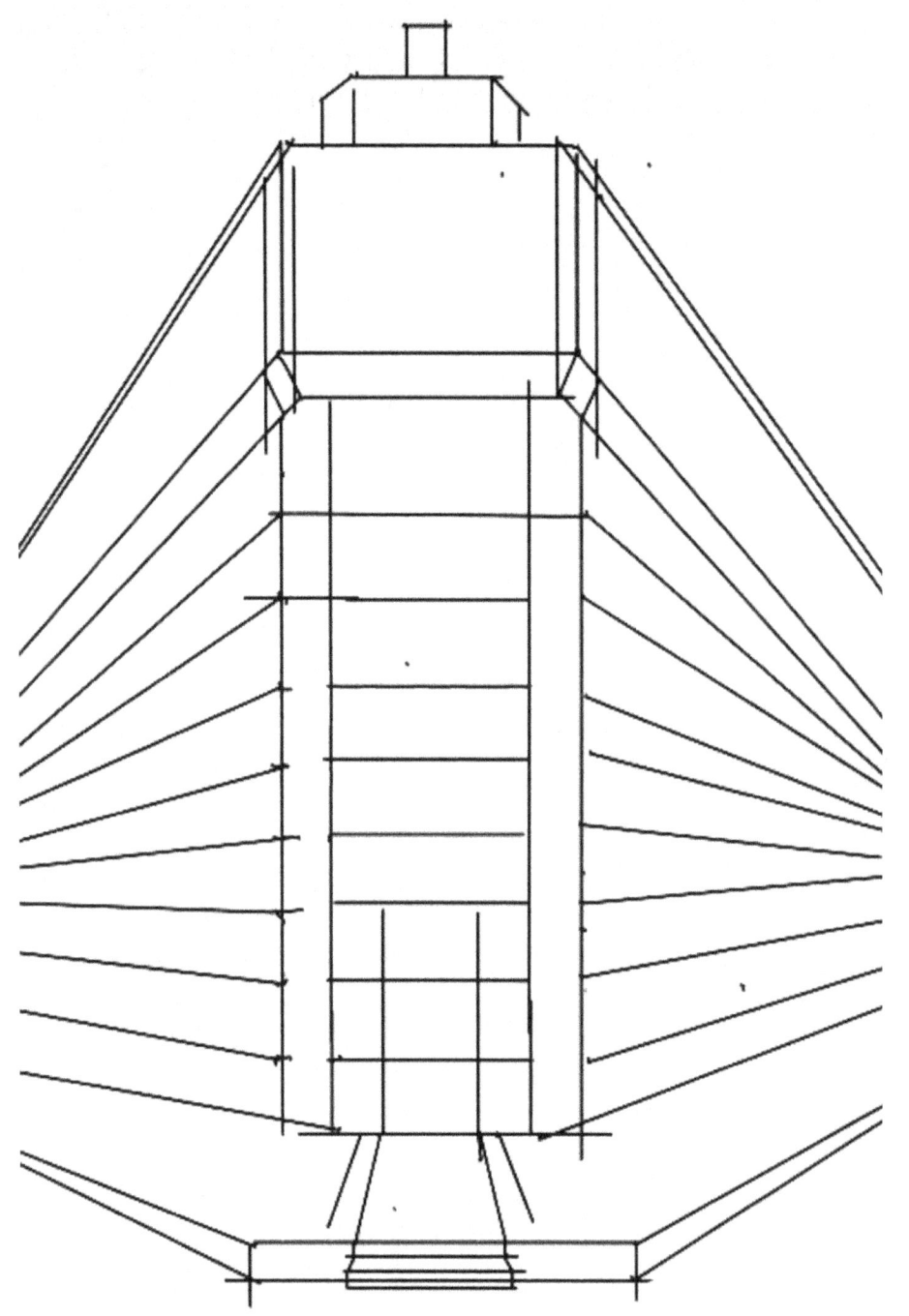

This is when it gets truly interesting and you get to start working with the top of the corporate building and the different architecture that makes the building unique. You'll also notice the completed door in the second image that demands proper attention.

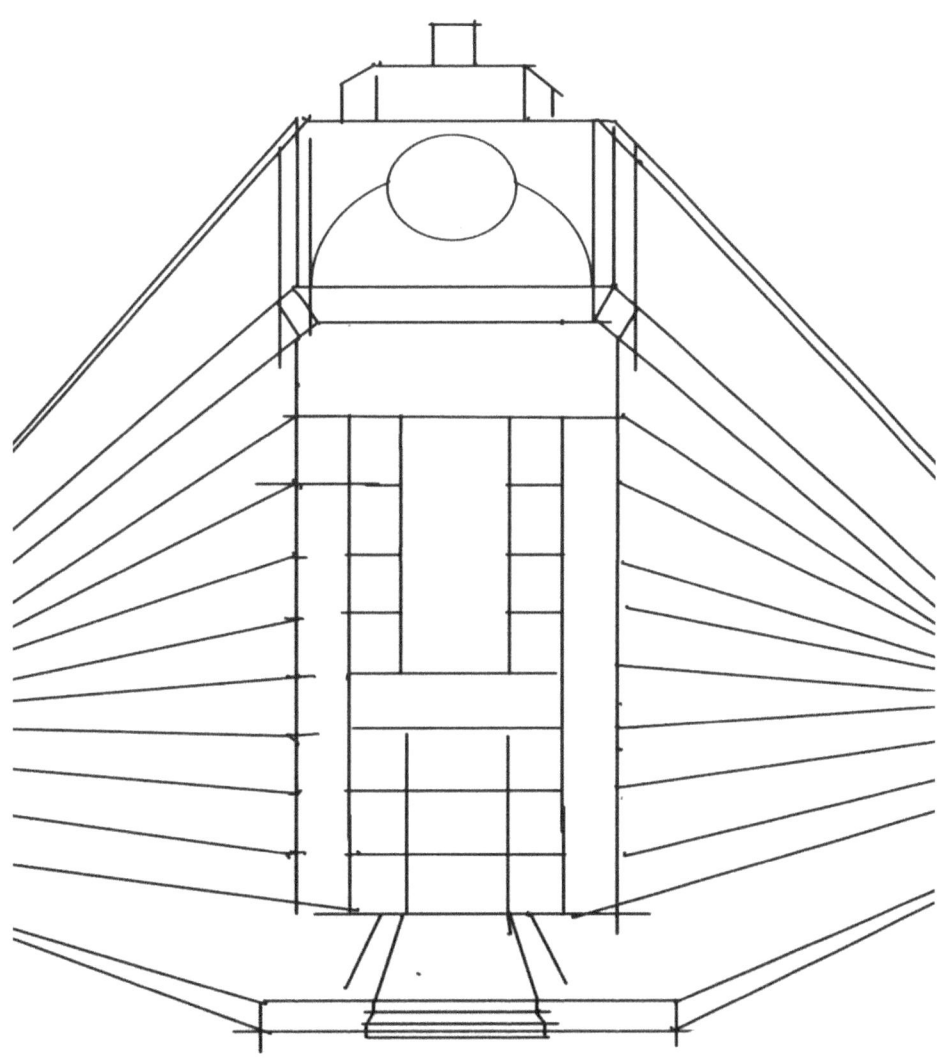

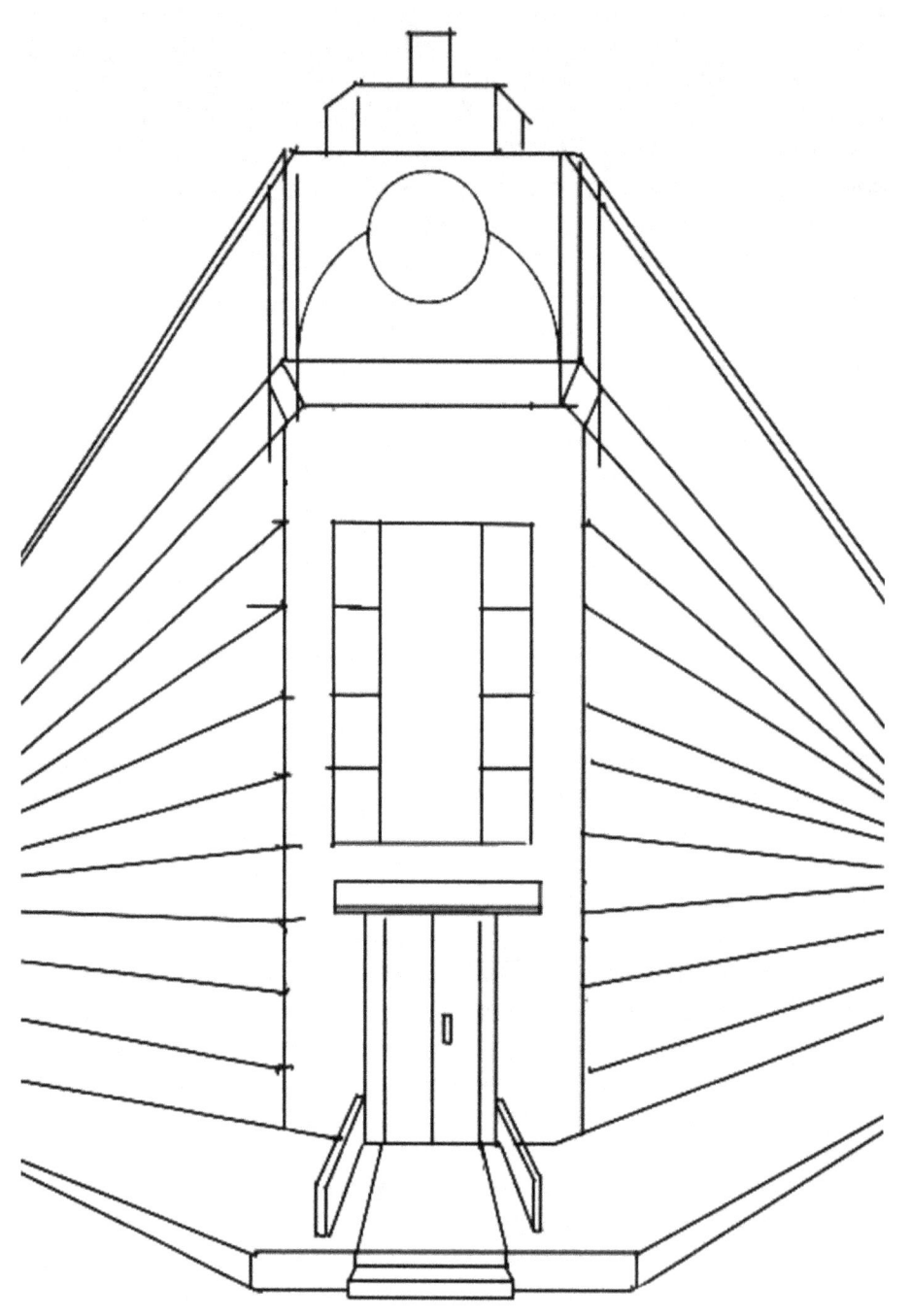

151

Once the front of the corporate building has been fine tuned, you then add even more lines to the sides of the building in order to make the installation of the windows much easier. As well you'll notice that most areas of the drawing itself are polished at this point and looking clear, keep up with your work and double check when you need to.

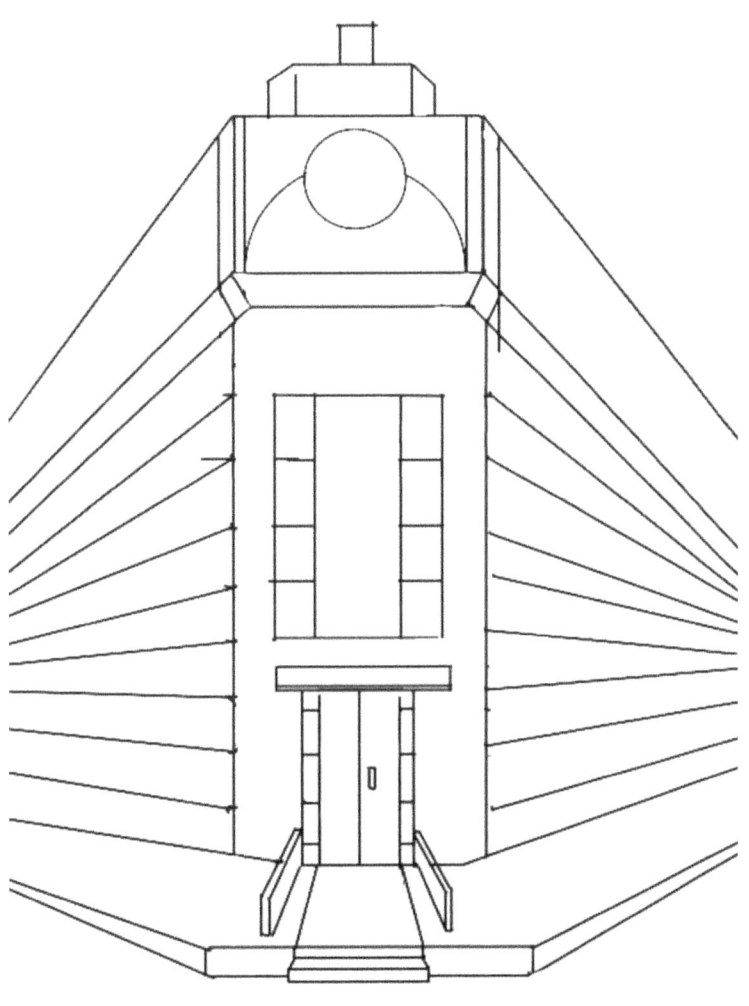

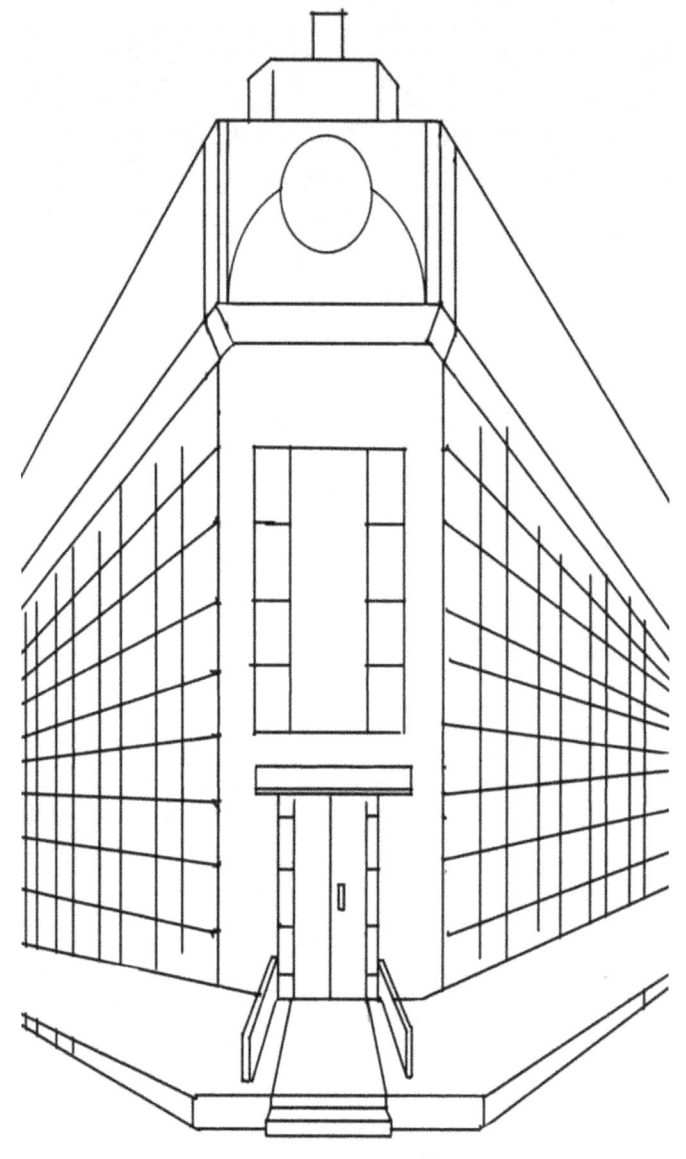

Now we perfect the windows. As you'll see in the first drawing the windows take a couple steps to complete. You start by erasing most of the intersecting lines except for the ones that do you actual favors, and then like in the second drawing you finally erase around the areas that are in your way.

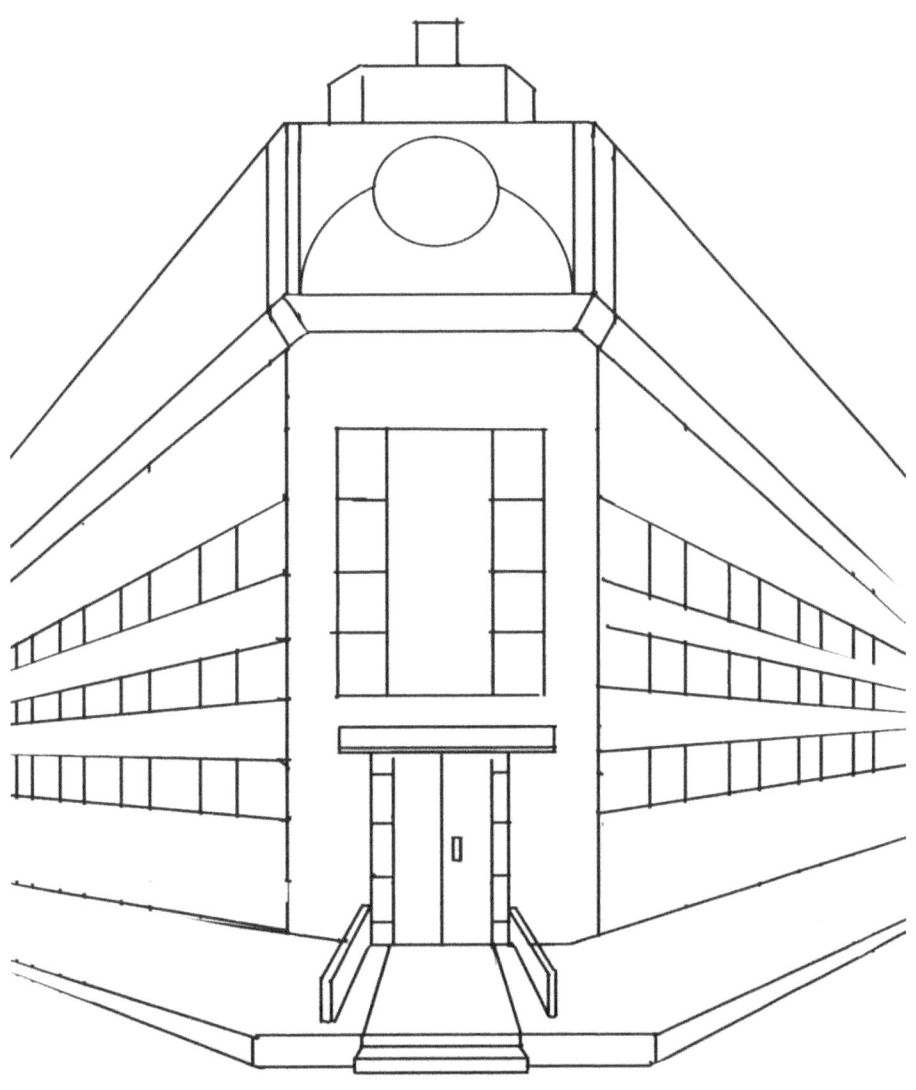

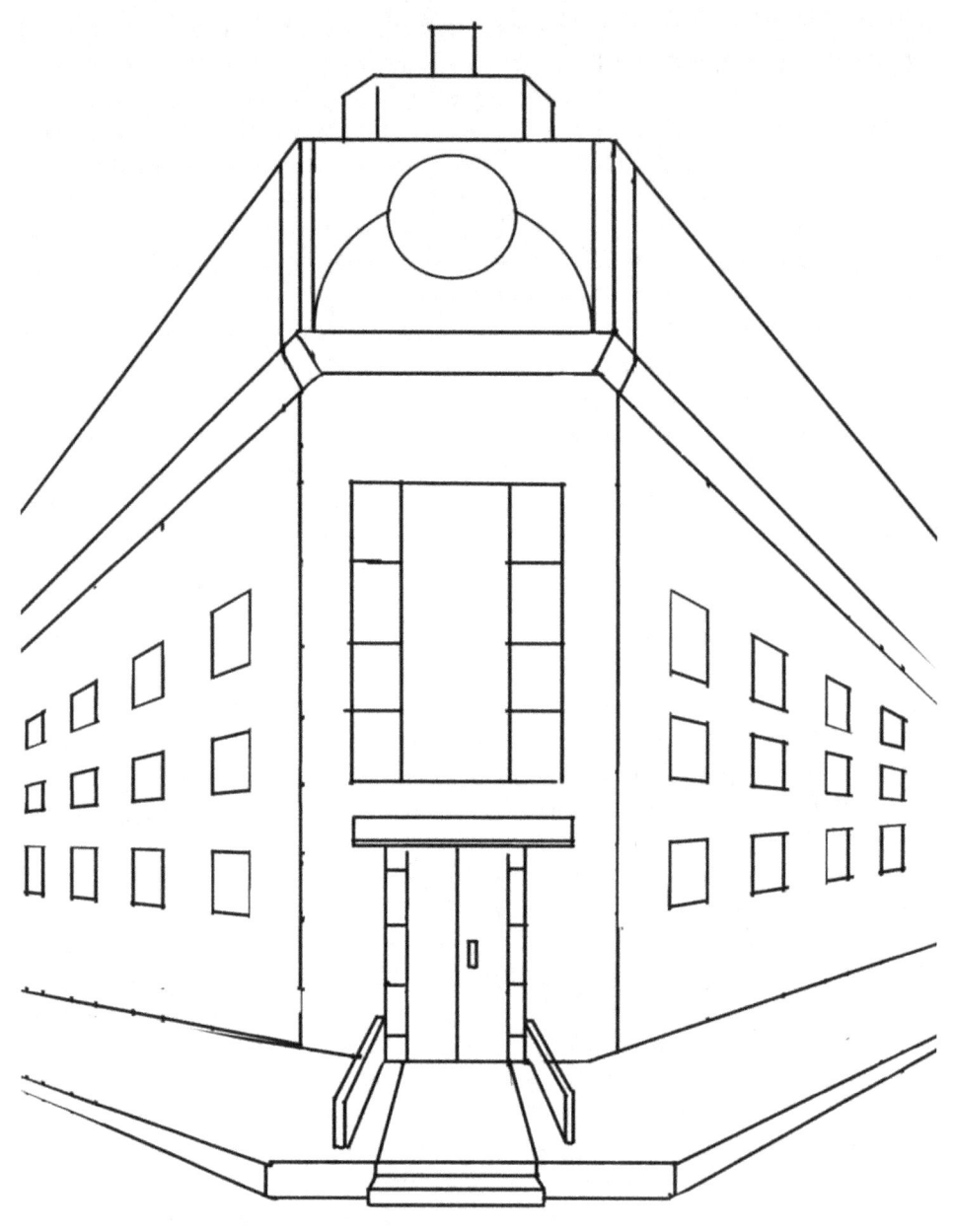

We start the shading as we always do, focusing on the
initial groupings of dark and light patches and then we add more as

we go. See how at least half of the image is shaded at this point.

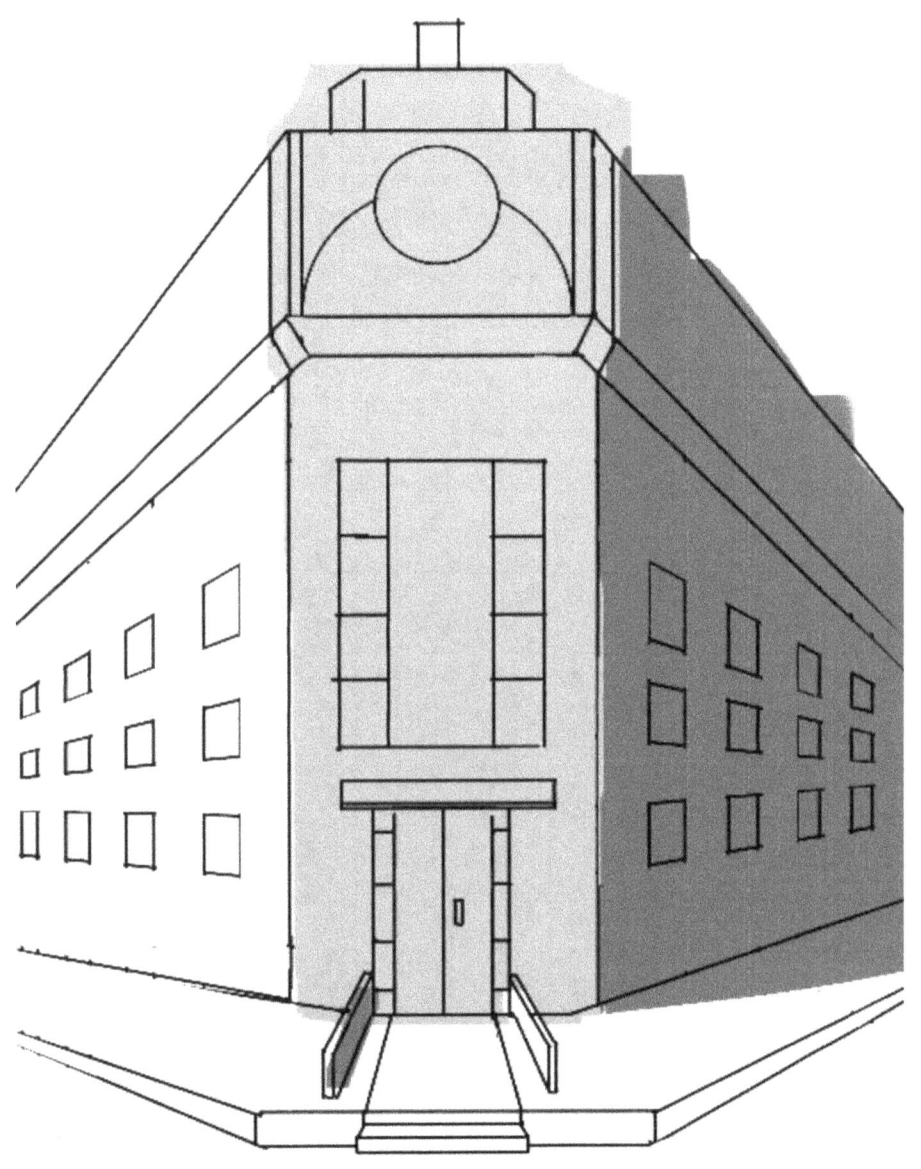

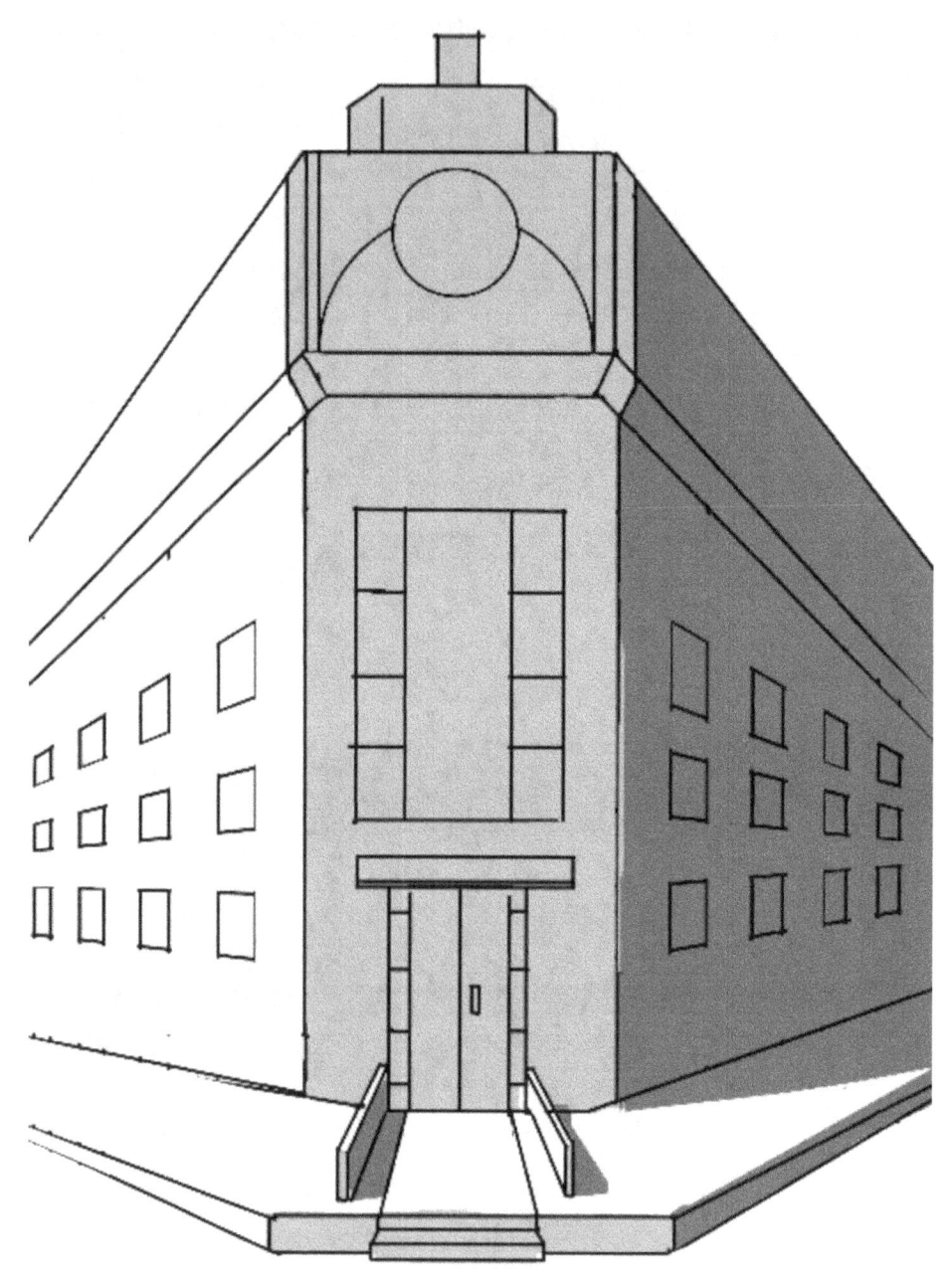

The last couple steps of shading are always the most crucial, showing the blending and actual precision this level of shading takes. Pay extra close attention to the door and the windows that surround the actual building.

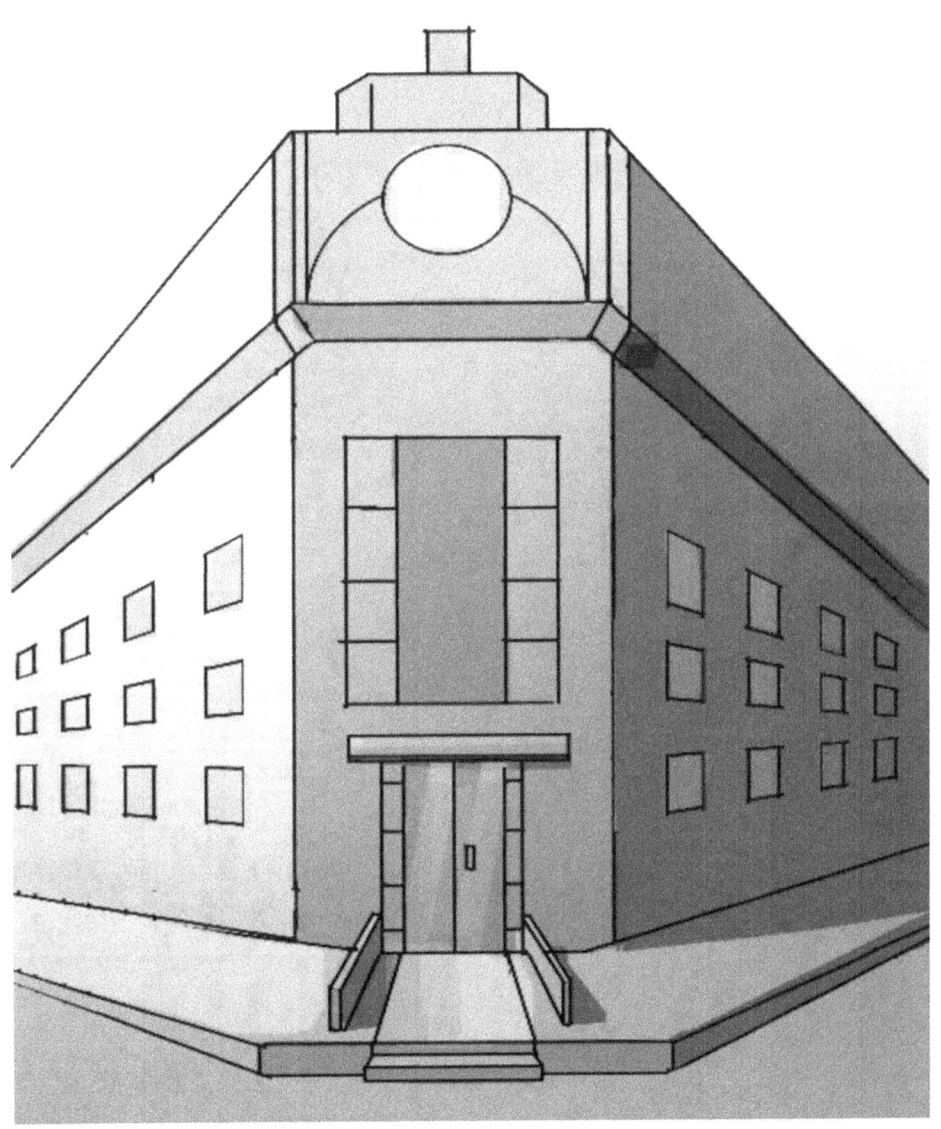

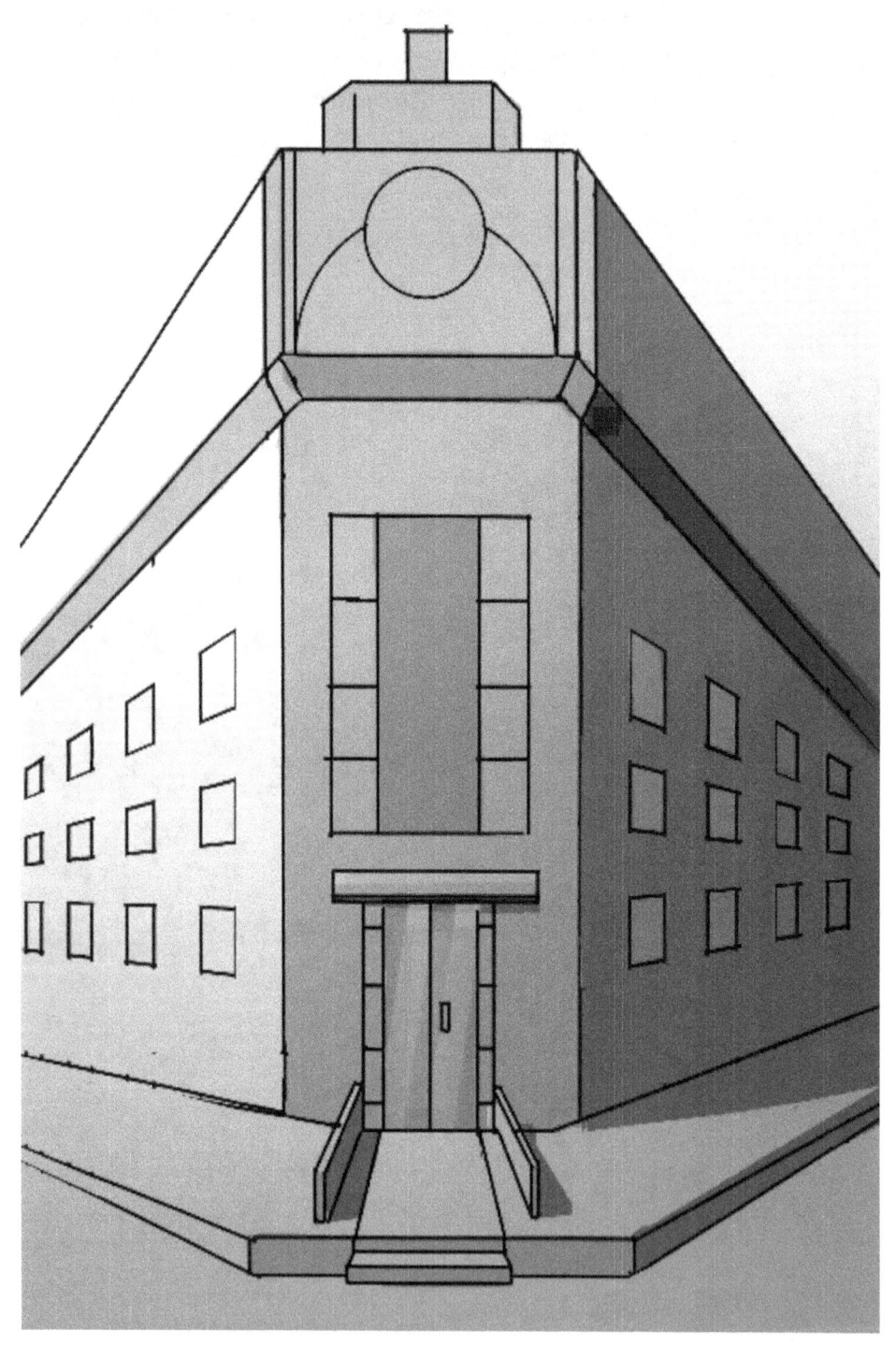

Here you have the finished product! Perfectly shaded and blended in such a way as to create an almost life like representation of a perspective beautifully captured through drawing. This now marks the final challenge in this book for you to face. Congratulations on completing your last challenge!

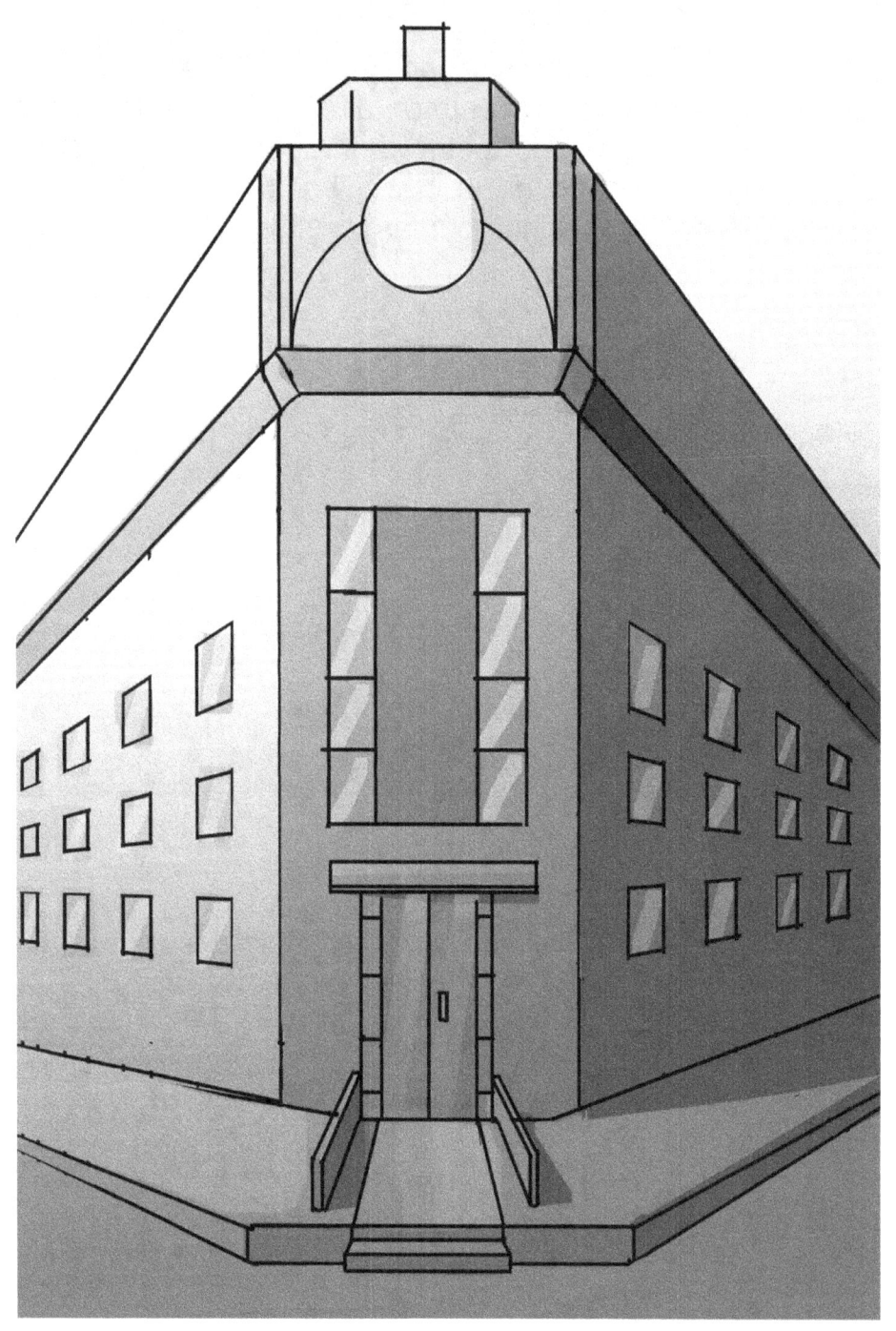

161

Conclusion

Now that you've made your way through these ten unique, intricate and challenging perspective drawings, you are ready to handle any perspective that may get thrown at you. Any image you see is now something that you could make a beautiful and hand crafted drawing out of if you set your mind to it. It doesn't need to be difficult, and now you've learned how to make sure it isn't.

If there are any challenges that face you in the future regarding this topic, you can always refer to these pages to help you through. I think an important message to take away from a project such as this, is that; "No matter what you see, there's a way to understand it". So go forth with your perspectives altered in a way to mirror acceptance and appreciation and conquer your world, and whatever resides in it.